CREDO SERIES

The Body of Christ: The Church

Based on the Curriculum Framework
Course IV: Jesus Christ's Mission
Continues in the Church

WRITERS
Joseph Draper, MA, PhD
(Chapters 1–5)
Daniella Zsupan-Jerome, MA, PhD
(Chapters 6–13)

GENERAL EDITOR
Thomas H. Groome, EdD

Professor Theology and Religious Education
Boston College

VERITAS

USA Office: Frisco, Texas

www.veritasreligion.com

The Subcommittee on the Catechism, United States Conference of Catholic Bishops, has found that this catechetical high school text, copyright 2014, is in conformity with the *Catechism of the Catholic Church* and that it fulfills the requirements of Core Course IV of the *Doctrinal Elements of a Curriculum Framework for the Development of Catechetical Materials for Young People of High School Age.*

CREDO SERIES CONSULTANT: Maura Hyland
PUBLISHER, USA AND THEOLOGICAL EDITOR:
Ed DeStefano
TEXT CONSULTANT: Annette Honan
COPY EDITOR: Elaine Campion
DESIGN: Lir Mac Cárthaigh
TYPESETTING: Heather Costello
COPYRIGHT RESEARCH: Emma O'Donoghue

INTERNET RESOURCES
There are internet resources available to support this text. Log on to *www.credoseries.com*

NIHIL OBSTAT
Rev. Msgr. Robert M. Coerver, S.T.L.
Censor Librorum

IMPRIMATUR
† Most Reverend Kevin J. Farrell, D.D.
Bishop of Dallas
March 8, 2012

The *Nihil Obstat* and *Imprimatur* are official declarations that the work contains nothing contrary to Faith and Morals. It is not implied thereby that those granting the *Nihil Obstat* or *Imprimatur* agree with the contents, statements or opinions expressed.

SEND ALL INQUIRIES TO:
Veritas, Customer Service
P.O. Box 789
Westerville, OH 43086
Tel. 866-844-0582
info@veritasreligion.com
www.veritasreligion.com

ISBN 978 1 84730 534 3 (Student Edition)
ISBN 978 1 84730 377 6 (Teacher Resource Edition)
ISBN 978 1 84730 536 7 (E-book: Student Edition)

Printed in the United States of America
1 2 3 4 5 6 7 / 17 16 15 14

CONTENTS

CHAPTER 1

Gathered to Be the People of God

JESUS CHRIST INSTITUTED THE CHURCH

THE HOLY SPIRIT IS ALWAYS PRESENT AND AT WORK IN THE CHURCH

THE CHURCH

THE NEW PEOPLE OF GOD

GOD'S GENEROUS GIFT TO HUMANITY

WE ARE BY NATURE COMMUNAL BEINGS

WE ARE IMAGES OF THE HOLY TRINITY, THE DIVINE COMMUNITY

THROUGH BAPTISM WE ARE MADE SHARERS IN THE WORK OF JESUS AND HIS CHURCH

THIS TEXT, *THE BODY OF CHRIST: THE CHURCH*, invites you to explore in detail the mystery of the Church, the new People of God, founded by Jesus Christ. 'The Father prepared for the Church through a series of covenant events described in the Old Testament. Jesus fulfilled the divine plan for the Church through his saving death and Resurrection' (*United States Catholic Catechism for Adults*, 122). The Holy Spirit works through the Church for the benefit not only of her own members but also of all people, bringing the saving light and work of Jesus Christ to the whole world.

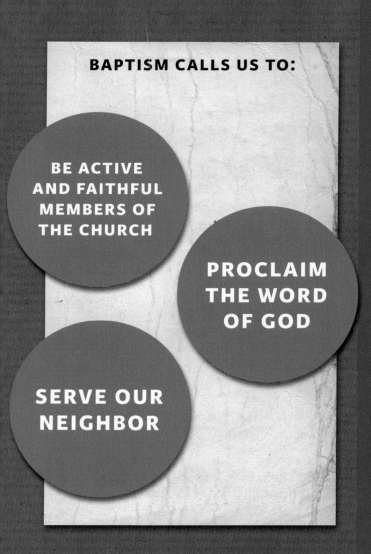

BAPTISM CALLS US TO:

BE ACTIVE AND FAITHFUL MEMBERS OF THE CHURCH

PROCLAIM THE WORD OF GOD

SERVE OUR NEIGHBOR

Faith Focus: The teachings of the Catholic Church that are the primary focus of the doctrinal content presented in this chapter include:
- ⊙ God created human beings to live in community with him and with one another.
- ⊙ God desires us to come to him as members of his family, his new people, so he established the Church to accomplish that purpose.
- ⊙ God the Father planned the Church from the beginning.
- ⊙ The Church, in her life and work, is the sign and the instrument of the communion of God and the human race.
- ⊙ The Church, the new People of God, was gradually revealed over time and prefigured in Noah's ark and in the covenant with the Israelites revealed in the Old Testament.
- ⊙ Jesus Christ, the Incarnate Son of God, is the new and everlasting covenant.
- ⊙ The Church is the means and goal of God's plan for the human race.
- ⊙ The Holy Spirit revealed the Church at Pentecost.

Discipleship Formation: As a result of studying this chapter and discovering the meaning of the faith of the Catholic Church for your life, you should be better able to:
- ⊙ be more aware of and value the role of the Church in your personal faith journey;
- ⊙ become more discerning of the Holy Spirit at work in your life;
- ⊙ strive to fulfill your baptismal calling to proclaim the Gospel;
- ⊙ identify actions you could take to bring the social justice of Jesus Christ to your community.

Scripture References: These Scripture references are quoted or referred to in this chapter:
OLD TESTAMENT: **Genesis** 1:26–27, 2:18, 9:1–17, 12:1–4, 17:4 and 7; **Exodus** 2:23, 3:7–8 and 10, 19:1–8, 20:18–21, 24:4; **Leviticus** 26:11–12; **Deuteronomy** 7:9; **Isaiah** 11:1–9; **Jeremiah** 31:33
NEW TESTAMENT: **Matthew** 5:17–19, 28:19–20; **Luke** 4:18; **John** 3:16; **Acts of the Apostles** 2:1–13; **Romans** 5:14, 10:17; **1 Corinthians** 15:22 and 45; **Ephesians** 6:10–11, 14–17; **1 Timothy** 3:15

Faith Glossary: Familiarize yourself with the meaning of these key terms. Definitions are found in the Glossary: **Apostles, charism, chrism, Church, consecrated life, covenant, Creator, divine Revelation, faith, hierarchy, Holy Trinity, laity, Messiah, new covenant, Paschal Mystery, Pentecost, People of God, prophet, redemption, sacrifice, salvation, Scripture, Tradition**

Faith Word: Church
Learn by Heart: Ephesians 6:10
Learn by Example: The early Church in Carthage

Why belong to a 'community' of faith?

Think about it. We all have a need and a desire to 'belong'. God has created every person to live with and for others. God the **Creator** said, 'It is not good for us to be alone' (based on Genesis 2:18). God created human beings to live in partnership. When we live as responsible members of a community, the community is better able to fulfill its purpose. Living as responsible members of a community also contributes to our growing and becoming the people God created us to be.

OPENING CONVERSATION
- What makes a community work well or achieve its goals?
- How different would your life be if you did not belong to a community?
- What do any of the communities you belong to contribute to your life? To your developing your talents? To your fulfilling your dreams?

OVER TO YOU
Think about your family and other communities to which you belong. How do each of those communities contribute to your life and well-being?

WE ARE WIRED FOR COMMUNITY
Our development as human persons depends on our connection to others—our relationships with others. In its own way, science teaches us the same truth. Neuroscientists—who study the brain—have produced a body of research that points to the ancient biblical truth that human beings are by nature created to live in community. Social scientists already attest that living in community enables us to achieve our full potential as human beings.

For example, neuroscientist Merlin Donald in his *A Mind So Rare* calls the human brain a 'hybrid brain'. By this Donald means that humans cannot acquire language or think complex thoughts—fundamentally human activities—*apart from* communities of family, tribe and civilization. Human growth requires the brain *plus* community. The human brain is the only brain on the planet that requires a community of others in order to know and develop.

To isolate a human child from others can permanently and irrevocably harm that child's capacity to develop and to master such basic 'human' capacities as language, complex thought or even social skills, which most of us take for granted. This is highlighted in the tragic cases of older children who, through abuse, abandonment or accidental separation, were isolated from others before learning to speak. When found, these children learned to communicate only with great difficulty.

This scientific research supports **divine Revelation** (the teachings of Sacred **Scripture** and Sacred **Tradition**) that the human person is by nature 'a communal being'. We are wired to live within nurturing relationships, in families,

The Holy Trinity is the mystery of one God in three distinct but inseparable divine Persons

THE HOLY TRINITY | ST. MAGNUS, WALDBURG, GERMANY

friendships and other social communities—and, most importantly, in communion with God—in order to grow, thrive and live in fullness of life. In short, we become who we are 'together'—in community.

OVER TO YOU

- Think of something you know or can do that you have learned only through your relationships with other people.
- Think of the people who have contributed to your becoming the person you are today.
- Decide on one way you can show your appreciation to them.

FROM THE WISDOM OF THE CHURCH
The Church is a communion. The starting point of this communion is our union with Jesus Christ. This gives us a share in the communion of the Persons of the Trinity and also leads to a communion among men and women.
—*United States Catholic Catechism for Adults* (USCCA), 123

IMAGES OF THE HOLY TRINITY: THE DIVINE COMMUNITY

Genesis teaches that God created us in the divine image and likeness. (Read Genesis 1:26–27.) Jesus has revealed that God is Father, Son and Holy Spirit. God the Creator is the **Holy Trinity**. The

Holy Trinity is the mystery of one God in three distinct but inseparable divine Persons. In other words, from the beginning God created human beings to live in community; God created us to live in right relationship with God and in right relationship with one another and with all creation. God created us to live *upward* toward God and *outward* toward others. '[The Church] is the sacrament of the Holy Trinity's communion with men' (*Catechism of the Catholic Church* [CCC], no. 747).

THINK, PAIR AND SHARE

- God the Holy Trinity creates each person in the divine image and likeness. Each one of us is an *imago dei,* an 'image of God'. What does this mean?
- What are some of the challenges for the Christian family to be an image of the Holy Trinity? For a Catholic school?

REFLECT AND DECIDE

- How might you be an image of God the Holy Trinity to others?

THE CHURCH: GOD'S GENEROUS GIFT TO HUMANITY

God desires us to come to him as members of his family, his new people, so he established the **Church** to accomplish that purpose. The Church

PREACHING CHRISTIANITY IN THE MIDDLE AGES | 19TH-CENTURY ENGRAVING

The Church is prefigured in the **People of God** of ancient Israel. The Church as the new People of God is a generous gift of God to humanity. She is the sign and instrument of the reconciliation of humanity with God (a vertical and an 'upward' communion) that enables human beings to relate to one another with justice and peace (a horizontal and an 'outward' communion) and to the divine plan of goodness for humanity.

WHAT ABOUT YOU PERSONALLY?

⊙ Reflect on your many God-given gifts. These are blessings from God. How will you cooperate with the free gift of God's grace to develop your gifts to build up the Church in the world?

⊙ Complete the statement 'I'm good at _____'. Include as many gifts and blessings as you can identify. Be generous!

⊙ Identify how you might use one or two of those gifts, right now, to build up the Church.

JOURNAL EXERCISE

⊙ Create a symbol that expresses the Church as an 'upward' and an 'outward' communion.

continues the mission of Christ. She is to call all people to live together in communion with God and with one another as the one people, the one family, of God. The Church, in her life and work, is 'the sign and the instrument of the communion of God and men' (CCC, no. 780). This has been part of the divine plan from the beginning:

Christians of the first centuries said, 'The world was created for the sake of the Church' [Pastor of Hermas]. . . . The gathering together of the People of God began at the moment when sin destroyed the communion of men with God, and that of men among themselves. The gathering together of the Church is, as it were, God's reaction to the chaos provoked by sin.

—CCC, nos. 760, 761

The covenant between God and his people in the making

In the Book of Deuteronomy we read, 'Know therefore that the LORD your God is God, the faithful God who maintains covenant loyalty with those who love him and keep his commandments, to a thousand generations' (Deuteronomy 7:9).

OPENING CONVERSATION

- ⊙ What do you think the inspired sacred human author means by the words 'maintains covenant loyalty'?
- ⊙ In what ways have you experienced God being 'loyal' to you?
- ⊙ In what ways have you been or are you 'loyal' to God?

PROMISES, PROMISES

We have been exploring the meaning of the truth that human beings, biologically and spiritually, are social, communal beings. We see this truth revealed in the **covenants**—solemn agreements—that God and his people entered. These covenants involve mutual commitments that define the relationships that bind God and his people, and the People of God with one another. The Bible speaks of covenants that God made with Noah and, through him, with every living creature (Genesis 9:1–17); with Abraham and his descendants (Genesis 12:1–3, 17:4, 7); and with Moses and the Israelites (Exodus 19:1–8,

20:18–21, 24:4; Leviticus 26:11–12). The **prophets** announced and pointed to the **new covenant** that God would establish with all humankind through the promised **Messiah**, whom we know and believe is Jesus Christ. Jesus Christ, the Incarnate Word of God, is the fullness of truth. In him the depth and truth of the relationship between God and humanity is fully revealed.

TALK IT OVER

- ⊙ Recall a time when someone made a promise to you that was conditional upon you doing something.
- ⊙ Would the promise have remained intact if you had not fulfilled your part?
- ⊙ What did you need to do to benefit from the promise?
- ⊙ What insights does this give you into the covenant loyalty that binds God and his people?

Great Old Testament Events in God's Plan for Humanity

Call of Abraham: To form a great people whose descendants will bless all people of the world.

Call of Moses: To reveal the name of God and liberate the Hebrews from slavery.

Covenant at Sinai: The covenant between God and Israel and the revealing of the Ten Commandments.

Call of the Prophets: God promises a new covenant with all people, one that is revealed in Jesus Christ and enacted in his Church.

Preparation: God Begins to Gather a People

The Church, the new People of God, was instituted by Jesus Christ by his preaching the Good News. This Church, which God the Father planned from the beginning, was slowly revealed and prefigured in the Old Testament in Noah's ark and the covenants between God and Abraham and his descendants, the Israelites. These covenants were fulfilled in Jesus Christ, the new and everlasting covenant. Through the Church, the new People of God and the Body of Christ, God invites all people into covenant. For 'all **salvation** comes from Christ the Head through the Church which is his body' (CCC, no. 846). The Church is the means and the goal of God's plan for humanity.

Let us briefly recall and explore who the one God is who *saves* (Noah), who *calls, promises and gathers* (Abraham), who *frees and liberates* (Moses and the Exodus), who *reveals the nature of the covenant* (Torah), and who *renews the divine promises* for all people (Prophets).

THE CALL OF ABRAHAM: GOD FORMS A PEOPLE THROUGH WHOM HE WILL BLESS THE WORLD

In Genesis 12:1–4 we read the story of God and Abraham entering into a covenant. The covenant that God and Abraham enter is the beginning of the story of God gathering his people. In this story the Church sees God preparing the world for the coming of Jesus Christ, the new and everlasting covenant, and for the Church that Christ would institute. In Eucharistic Prayer I the Church professes Abraham to be our father in **faith**.

LET'S PROBE DEEPER
- Read Genesis 12:1–4.
- What does the passage say about Abraham's faith?
- Role-play a conversation between Abraham and Sarah as they discuss their response to God's invitation.

OVER TO YOU
- Imagine yourself in Abraham's sandals. How would you have responded?
- What kind of faith would it take for you to say 'yes' to God?

JOURNAL EXERCISE
- Recall that faith is both a gift and a free response to God's invitation to come to know him more deeply.
- When have you said 'yes' to God?
- Write about how your faith has influenced your choices.

THE CALL OF MOSES: GOD FREES AND LIBERATES HIS PEOPLE

Within a few generations after the death of Abraham and Sarah, which biblical scholars say was sometime during the nineteenth century BC, many of the Israelites had to leave Canaan, the land God promised them, and they settled in Egypt to escape the ravages of a famine. While God's people were in Egypt, the Egyptians took them into slavery because they had grown so large in number that they were seen as a threat to Pharaoh. The Book of Exodus tells us that God's people were so greatly oppressed that they 'groaned under their slavery, and cried out' to God (Exodus 2:23). God, faithful to his people, *heard* their cry, *saw* their oppression, *knew* their misery, and decided to *act* to bring about freedom and justice for the enslaved Hebrews. The author of Exodus tells us:

Then the LORD said, 'I have observed the misery of my people who are in Egypt; I have heard their cry on account of their taskmasters. Indeed, I know their sufferings, and I have come down to deliver them. . . . So come [Moses], I will send you to Pharaoh to bring my people, the Israelites, out of Egypt.'
—Exodus 3:7–8, 10

This part of the Exodus account repeats a common theme in Sacred Scripture: God acts on behalf of suffering human communities *through people*. God does not wave a magic wand; rather, he calls, equips and sends human beings to carry out his work in the world. God continues to do the same today as he has done in the past.

WHAT ABOUT YOU PERSONALLY?

- ⊙ Read the story of Moses at the burning bush in Exodus 3.
- ⊙ What connection can you see between Moses' initial response and your response to God's invitation to faith? Explain.
- ⊙ Name your own strengths that you might use to work with the Holy Spirit to bring about God's work in the world.
- ⊙ How might both your strengths and weaknesses become something God works with to benefit you and the world?

The Ten Commandments guided God's people in living in covenant loyalty to God and to one another

THE TEN COMMANDMENTS | COLORED ENGRAVING AFTER PHILIPPE DE CHAMPAIGNE

THE PROPHET MICAH ADDRESSING THE ISRAELITES | GUSTAVE DORÉ

THE COVENANT AT SINAI: THE NATURE AND LAW OF THE COVENANT

After God brought the ancient Israelites out of their slavery in Egypt, he revealed the Law of the covenant to his people. The Ten Commandments were a central part of the Law and they guided God's people in living in covenant loyalty to God and to one another. God promised the Israelites that he would always be their God, and the Israelites promised that the Lord alone would be their God. Tragically, the ancient Israelites were not as faithful to the covenant as God was. The history of God's people reveals a pattern of the Israelites' infidelity to God and their acts of injustice toward one another.

THINK, PAIR AND SHARE
⊙ Pair up and review the Ten Commandments on page 263 of this text.
⊙ Why do human communities need to live by each of the Ten Commandments?

THE CALL OF THE PROPHETS: GOD PROMISES A NEW COVENANT WITH ALL PEOPLE

The Israelites were taken into exile as a consequence of their infidelity to God and to one another. Once again God, faithful to his people, *heard* their cry, *saw* their oppression, *knew*

their misery and decided to *act* to bring about freedom and justice for his people. God called and sent prophets through whom he promised a new outpouring of God's love onto the whole world. The prophet Jeremiah proclaimed, '[This] is the covenant that I will make with the house of Israel after those days, says the LORD: I will put my law within them, and I will write it on their hearts; and I will be their God, and they shall be my people' (Jeremiah 31:33). The Church recognizes in this message the anticipation of the new covenant uniting God and humanity, Jesus Christ, into which we are reborn at Baptism.

READ AND DISCUSS
⊙ Read Matthew 5:17–19.
⊙ What connection can you see between the words of Jeremiah and the words of Jesus? Explain.
⊙ What do you think is the 'law' within us, written on our hearts?

WHAT ABOUT YOU PERSONALLY?
⊙ From your study of this section of the chapter, what new insights did you get into how God relates to his people?
⊙ What do these insights tell you about God's relationship with you? About living out your relationship with God?

God fulfills his promise in Jesus Christ

OPENING CONVERSATION

- Recall and reflect on a time when you were invited to join a team, a project, or to participate in some event. Who called? What were you called to?
- What was expected of you?
- How did you do?

COMPARE AND ANALYZE

- How does what you described in the 'Opening Conversation' compare with your baptismal call to live as a disciple of Jesus Christ?

The Church Celebrates the Great New Testament Events in God's Plan for Humanity

Incarnation: The Son of God assuming human nature and becoming fully human in Jesus Christ without giving up his divinity. We prepare ourselves for this mystery in Advent and celebrate it during the Christmas season.

Public Life and Ministry of Jesus: Jesus taught people; he healed the sick and lifted up the broken hearted. We celebrate this in the first part of Ordinary Time.

Death and Resurrection of Jesus Christ: We prepare ourselves for this mystery in Lent; we celebrate it during the Easter Triduum, which begins with the Evening Mass of the Lord's Supper on Holy Thursday and concludes with Evening Prayer on Easter Sunday. Our celebration of the Resurrection continues throughout the fifty days of the Easter season.

Ascension: We celebrate the return of the risen Christ to his Father on the fortieth day of the Easter season.

Pentecost: We celebrate the outpouring of the Holy Spirit on the disciples, the revealing of the Church and the beginning of the work of the Church on the fiftieth day of the Easter season.

THE ASCENSION

Jesus began his public life and ministry by announcing the Kingdom of God that Isaiah so clearly foretold

ISAIAH | ST. MICHAEL'S CHURCH, UNTERGRIESBACH, GERMANY

GOD GATHERS . . . WE RESPOND

During the Assyrian conquest of Israel, which began around 735 BC, the prophet Isaiah (a Hebrew name meaning 'God is salvation') proclaimed the coming of a new creation, a new kingdom in which God's reign would prevail. (Read Isaiah 11:1–9.) At God's appointed time the Son of God, out of sheer love, 'came down from heaven, / and by the Holy Spirit was incarnate of the Virgin Mary, / and became man' (Nicene Creed). Jesus began his public life and ministry by announcing that 'the Spirit of the Lord is upon me' and that the Spirit had anointed him to inaugurate the Kingdom of God that Isaiah so clearly foretold. (See Luke 4:18.) Jesus preached and brought about that kingdom in his Person and through his ministry, especially through his total self-giving in the events of his **Paschal Mystery**. The Paschal Mystery is 'Christ's work of redemption accomplished principally by his Passion, death, Resurrection, and glorious Ascension' (CCC, Glossary).

Jesus is the 'New Adam' in and through whom the re-creation of the world began and is now taking place. Because of his love for his Father and for all humanity, Jesus freely accepted death on the Cross. Jesus said 'yes' to his Father on behalf of all humanity. His 'yes' overcame and wiped out the power of sin and death and reconciled human beings with God and one another. Through the outpouring of Jesus' Blood on the Cross the Church was born. As Adam's choice enslaved us all, Jesus' **sacrifice** on the Cross liberates us to share in new life in Christ.

From the very beginning Jesus gathered around himself the Apostles and many other disciples, both men and women, to work with him to bring about the Kingdom of God. He sent them into the world to spread his message and invite all peoples into discipleship. Jesus continues that work today in and through his Church.

The Church is the seed and the beginning of the Kingdom of God. As members of the Church we are called to work toward bringing about that Kingdom, here and now, and preparing for its fullness when Christ comes again at the end of time. In his divine wisdom and love, God calls, gathers and forms the Church into the one People of God. He invites us to grow in living together as Jesus' disciples by learning, by praying, by celebrating and by doing good works of charity and justice.

The Church *calls* the whole human family to partake of and celebrate our **redemption** in Christ. The Spirit of Christ, the Holy Spirit, *sends* us into the world to transform cultures of injustice with the leaven of the Gospel. The Holy Spirit *sustains and empowers* the Church from age to age. It is the Spirit of Christ who animates both the invisible and the visible patterns of relationships that make up the Body of Christ to carry on the work of God in the world. 'The Holy Spirit is the protagonist, "the principal agent of the whole of the Church's mission [Pope John Paul II, encyclical, *The Mission of the Redeemer*, no. 21]" ' (CCC, no. 852).

REFLECT AND DISCUSS

⊙ Read this well-known Gospel passage: 'God so loved the world that he gave his only Son, so that everyone who believes in him may not perish but may have eternal life' (John 3:16).
⊙ Where do you see the Church today proclaiming this same message?
⊙ How does your school proclaim this message?

OVER TO YOU

⊙ Why is belonging to the Church important to you?
⊙ How does belonging to the Church influence your life the most? The least? Why the difference?

Pentecost and the Church's call to mission

OPENING CONVERSATION

Read the account of Pentecost in Acts of the Apostles 2:1–13.

- ◉ Share what you know about the work of the Holy Spirit.
- ◉ Where do you see Christians acting boldly for their faith as St. Peter did at Pentecost?

WHAT ABOUT YOU PERSONALLY?

- ◉ How do you experience the Holy Spirit at work in your life?

> **FROM THE WISDOM OF THE CHURCH**
> 'What the soul is to the human body, the Holy Spirit is to the members of Christ, that is, the body of Christ, which is the Church' (St. Augustine).
> —*Compendium of the Catechism of the Catholic Church*, no. 159

CONSTANTINE THE GREAT | 4TH-CENTURY ROMAN

THE HIDDEN WORK OF THE HOLY SPIRIT GOES PUBLIC

The power of the Holy Spirit burst forth upon the Church at **Pentecost**, ten days after the Ascension and fifty days after the Resurrection. That same Spirit was always at work and active in the world from the moment of creation and will remain at work in the world until Christ comes again in glory at the end of time, when the plan of God for humanity will come about in its fullness.

Some argue that the change introduced to the Roman Empire through the work of the Holy Spirit in the Church was the most radical and sustained transformation any culture had experienced in history up to that time. Within a few centuries, Christianity, a faith whose members had experienced both sporadic and systematic persecution, had become the religion of the Empire. In AD 313 Emperor Constantine the Great and Co-emperor Lucinius granted Christians and all other citizens of the Empire the right and freedom to worship publicly. And in 391 Emperor Theodosius I, Roman Emperor in the East from AD 379 to 392, decreed Christianity to be the official religion of the Empire.

One explanation some historians might give for this major transformation is the genius of the leaders of the visible organization of the Church. Another reason is that the Church is a people gathered, organized and gifted by the Holy Spirit, who is 'the principal agent of the whole of the Church's mission' (CCC, no. 852) and 'whom Christ the head pours out on his members, builds, animates, and sanctifies the Church' (CCC, no. 747) as she unfolds the mission of Christ.

The Church is the temple of the Holy Spirit. She is the visible sign of the hidden mystery of the Spirit at work in the world. The Holy Spirit is always present within the Church as Jesus promised. The Spirit of Christ is always offering

The power of the Holy Spirit burst forth upon the Church at Pentecost

DESCENT OF THE HOLY SPIRIT | EASTERN ORTHODOX ICON

the **charisms**, or graces, the Church needs for the building up of the Church. These graces guide and strengthen the whole Church and individual members of the Church to unfold the mission of Christ according to one's role in the Church. The Holy Spirit is always at work in every culture, in every age, until the end of time.

REFLECT AND SHARE

⦿ What truth might the Holy Spirit be calling you to proclaim right now to give witness to the Gospel?

⦿ What action might the Holy Spirit be calling you to take to participate in the mission of Christ and build up the Church?

FROM THE WISDOM OF THE CHURCH

'When the work which the Father gave the Son to do on earth was accomplished, the Holy Spirit was sent on the day of Pentecost' [Vatican II, *Dogmatic Constitution on the Church*, no. 4]. Then 'the Church was openly displayed to the crowds and the spread of the Gospel among the nations, through preaching, was begun' [*Decree on the Church's Missionary Activity*, no. 4].

—CCC, no. 767

PENTECOST—THE WORK OF THE CHURCH BEGINS

St. Peter, having been graced with the 'fire' of the Holy Spirit and accompanied by the other disciples, left the upper room and went out into the marketplace of Jerusalem. There he fearlessly and boldly began to fulfill the commission that the risen Lord had given him and the other **Apostles**:

'Go therefore and make disciples of all nations, baptizing them in the name of the Father and of the Son and of the Holy Spirit, and teaching them to obey everything that I have commanded you. And remember, I am with you always, to the end of the age.'

—Matthew 28:19–20

St. Luke tells us that the people's response to Peter's preaching was overwhelming. He writes: '[T]hose who welcomed his message were baptized, and that day about three thousand persons were added' (Acts of the Apostles 2:41). By the grace of the Holy Spirit, the Apostles and the other disciples were ready to take this great mission to the four corners of the world.

A PRIEST BLESSES A CHILD DURING A BAPTISMAL MASS, VICTORIA, SEYCHELLES

Reborn and Anointed with the Spirit and Water

As the Church, 'we're all in this together'. In the Sacrament of Baptism the newly baptized are anointed with sacred **chrism**. This anointing shows that they have been made sharers in the threefold mission of Jesus the Priest, Prophet and King. In Baptism the Spirit calls all the faithful to work with others to fulfill this mission. The Church, in her Code of Canon Law, outlines the obligations and rights that flow from Baptism. These include:

⊙ First, the baptized have the responsibility to be active and faithful members of the Church. We fulfill this responsibility according to our state of life, namely, as a member of the **hierarchy**, of the **consecrated life** or of the **laity**.

⊙ Second, the baptized have the responsibility to proclaim the Word of God. Guided by the Spirit of Truth, we are to proclaim the teachings of Jesus. This means we have the responsibility to become intimately familiar with the Gospel of Jesus Christ through studying the Bible and the teachings of the Church. The apostle Paul teaches, '[F]aith comes from what is heard, and what is heard comes through the word of Christ' (Romans 10:17).

⊙ Third, Baptism calls every Christian to serve their neighbors, and all people in need, including those who are not members of the Church.

—Based on *Code of Canon Law*, cc. *208–223*

WHAT ABOUT YOU PERSONALLY?

⊙ How are you doing at sharing the Word of God?

⊙ How boldly do you let others come to know who you are—a disciple of Jesus Christ?

⊙ How are you doing at reaching out to people in need?

THE CALL TO BOLDNESS

Proclaiming the Gospel requires a Peter-like boldness and a Paul-like zeal. Those engaged in that work need to be prepared and sustained by the Holy Spirit. To Timothy, his companion in preaching the Gospel, St. Paul wrote, '[The Church is] the pillar and bulwark of the truth' (1 Timothy 3:15) revealed in Jesus.

Paul used military metaphors to share his own experiences in proclaiming the Gospel. In the New Testament letter written to the Church in Ephesus, we read:

[B]e strong in the Lord and in the strength of his power. Put on the whole armor of God, so that you may be able to stand against the wiles of the devil. . . . Stand therefore and fasten the belt of truth around your waist, and put on the breastplate of righteousness. As shoes for your feet put on whatever will make you ready to proclaim the gospel of peace. With all of these, take the shield of faith, with which you will be able to quench all the flaming arrows of the evil one. Take the helmet of salvation, and the sword of the Spirit, which is the word of God.

—Ephesians 6:10–11, 14–17

THINK, PAIR AND SHARE
- Reflect on the passage from Ephesians.
- What do the images that St. Paul uses—a belt, shoes, breastplate, shield, a helmet and sword—say about the work of proclaiming the Gospel?

OVER TO YOU
- What might be the 'armor of God' you need to fulfill your baptismal calling to proclaim the Gospel?

JUDGE AND ACT

REFLECT ON WHAT YOU HAVE LEARNED IN THIS CHAPTER

As you come toward the end of this first chapter, pause and reflect on what you have come to understand to be the role of the Church in God's plan for humanity. Share the teachings of the Catholic Church on these statements:

- God created human beings to live in community with him and with one another.
- God desires us to come to him as members of his family, his new people, so he established the Church to accomplish that purpose.
- God the Father planned the Church from the beginning.
- The Church is the sign and instrument of the communion of God and the human race; she is the means and the goal of God's plan for humanity.
- The Church was gradually revealed over time and was prefigured and revealed in the Old Testament.
- Jesus Christ, the Incarnate Son of God, is the new and everlasting covenant.
- The Holy Spirit revealed the Church at Pentecost.
- The Church is the pillar and foundation of truth.

OVER TO YOU

- What have you learned about your role in the Church? How might you make that wisdom part of your daily life?

CALLED TO TRANSFORM THE WORLD IN CHRIST

Christ gave the Apostles, their successors and the whole Church the commission to preach the Gospel to the whole world. The early Church took up this mission and transformed the world in which she lived. The Church has the mission to continue this work of transformation begun by Jesus Christ. She is the seed and the beginning of the Kingdom. This mission is not limited to calling individuals to personal transformation and reconciliation with God; it also includes the transformation of the local communities and the global community in which the Church lives. Personal reconciliation and social transformation go together. To be reconciled to God in Christ is to participate in the transformation of the world.

In *A Catholic Framework for Economic Life* (1966), the bishops in the United States addressed this work of the Church. They taught:

> All economic life should be shaped by moral principles. Economic choices and institutions must be judged by how they protect or undermine the life and dignity of the human person, support the family, and serve the common good.

DECIDE FOR YOURSELF

- What is the connection between discipleship and citizenship?
- What can you do to be a responsible disciple-citizen?

LEARN BY EXAMPLE

The early Church in Carthage, North Africa

By the early third century, the Church in Carthage already had a clear public structure consisting of orders of virgins, widows, deacons, priests, and one bishop, Cyprian. A widespread persecution of Christians began in AD 248. Decius, who was Roman Emperor from 249 to 251, decided that the barbarian invasions, sporadic famines and other ills facing the Empire were a result of the people no longer honoring the traditional Roman gods. Christians were the worst offenders because they rejected every god but their own.

Decius decreed that everyone had to show their loyalty to the gods of the Empire, which included the Emperor, by performing a simple act of worship, after which they would receive a certificate of compliance. Failure to comply meant painful and prolonged torture. More than half of the Christians abandoned the faith in order to avoid torture and the confiscation of their property. Some Christians, however, were able to purchase phony certificates of compliance to avoid imprisonment, torture and even death. Many others fled into hiding, including Cyprian.

A minority of Christians boldly resisted the edict of the Emperor; they were imprisoned and some died under torture for 'confessing' Christ. The persecution was so devastating that there was a near total collapse of the structure of the Church. Gathering spaces were raided, sacred writings were confiscated

ST. CYPRIAN OF CARTHAGE | MASTER OF MESSKIRCH

and burned, and the majority of leaders were dispersed.

When Emperor Decius died in AD 251, the persecution ended. Almost instantly the Church re-emerged battered but not defeated. Through it all the Holy Spirit was at work.

TALK IT OVER
- ⊙ How might you explain the diversity of responses by Christians to Decius' edict?
- ⊙ What diversity of responses do you see among Christians today to the challenges they face in living the Gospel? Give examples.

WHAT ABOUT YOU PERSONALLY?
- ⊙ How boldly do you share your faith in Christ? What motivates you to do so?
- ⊙ What have you learned from the story of

the early Church in Carthage for your own discipleship?

RESPOND WITH FAMILY AND FRIENDS
- ⊙ What situations challenge Christians today to live their faith in Christ?
- ⊙ Choose one of the situations. Decide upon a concrete way you can work together to bring the Gospel to that situation.

WHAT WILL YOU DO NOW?
- ⊙ What commitments are you willing to make to respond to the call of the Holy Spirit to proclaim the Gospel?

LEARN BY HEART

[B]e strong in the Lord and in the strength of his power.

EPHESIANS 6:10

PRAYER REFLECTION

Pray the Sign of the Cross together.

LEADER
In the quiet of our heart, let us pray:

ALL
Lord, make me an instrument of your peace;
  where there is hatred, let me sow love;
  where there is injury, pardon;
  where there is doubt, faith;
  where there is despair, hope;
  where there is darkness, light;
  where there is sadness, joy.

LEADER
Lord, help us make those changes that will
enable us to be instruments of your peace in the
world.
Come, Holy Spirit, help us to sow:
  love where there is hatred;
  pardon where there is injury.

*All quietly reflect on how you can be sowers of love
and pardon (forgiveness).*

LEADER
Lord, help us make those changes that will
enable us to be instruments of your peace in the
world.
Come, Holy Spirit, help us to sow:
  faith where there is doubt;
  hope where there is despair.

*All quietly reflect on how you can be sowers of faith
and hope.*

LEADER
Lord, help us make those changes that will
enable us to be instruments of your peace in the
world.
Come, Holy Spirit, help us to sow:
  light where there is darkness;
  joy where there is sadness.

*All quietly reflect on how you can be sowers of light
and joy.*

LEADER
Let us join together and pray.

ALL
O divine Master, grant that I may not so much
seek
  to be consoled as to console;
  to be understood as to understand;
  to be loved as to love;
for it is in giving that we receive,
  it is in pardoning that we are pardoned,
  and it is in dying that we are born to eternal
    life.

*Exchange a sign of peace and then pray the Sign of
the Cross together.*

All quietly reflect on how you can be sowers of faith and hope

Filled with the Holy Spirit

GOD **LOVES** THE WORLD

GOD HAS **SAVED** THE WORLD IN CHRIST

THE BLOOD OF MARTYRS IS **THE SEED** OF THE CHURCH

THE SPIRIT OF TRUTH AND LOVE IS AT WORK IN THE CHURCH

THE HOLY SPIRIT **BLESSES THE CHURCH** WITH SPECIAL GIFTS, CALLED CHARISMS

THE SEVEN GIFTS OF THE HOLY SPIRIT HELP US **LIVE AS DISCIPLES** OF JESUS

THE FRUITS OF THE HOLY SPIRIT ARE SIGNS THAT **WE ARE COOPERATING** WITH THE HOLY SPIRIT

THE HOLY SPIRIT IS ALWAYS PRESENT AND WORKING in the whole Church and in every one of her members. In this chapter we continue our exploration of the teachings of Scripture and Tradition on this truth of faith. The Holy Spirit, the third divine Person of the Holy Trinity, is the giver of life and our Advocate and Teacher. The Spirit of Christ builds, animates and sanctifies the Church with spiritual gifts. These gifts, or graces, serve the common good of building up the Church.

GIFTS OF THE SPIRIT

GIFTS FOR GROWING OUR MINDS

GIFTS FOR MAKING GOOD AND WISE JUDGMENTS

GIFTS FOR IMPLEMENTING GOOD AND WISE DECISIONS

Faith Focus: The teachings of the Catholic Church that are the primary focus of the doctrinal content presented in this chapter include:

- ◉ The Holy Spirit is present in the entire Church.
- ◉ The Holy Spirit blessed the Church with leadership and other charisms to help her accomplish her mission.
- ◉ The Holy Spirit's gifts help the Church fulfill her mission.
- ◉ The Holy Spirit inspired the Apostles' mission.
- ◉ The Holy Spirit's gifts strengthen and guide the baptized to live as faithful disciples of Jesus and of the Church, the community of Jesus' disciples.
- ◉ The fruits of the Holy Spirit are signs that we are cooperating with the Holy Spirit.
- ◉ The blood of martyrs is the seed of the Church.

Discipleship Formation: As a result of studying this chapter and discovering the meaning of the faith of the Catholic Church for your life, you should be better able to:

- ◉ be more discerning of the presence and activity of the Holy Spirit in your life;
- ◉ value your role in God's ongoing work of salvation and redemption;
- ◉ nourish and strengthen your faith from the example of the first disciples;
- ◉ identify the graces you have been given to take up the work of the Church;
- ◉ recognize and respond to situations in need of the fruits and gifts and of the Holy Spirit.

Scripture References: These Scripture references are quoted or referred to in this chapter:
OLD TESTAMENT: 2 Samuel 7:14, 16, 30–34; **Psalms** 4:2, 6:3, 9:14, 25:11, 119:7, 62 and 106, 121:3; **Isaiah** 33:2; **Tobit** 8:10
NEW TESTAMENT: Matthew 7:20, 9:27, 15:22, 20:3; **Mark** 10:47; **Luke** 1:4, 16:24, 17:13; **John** 1:14, 3:1–21, 10:10, 12:24, 13:31–35, 20:19; **Acts of the Apostles** 1:3–5, 8–9, 12–13, and 21–26, 2:2–4, 14–36, 39 and 47, 4:13, 32–36 and 38–39, 6:1—7:53, 8:1, 9:19b–22, 11:19, 12:1–2, 18:12;
1 Corinthians 13:4–7; **1 Timothy** 2:4; **1 John** 3:11, 13–14 and 18, 4:8 and 16

Faith Glossary: Familiarize yourself with the meaning of these key terms. Definitions are found in the Glossary: **charism, conscience, fruits of the Holy Spirit, gifts of the Holy Spirit, grace, Holy Spirit, Holy Trinity, martyr, mercy, passions (moral), Pentecost, salvation**

Faith Word: charism
Learn by Heart: Acts of the Apostles 2:39
Learn by Example: Blessed Mother Teresa of Calcutta

What is God's relationship with the world?

Many people in the 1980s joined in singing the popular song 'Kyrie'. The praying of the supplication *Kyrie, eleison* at the beginning of Mass has a long tradition in the Liturgy of the Church. We find its earliest use in the late-fourth-century collection of treatises, the *Apostolic Constitutions*. This same supplication can be found in the Old Testament (see Psalms 4:2, 6:3, 9:14, 25:11, 121:3; Isaiah 33:2; Tobit 8:10) as well as in the New Testament (see Matthew 9:27, 15:22, 20:30; Mark 10:47; Luke 16:24, 17:13). We continue this tradition today during the Penitential Act of the Introductory Rites of the Mass. The words *Kyrie, eleison* mean 'Lord, have mercy'. When we sing or pray aloud *Kyrie, eleison*, we acknowledge God's presence with us and seek his direction and guidance for our lives. We petition God for all we need to turn our lives toward him and respond to his loving mercy.

OPENING REFLECTION

⊙ When might you have called out, 'Lord, have mercy'?

⊙ What moves you to reach out to God at those times in your life?

REBORN OF THE HOLY SPIRIT

In John's Gospel we read about Nicodemus, a Pharisee, who came to speak with Jesus in the darkness of the night. Obviously something was stirring in Nicodemus and he wanted to come to know more about the rabbi Jesus.

NICODEMUS SEEKS JESUS BY NIGHT | ENGRAVING AFTER ALEXANDRE BIDA

POPE BENEDICT XVI IN 2013

LET'S PROBE DEEPER

⊙ Read John 3:1–21, the Gospel narrative describing the encounter between Jesus and Nicodemus.

⊙ What did Jesus say about the meaning of his words 'being born of water and the Spirit'?

⊙ What spiritual wisdom for your life did you learn from the conversation between Jesus and Nicodemus?

WHAT ABOUT YOU PERSONALLY?

⊙ What might the **Holy Spirit** be 'stirring' you to do and to be?

⊙ What do you find most challenging?

GOD'S SPIRIT IN THE WORLD

Salvation in Christ is God's greatest work of **mercy**. While we attribute the divine work of salvation to Christ, it is really the work of the **Holy Trinity**. God the Holy Trinity is the God of mercy. The three divine Persons of the Holy Trinity are one God. While the three divine Persons of the Holy Trinity are distinct from one another, they are inseparable in their work.

One striking point from Jesus' conversation with the Pharisee Nicodemus is that God's love and mercy extend to the whole human race. God saves the whole world, all he created—everyone and everything, every person and every culture—in Christ, who is the fullness of '**grace** and truth' (John 1:14). God 'desires everyone to be saved and to come to the knowledge of the truth' (1 Timothy 2:4) and 'God wills the salvation of everyone through the knowledge of the truth' (*Catechism of the Catholic Church* [CCC], no. 851).

Salvation is God's greatest work of 'mercy'. The biblical words (both Hebrew and Greek) that are translated into the English word 'mercy' have multiple meanings. At the heart of all these meanings is the undeserved love of God for humanity and that the merciful love of God is the foundation of the covenant relationship that God freely entered into with his people and with all of humanity in Christ.

While salvation is already accomplished through the merciful events of Jesus' life, and of his Paschal Mystery, namely, his Passion, Death, Resurrection and Ascension, the saving work of God is 'not yet' complete. The 'not yet' refers to the reality that history is still moving toward its final fulfillment, when the reign of God will be fully realized 'on earth as it is in heaven'. Reflecting on this truth of our faith, Pope Benedict XVI wrote: 'The kingdom of Jesus, Son of David, knows no end because in him God

What experiences or situations reflect an 'unredeemed' world?

is reigning, in him God's kingdom erupts into this world' (*Jesus of Nazareth: The Infancy Narratives*).

Christ has willed that the Catholic Church be his sacrament of salvation, the sign and instrument of the communion of God and the human race. Christ has sent the Church on mission to the whole world. The Spirit of Christ now fills the Church and the world and invites all people to the living waters of salvation and to the fullness of life in the Kingdom of God.

THINK, PAIR AND SHARE
- When you look around at the 'unredeemed' state of things, it can be difficult to understand that God has saved and redeemed the world in Christ.
- Name one or two experiences or situations that reflect an 'unredeemed' world. What reasons can you identify for this?
- God has saved the world in Christ. Why then is so much of the world 'seemingly' unsaved?

- What do you think the role of young Catholics and of other Christian youth is in God's ongoing work of salvation and redemption?

OVER TO YOU
- Reflect on these words from the Fourth Gospel: 'The thief comes only to steal and kill and destroy. I came that they may have life, and have it abundantly' (John 10:10).
- What could the Holy Spirit be stirring you to do to 'be a giver of life' to others?
- Who can you invite to join you in that work?

JOURNAL EXERCISE
- There is also much in the world that manifests the saving grace of God in Jesus. Think of experiences of goodness and joy.
- Describe how you think the Spirit of mercy might be moving in your family or in your school or in our culture and society.
- What is your response to that movement?

The power and guidance of the Spirit

St. Peter and the other Apostles were, on the surface, not the most promising group for Jesus to choose to lead the transformation of the world that he inaugurated. You will recall that after the Death and burial of Jesus, his disciples, fearful that they too might be arrested, suffer and even be killed, had locked themselves in an upper room of a home in Jerusalem (see John 20:19). The disciples' experience of **Pentecost**, as we saw in chapter 1, turned that fear into a courage which the Acts of the Apostles describes as 'bold'.

OPENING REFLECTION
⊙ When was the last time you felt afraid? What did you fear?
⊙ Do you ever fear to live your faith in Christ? Why is that?
⊙ What can you do to overcome your fear?

The Rushing Wind: Pentecost

Let us look more deeply into that Pentecost event. Following the Resurrection, there was a forty-day period when the risen Christ appeared to the Apostles and other disciples on a number of occasions. During those forty days before the Ascension, he prepared the Apostles for the mission he was to give them. Luke tells us:

After his suffering he presented himself alive to them by many convincing proofs, appearing to them over the course of forty days and speaking to them about the kingdom of God. While staying with them, he ordered them not to leave Jerusalem, but to wait there for the promise of the Father. 'This', he said, 'is what you have heard from me; for John baptized with water, but you will be baptized with the Holy Spirit not many days from now. . . . [Y]ou will receive power when the Holy Spirit has come upon you; and you will be my witnesses in Jerusalem, in all Judea and Samaria, and to the ends of the earth.' When he had said this, as they were watching, he was lifted up, and a cloud took him out of their sight. . . . Then they returned to Jerusalem from the mount called Olivet, which is near Jerusalem, a sabbath day's journey away. When they had entered the city, they went to the room upstairs where they were staying.
—Acts of the Apostles 1:3–5, 8–9, 12–13

For the next ten days the Apostles, Mary the Mother of Jesus and other disciples devoted themselves to prayer while they were awaiting the fulfillment of Jesus' promise to send them the Holy Spirit. They also chose Matthias to take the place of Judas Iscariot in ministry as an apostle. (Read Acts of the Apostles 1:21–26.) Then at nine o'clock in the morning on the Jewish feast of Pentecost, there 'came a sound like the rush of a violent wind, and it filled the entire house where they were sitting. Divided tongues, as of fire, appeared among them, and a tongue rested on each of them. All of them were filled with the Holy Spirit and began to speak in other languages, as the Spirit gave them ability' (Acts of the Apostles 2:2–4).

THE HOLY SPIRIT AT PENTECOST | 17TH-CENTURY ROMAN COIN

PENTECOST | PERE NICOLAU

LET'S PROBE DEEPER

- ⊙ Read Acts of the Apostles 2:4–13.
- ⊙ Now, imagine yourself being in the upper room. Describe your experience of the Holy Spirit.
- ⊙ How can the Holy Spirit help you face your fears with confidence and imagine creative ways of dealing with them?

FROM THE WISDOM OF THE CHURCH

'The Holy Spirit' is the proper name of the third Person of the Most Holy Trinity. Jesus also called him the Paraclete (Consoler or Advocate) and the Spirit of Truth. The New Testament also refers to him as the Spirit of Christ, of the Lord, of God—the Spirit of Glory and the Spirit of the Promise.

—*Compendium of the Catechism of the Catholic Church*, no. 138

THE ADVOCATE AND TEACHER

Recall Pope St. John Paul II's teaching that the Holy Spirit 'is the principal agent of the whole of the Church's mission' (*The Mission of the Redeemer*, no. 21). Transformed by the Holy Spirit, St. Peter and the others left the upper room. They fearlessly entered the marketplace, which was filled with Jewish pilgrims from all over the then-known world who had come to Jerusalem to celebrate Pentecost. This feast is known to Jews as *Shavu'ot*. On *Shavu'ot* Jews commemorate both the giving of the Torah to Moses and the harvest of the first fruits.

It was during the celebration of Pentecost, you will recall from chapter 1, that St. Peter and the other Apostles began the work Jesus had given them. They boldly faced their fellow Jews whom they had feared just fifty days earlier. Peter, referring to the Hebrew Scriptures as evidence for the claims he was making about Jesus, proclaimed the crucified Jesus to be the descendant of King David—the One spoken of beforehand in their Scriptures (check out 2 Samuel 7:14, 16, 30–34), and who now had risen from the dead. Peter declared:

This Jesus God raised up, and of that all of us are witnesses. Being therefore exalted at the right hand of God, and having received from the Father the promise of the Holy Spirit, he has poured out this that you both see and hear. . . . Therefore let the entire house of Israel know with certainty that God has made him both Lord and Messiah.

—Acts of the Apostles 2:32–33, 36

And when Peter and the other Apostles were asked, 'Brothers, what should we do?', Peter responded:

'Repent, and be baptized every one of you in the name of Jesus Christ so that your sins may be forgiven; and you will receive the gift of the Holy Spirit. For the promise is for you, for your children, and for all who are far away, everyone whom the Lord our God calls to him.'

—Acts of the Apostles 2:38–39

Luke's Gospel begins in Bethlehem and concludes with the Death, Resurrection and Ascension of Jesus in Jerusalem. Luke's Acts of the Apostles reports the preaching of Peter and Paul from Jerusalem, the center of Judaism, to Rome, the center of the world in the first century AD.

READ, REFLECT AND SHARE
- Read and reflect on St. Peter's address to the crowd in Acts of the Apostles 2:14–36.

- What stands out for you in this passage?
- How did the opinion of the crowd about Peter and the disciples change during Peter's address to them?
- Share your reflections with a partner or small group.

OVER TO YOU
In Baptism we are reborn of water and the Spirit and we first receive the gift of the Holy Spirit. But some see the celebration of the Sacrament of Confirmation as a 'Pentecost' event, the coming of the Holy Spirit into our lives. In Confirmation the graces of our Baptism are strengthened.
- Recall your understanding of your Confirmation. How did you experience the gift and presence of the Holy Spirit?
- Did your Confirmation empower you to give witness to Jesus? Explain.
- How often do you pray to the Holy Spirit, your Advocate and Teacher? Why is that?

ST. PETER PREACHING IN THE PRESENCE OF ST. MARK | FRA ANGELICO

TO THE ENDS OF THE EARTH AND TO ALL PEOPLE

Luke wrote his account of the Gospel and his Acts of the Apostles so that we might know the truth about Jesus (see Luke 1:4). Luke–Acts is the account of the Son of God becoming incarnate of the Virgin Mary by the power of the Holy Spirit, and how that same Spirit transformed a group of sometimes fearful folk into a bold, focused community of visionaries and missionaries. Luke–Acts is the inspiring adventure story of the early Church's love for the Lord and for one another. It announces the beginning of the final stage, the final days, of the transformation of the world. Pope Benedict XVI, reflecting on the teaching in Luke's account of the Gospel, wrote: 'Jesus takes upon himself the whole of humanity, the whole history of man, and he gives it a decisive reorientation toward a new manner of human existence' (*Jesus of Nazareth: The Infancy Narratives*).

WHAT ABOUT YOU PERSONALLY?

- How does your faith in Christ give meaning to your life?
- What have you done so far to take part in the Church's work of transforming the world?

Luke wrote his account of the Gospel and his Acts of the Apostles so that we might know the truth about Jesus

LUKE THE EVANGELIST | ENGRAVING AFTER JULIUS SCHNORR VON CAROLSFELD

The Spirit of Truth and Love

What drove Saints Peter and Paul, their companions and the early Church to proclaim Jesus so boldly and with such zeal, even when threatened with death? Tertullian (c. AD 160–c. 220), the first Christian writer to write in Latin, explained it this way in his treatise *Apologetics*: '*Vide, ut invicem se diligant*', which means, 'See, how they love one another'. The early Church clearly took to heart Jesus' New Commandment: '[L]ove one another. Just as I have loved you, you also should love one another. By this everyone will know that you are my disciples, if you have love for one another' (John 13:34–35).

OPENING REFLECTION

⊙ From your personal experiences, how would you define love?
⊙ Where in your own life do you experience love as you define it?

PROBE DEEPER

⊙ Now, read 1 Corinthians 13:4–7 and 1 John 3:11, 13–14, 18.
⊙ How does your understanding of love stack up against the descriptions in 1 Corinthians and 1 John?
⊙ Where are you strongest in your own capacity to love in this way? Where are you in need of growth?

FROM THE WISDOM OF THE CHURCH

God revealed himself to Israel as the One who has a stronger love than that of parents for their children or of husbands and wives for their spouses. God himself 'is love' (1 John 4:8, 16), who gives himself completely and gratuitously, who 'so loved the world that he gave his only Son so that the world might be saved through him' (John 3:16–17). By sending his Son and the Holy Spirit, God reveals that he himself is an eternal exchange of love.

—*Compendium of the Catechism of the Catholic Church*, no. 42

STUDY IN CONTRASTS: CHRISTIAN LOVE IN A CRUEL WORLD

The Church is the way of salvation willed by God. God desires and wills that all humanity form and live as the one family, the one People of God. The same Spirit of Truth and Love who animated and guided and strengthened St. Peter, St. Paul and the early Church continues to work in and through the Church today to bring about God's will for humanity. Christ's New Commandment of love (see John 13:34–35) drives that work of the Church. The Christ-like love that distinguished the early Church from other societies was practical, authentic and self-sacrificing. Luke writes:

> There was not a needy person among [the Christians], for as many as owned lands or houses sold them and brought the proceeds of what was sold. They laid it at the apostles' feet, and it was distributed to each as any had need. . . . And day by day the Lord added to their number those who were being saved.
> —Acts of the Apostles 4:34–35; 2:47

The Spirit of Christ at work in the early Church stood in stark contrast to the harshness of the first-century Greco-Roman world. In this historical period the majority of the citizens of the Empire lacked many of the basic necessities of life, things that most people living in the United States of America have come to expect. One biblical scholar, Justin Meggitt, proposes that ninety-nine percent of the population of that first-century Greco-Roman society was destitute. They 'lived subsistence or near subsistence lives, in which access to necessities was inadequate and precarious' and their lives were 'dominated by the struggle for physical survival'. These desperate realities of everyday life encouraged people to develop three survival attitudes, namely:

- an intense competition for scarce resources;
- a 'zero-sum' belief that 'your gain is my loss', and the corollary, 'for me to win, you have to lose';
- an attitude of self-interest, creating a society of opportunists seeking the fulfillment of their own needs and interests.

Seven Popular Survival Rules in the Greco-Roman World

GLADIATORIAL COMBAT | ROMAN MOSAIC

- Help your friends, harm your enemies.
- Ritually curse important rivals.
- Seek first your own needs and interests.
- Do not meet the needs of others unless there is profit in it for you.
- To have nothing is to be nothing.
- To have status and wealth is to have honor.
- Do to others as they do to you.

Gospel Values for a Thriving World

- Love your enemies.
- Do good to those who hate you.
- Bless those who curse you.
- Forgive those who harm you.
- Give to everyone who reaches out for help.
- Seek the advantage of others before seeking your own advantage.
- Honor is not in having (things) but in being (a child of God).
- Do unto others as you would have them do to you.

JESUS HEALS A LEPER | ENGRAVING AFTER ALEXANDRE BIDA

TALK IT OVER

- Where do you see the three 'survival' attitudes and policies of the Greco-Roman world mirrored in the world today?
- Where do you see the Church working against attitudes and policies that result in people not having the basic necessities of life? Be as specific as possible?
- How and where are Catholic youth joining in those efforts?

WHAT ABOUT YOU PERSONALLY?

- Think about situations in your life that involve you in competition. The English word 'competition' comes from the Latin *cum* and *petire*, which means 'to seek with'. Does that seem like an 'unreal' description of competition? Explain.
- When have you had a choice either to compete against someone or cooperate with that person? What was your choice? And how did it work out?

The blood of martyrs, the seed of the Church

THE STONING AND BURIAL OF ST. STEPHEN (DETAIL) | MARIOTTO DI NARDO

Recall Tertullian's description of the hallmark of the life of the early Church, 'See, how they love one another'. Tertullian lived at a time when many Christians willingly chose to die for their faith in and love for Christ. Tertullian identified this self-sacrificing love as the reason for the growth of the Church. He wrote, 'The blood of **martyrs** is the seed [of the Church].'

OPENING CONVERSATION
- What is 'blood' a symbol for?
- Why did the example of martyrs lead so many others to Christ?

OVER TO YOU
- What do you see as the most difficult challenge of living Jesus' command '[L]ove one another. Just as I have loved you, you also should love one another. By this everyone will know that you are my disciples, if you have love for one another' (John 13:34–35)?
- What sacrifices would you be prepared to make to meet that challenge?

THE BLOOD OF MARTYRS, THE SEED OF THE CHURCH

The early Church emerged in two societies, Jewish and Roman, whose leaders actively and aggressively sought to persecute and suppress the Church. For example, we read of two such incidents in the Acts of the Apostles: the martyrdom of St. Stephen and of St. James the Apostle.

Acts of the Apostles 6:1—7:53 tells the story of St. Stephen, deacon and first martyr of the Church, whose feast the Catholic Church celebrates each year on December 26. When he steadfastly refused to deny Christ and boldly professed his faith in Christ, Stephen was arrested, dragged out of Jerusalem and stoned to death.

Acts 12 gives the account of the violent death of St. James the Apostle—also known as James the Greater, or James the Elder, the son of Zebedee and brother of St. John—at the hand of Herod Agrippa I, King of Judea from AD 41 to 44. We read:

King Herod laid violent hands upon some of who belonged to the church. He had James, the brother of John, killed with a sword. After he saw that it pleased the Jews, he proceeded to arrest Peter also.

—Acts of the Apostles 12:1–2

The Roman historian Suetonius (b. AD 69) tells us that when Jewish disciples of Jesus began preaching the Gospel in Rome, the larger Jewish community considered them to be heretics and a threat to Judaism. (The Evangelist Luke also tells about this situation in Acts of the Apostles 18:12.) Suetonius wrote: 'Because the Jews at Rome caused continuous disturbances at the instigation of *Chrestus*, he [Emperor Claudius] expelled them from the city.' *'Chrestus'* is Suetonius' transliteration of 'Christ'. Opposition to Christians was further strengthened because many Christians also publicly refused to worship and offer sacrifice to the Emperor and the other gods of the Roman Pantheon. These acts of civil disobedience and defiance of Roman law were another major source for persecution of the early Church. Historians identify at least eight periods of persecution of the early Church.

Despite these early persecutions, the Church continued to spread throughout Judea and Samaria (see Acts of the Apostles 8:1), to Damascus (see Acts of the Apostles 9:19b–22), and as far as Phoenicia, Cyprus and Antioch (see Acts of the Apostles 11:19) and Rome. The blood of the martyrs, which flowed from their self-sacrificing love, was the seed of the Church.

NERO | 1ST CENTURY ROMAN COIN

Persecution Of The Early Church

Historians name ten periods of persecution of the early Church under the Emperors:
- Nero (c. 64–88)
- Domitian (c. 81–96)
- Trajan (112–117)
- Marcus Aurelius (161–180)
- Septimus Severus (202–210)
- Decius (250–251)
- Valerian (257–259)
- Maximinus the Thracian (235–238)
- Aurelian (270–275)
- Diocletian and Galerius (303–324)

READ, REFLECT AND SHARE
- Compare Tertullian's statement 'The blood of martyrs is the seed of the Church' with the words of Jesus to his disciples, 'Very truly, I tell you, unless a grain of wheat falls into the earth and dies, it remains just a single grain; but if it dies, it bears much fruit' (John 12:24).
- Why is dying for one's faith in Christ a sign of Christ-like love?

CHARISMS, GRACES OF THE HOLY SPIRIT
Strengthened and guided by the Spirit of Truth and Love, the Church lives out Jesus' radical New Commandment to love others, even one's enemies. Meeting the day-to-day practical challenges of living this commandment requires the help and **gifts of the Holy Spirit**. (*Turn to page 262 of this text and review your understanding of the gifts of the Holy Spirit.*)

Let us draw on an analogy from nature to explore the meaning of the role of the sevenfold Gift of the Holy Spirit in our lives. A fruit tree exists to bear fruit. But it cannot do so without certain gifts that it has no control over receiving. Among these gifts are sunlight, rain and fertile soil. The orchard farmer does not provide the sun, rain and soil—these come from God, as does the very life of the tree and of the farmer. But the

Charism

A specific gift or grace of the Holy Spirit which directly or indirectly benefits the Church, given in order to help a person live out the Christian life, or to serve the common good in building up the Church.

—CCC, Glossary

farmer can increase the stability and quality of the gifts and so ensure a good harvest of fruit. The farmer can provide water through irrigation during dry spells, and manage land in other ways that keep the soil healthy and vibrant. Given the right balance of these and other 'gifts', the tree can thrive and produce abundant fruit.

The Church, the new People of God, is *both* the tree and the farmer. The faithful are stewards of the gift of spiritual life that we receive from God. God provides the gifts that we need in order to grow and thrive and bear fruit. The Holy Spirit blesses the Church and her members with **charisms**, or special graces, that enable the members of the Church to build up the Church. The Spirit gives unique charisms to the hierarchy; to members of the consecrated life; and to the laity, single and married. All members of the Church are responsible for bearing 'fruit'. Each one of us is responsible for cultivating the soil of our heart, for letting cool waters nourish the roots of our soul, and for letting the sun shine into our mind for the renewing of our whole person.

JOURNAL EXERCISE

⊙ Write about the special graces you have been given to take up your work in the Church.

The Seven Gifts of the Holy Spirit at Work in Our Lives

At Baptism we are joined to Christ and become adopted sons and daughters of the Father and temples of the Holy Spirit. Every member of the Church is blessed at Baptism with the sevenfold Gift of the Holy Spirit. These seven gifts are special graces that help us live our daily lives as disciples of Jesus. They are the gifts of Wisdom and Understanding, of Counsel (Right Judgment) and Fortitude (Courage), of Knowledge and of Piety (Reverence), and of Fear of the Lord (Wonder and Awe). These seven gifts help us live holy and just lives—to bring us into 'right and loving relationship' with God, with ourselves and with others.

St. Thomas Aquinas taught that grace perfects nature. This principle helps us understand the working of the Holy Spirit in our life. Grace sanctifies and restores nature and enables it to attain what it cannot attain on its own. The Holy Spirit both dwells in us and works through us. The gifts of the Holy Spirit work through the ordinary functions of our minds and hearts in the ordinary issues of life.

Let us take a brief look at the seven gifts of the Holy Spirit as they are named by the Church and explained by St. Thomas Aquinas in his

Summa Theologiae. Aquinas teaches that two of the gifts have to do with growing our minds, two with understanding and good judgment, the last three with carrying out good decisions.

GIFTS FOR GROWING OUR MINDS

Counsel (Right Judgment) and Understanding: These two gifts have to do with insight, with 'getting it', or seeing things for ourselves. *Counsel* enables us to function in the midst of practical, everyday experiences, something similar to common sense. *Understanding* helps us to probe and go beyond the obvious and comprehend the deeper meaning of things. We collaborate with the Holy Spirit and use the gifts of Counsel and Understanding when we pay attention to everyday experiences and 'use our heads' to understand ourselves and what's going on around us.

GIFTS FOR MAKING GOOD AND WISE JUDGMENTS

Wisdom and Knowledge: These two gifts move us beyond Understanding and Counsel and strengthen our ability to figure out what is wise and what is true. While Understanding and Counsel help us answer such questions as 'Who?', 'What?', 'Where?', 'When?', 'How?' and 'Why?', they do not strengthen us to answer questions such as 'Is it true?', 'Is it real?', 'Is it right or wrong?', 'Is it good?'. These are questions for Wisdom and Knowledge. These two gifts sharpen our mind and our **conscience** to discern good from evil so that we may walk in the path of righteousness and live holy and just lives. (Read Psalm 119:7, 62, 106.)

Wisdom and Knowledge work hand in hand, helping us make good judgments and decisions.

The gifts of the Holy Spirit work through the ordinary functions of our minds and hearts in the ordinary issues of life

Informed by Christian faith, we try to make the best judgments and decisions

We use these two gifts and collaborate with the promptings of the Holy Spirit when we deliberate, weigh evidence, calculate consequences, seek good advice, and recognize what is right and wrong, good and evil, true and false. Informed by Christian faith, we try to make the best judgments and decisions.

GIFTS FOR IMPLEMENTING GOOD AND WISE DECISIONS

Courage (Fortitude), Piety (Reverence) and Fear of the Lord (Wonder and Awe): These three gifts have to do with implementing good decisions. *Courage* enables us to stand up for what is true and good in the face of fear and danger and enhances our sense of self-worth and dignity. It helps us always to do what will be most pleasing to God. *Piety* directs our hearts to respond to the image of God in every human being and generates a sense of reverence for others. *Fear of the Lord* does not mean being 'afraid' of God. The biblical expression 'fear of the Lord' means having great reverence for God, being awestruck at the amazing gift of God's unconditional love. In this sense, Fear of the Lord enhances our reverence for God and for all of God's people. It helps us discipline our **passions** (our emotions and feelings) and our desires out of a heartfelt concern not to offend God and his love for us.

OVER TO YOU

- ⊙ Which of the gifts of the Holy Spirit do you need to deepen your relationship with God? Why?
- ⊙ What gifts of the Spirit do you need to improve your relationships with family, friends and others? Why?
- ⊙ What gifts of the Spirit do you need to love yourself appropriately? Why?

REFLECT ON WHAT YOU HAVE LEARNED IN THIS CHAPTER

As you come toward the end of this chapter, pause and reflect on what you have come to understand to be the mission of the Holy Spirit in the life of the Church. Share the teachings of the Catholic Church on these statements:

- Salvation is the work of the Holy Trinity.
- The Spirit of Christ, the Holy Spirit, fills the Church and the world.
- The Holy Spirit is the principal agent of the Church's mission.
- The Holy Spirit blesses the Church with charisms to fulfill her mission.
- The seven gifts of the Holy Spirit help us live as disciples of Jesus Christ.
- Jesus' New Commandment, '[L]ove one another. Just as I have loved you, you also should love one another' (John 13:34), is the heart of living as his disciples.
- The blood of martyrs is the seed of the Church.

OVER TO YOU

- What one important decision might you make based on what you have learned in this chapter?

YOU WILL KNOW THEM BY THEIR FRUITS (MATTHEW 7:20)

Jesus used the example of fruit trees to teach that we can come to know the quality of people's lives, beginning with our own, by the 'fruits' that they bring forth. When we collaborate with the Holy Spirit, we inevitably bear good fruit.

St. Paul contrasted the 'fruits of the Spirit' with the 'works of the flesh'. By this comparison he did not intend to demean the human body, which he valued as a 'temple of the Holy Spirit' (1 Corinthians 6:19). Paul refers to 'the flesh' to name the times when we act only out of self-interest and not with the strength and guidance of the Spirit of Truth and Love—when we turn our backs on God's grace.

What are these good fruits? Building on the 'fruits' that St. Paul names in Galatians 5:22, the Catholic Church names twelve **fruits of the Holy Spirit**. They are love, joy, peace, patience, kindness, goodness, generosity, faithfulness, gentleness, modesty, self-control and chastity. These are the signs that we are cooperating with the Holy Spirit.

ST. PAUL | VATICAN CITY

OVER TO YOU

⊙ Where do you see evidence of the fruits of the Holy Spirit in your life? Rank the fruits of the Holy Spirit according to how you see them in your own life. Give reasons for the order in which you ranked them.

LEARN BY EXAMPLE

Blessed Mother Teresa of Calcutta, who showed the fruits of the Spirit of Love at work among the poorest of the poor

The Christ-like love that drove the early Church was both practical and authentic. Guided by the Holy Spirit, Christians today continue to demonstrate this practical and authentic love. Blessed Mother Teresa of Calcutta is one such example.

Agnes Gonxha Bojaxhiu was born in Macedonia, a small country in Eastern Europe, in 1910. As a young girl Agnes became interested in the work of missionaries and, when she was eighteen, she responded to the call of the Holy Spirit to become a missionary nun. She joined the Sisters of Loreto, an Irish community of nuns with missions in India. After a few months' training in Dublin, Ireland, she was sent to India, where on May 24, 1931 she took her initial vows as a nun. From 1931 to 1948 Mother Teresa—as she came to be known—taught geography and theology at St. Mary's High School, Calcutta, India, but she soon realized that the Holy Spirit was calling her to serve the Church in a different way. She obtained permission from her superiors to leave the convent school and devote herself to working among the poorest of the poor. So, together with a group of her former pupils, she started an open-air school in the slums of Calcutta. There she found people living in absolute destitution, with no healthcare facilities, and many were often left to die on the street.

Mother Teresa and her companions were compelled to action by the grace for making good and wise judgments and the grace for implementing good and wise decisions. They began 'Homes for the Dying' and committed themselves to caring for people whom nobody else was prepared to look after. More and more women came to join them in their efforts and, in 1950, the Church officially established them as a religious congregation, to be known as the Missionaries of Charity.

By the time of Mother Teresa's death in 1997, there were over four thousand sisters in the Missionaries of Charity. Today, the Missionaries of Charity comprises Active and Contemplative branches of Sisters and Brothers in more than one hundred countries, caring for the poor, people with HIV/AIDS and other illnesses, and running schools, orphanages and soup kitchens.

During her lifetime, Mother Teresa was awarded numerous accolades for her work, including the Nobel Peace Prize in 1979. She was beatified by Pope St. John Paul II in 2003, and is now known as Blessed Mother Teresa of Calcutta.

TALK IT OVER

- What do you find most inspiring for your own life from the example of Blessed Mother Teresa of Calcutta?
- Where do you see signs that people are cooperating with the Holy Spirit and responding to situations of injustice?
- What gifts of the Holy Spirit might help you in such situations?

WHAT ABOUT YOU PERSONALLY?

- When did you ever feel moved by the Spirit of Truth and Love to act when you faced situations of injustice?
- What gift or gifts of the Holy Spirit would empower you to act in such situations?
- Pray together, 'Come, Holy Spirit, fill us with the fire of your love.'

RESPOND WITH FAMILY AND FRIENDS

- What one gift of the Holy Spirit would help deepen the transformation of your lives into living as a more authentic community of Jesus' disciples?
- Share how you would put that gift of the Spirit into action.

DECIDE AND ACT

- Identify a situation in your neighborhood or school in need of the transforming power of the gifts of the Holy Spirit. Share how responding to the Holy Spirit might lead to the transformation of that situation.
- Which of the fruits of the Holy Spirit would show that the Holy Spirit is at work transforming the situation?

LEARN BY HEART

[T]he promise is for you, for your children, and for all who are far away, everyone whom the Lord our God calls to him.

ACTS OF THE APOSTLES 2:39

PRAYER REFLECTION

Pray the Sign of the Cross together.

LEADER

The Holy Spirit, our Advocate and Teacher, is always at work in the Church. The Spirit of Truth and Love dwells within the whole Church and within every member of the Church.

Let us place our self in the presence of the Holy Spirit and
- give thanks for the gift of this past day; (*Pause*)
- recognize where the Holy Spirit was active in our life; (*Pause*)
- review how we responded to the Spirit's promptings. (*Pause*)

Let us now ask the Spirit of Truth and Love to help us raise up our minds and hearts in prayer.

GROUP 1

O Lord, you have searched me and you know me.
You know when I sit down and when I stand up.

GROUP 2

You discern my innermost and most secret thoughts.
You are acquainted with all my ways.

ALL

Come, Holy Spirit,
fill me with the fire of your love.

GROUP 1

Even before a word is on my tongue, O Lord, you
    know it completely.
You lay your hand on me.

GROUP 2

Where can I go and be away from you?
Where can I flee from your presence?

ALL

Come, Holy Spirit,
fill me with the fire of your love.

GROUP 1

You formed my inmost parts.
You knit me together in my mother's womb.

GROUP 2

I praise you.
I am wonderfully made.

ALL

Come, Holy Spirit,
fill me with the fire of your love.

LEADER

Let us pray. (*Pause*)
O God, by the light of your Holy Spirit
    you instruct the hearts of your faithful.
Grant that by the same Holy Spirit
    we may be truly wise and ever rejoice in your
        love.
We ask this in the name of Christ our Lord.

ALL

Amen.

Conclude by praying the Sign of the Cross together.

Come, Holy Spirit, fill me with the fire of your love

CHAPTER 3

God Loves All People

THE MYSTERY OF GOD'S UNCONDITIONAL LOVE

GOD'S LOVE IS INFINITE

GOD'S LOVE EXTENDS TO ALL

GOD'S LOVE IS A FREE AND PERMANENT GIFT

WE ARE ALWAYS GOD'S 'BELOVED CHILDREN'

GOD'S LOVE FOR US IS ASSURED IN JESUS

GOD IS LOVE 'EVERLASTING' (ISAIAH 54:8). THE mystery of the universal saving and merciful love of God for all people is revealed most fully in Jesus, the Incarnate Son of God. In this chapter we explore Christ's commissioning of his Apostles and his Church to bring the good news of the mystery of divine love to all people. We explore our need to open our minds, hearts and souls to God so that we can be living images and signs of our God, who is love, to our family, friends and neighbors—and even to those who consider us to be their enemies.

THE GIFT OF CHRISTIAN CONVERSION

CONVERSION OF THE SOUL (RELIGIOUS CONVERSION)

CONVERSION OF THE HEART (MORAL CONVERSION)

CONVERSION OF THE MIND (INTELLECTUAL CONVERSION)

PASSING ON THE APOSTOLIC TRADITION

MISSIONARY JOURNEYS

COUNCIL AT JERUSALEM

THE FOUR WRITTEN ACCOUNTS OF THE GOSPEL

Faith Focus: The teachings of the Catholic Church that are the primary focus of the doctrinal content presented in this chapter include:

⊙ God's very being is truth and love.
⊙ Jesus Christ, the Incarnate Son of God, most fully reveals God and his loving plan of goodness and salvation.
⊙ Christ established his Church to continue his presence and work.
⊙ The Church is the sacrament of the Holy Trinity's communion with humanity.
⊙ The Church in this world is the sacrament of salvation, the sign and instrument of the communion of God and humanity.
⊙ All people are called to belong to the People of God by faith and Baptism.
⊙ God desires all people to come to knowledge of the truth and be saved.

Discipleship Formation: As a result of studying this chapter and discovering the meaning of the faith of the Catholic Church for your life, you should be better able to:

⊙ value mission as integral to giving witness to Christ;
⊙ realize your need for conversion of your soul, heart and mind;
⊙ be inspired by the witness of St. Peter to his faith in Jesus Christ;
⊙ be motivated by the life, ministry and mission of St. Paul;
⊙ discern the presence and activity of the Holy Spirit in your life and in the world around you;
⊙ respond to people who are marginalized and neglected by society.

Scripture References: These Scripture references are quoted or referred to in this chapter:
OLD TESTAMENT: Psalms 51:17; **Isaiah** 54:8
NEW TESTAMENT: Matthew 1:1–17, 22:34–37; **Luke** 3:23–38, 15:11–32; **John** 6:44, 12:32, 14:25–26; **Acts of the Apostles** 2:22–36, 9:1–22, 10:1—11:18, 13:1—14:28, 15:7–9, 13, 19–20, 15:36—18:22, 18:23—21:15, 22:4–16, 26:9–18; **Romans** 1:16, 8:38–39, 12:1–2; **1 Corinthians** 11:25; **2 Corinthians** 1:20, 3:16—4:6, 5:16–17 and 19; **Galatians** 1:13–17, 2:11–21; **Ephesians** 1:9, 2:18; **2 Peter** 1:4; **1 John** 4:10; **Revelation** 7:9

Faith Glossary: Familiarize yourself with the meaning of these key terms. Definitions are found in the Glossary: **apostolic succession, Apostolic Tradition, conversion, Ecumenical Council, Gospel, inspiration, oral tradition, parable, Passion**

Faith Word: conversion
Learn by Heart: Romans 8:38–39
Learn by Example: Pope St. John Paul II

What is the nature of divine love?

When the boy steps up to the counter, he reaches into his pocket and discovers that his two dollars are not there. He begins to cry inconsolably and steps out of the line. Meanwhile, the young man, now with three dollars, orders a triple-scoop cone and sits down to eat it as he watches the boy cry his heart out.

OPENING CONVERSATION

⊙ What is your response to the young man's action?

⊙ How difficult is it for you to look past a person's cruel words or actions and still 'love' him or her as God loves all people, both 'saints' and 'sinners'? Why?

GOD'S INFINITE LOVE

Recall the **parable** of the two sons and the forgiving father in Luke 15:11–32. Jesus told this parable to help people come to understand and be open to experience the mystery of the depth and true nature of divine love. Jesus would most fully reveal God's love by the sacrifice of his life on the Cross for all people.

It is a hot summer day and people are gathering around the Tasty Ice Cream shack. Standing in line is a young man who is poorly dressed. He has one dollar, enough money for a single scoop. Standing in front of him is a six-year-old boy whose mother is watching from the car. She has given her son permission to stand in line by himself for the first time.

Several times the boy checks to make sure that the two dollars his mother has given him are still in the pocket of his pants. Nearing the counter the six-year-old checks one last time, and as he pulls his hand out of the pocket the bills fly out and land on the ground. The man standing behind the boy sees what happens and he quickly picks up the two dollar bills and puts them into his own pocket.

REFLECT AND DISCUSS

Look up Luke 15:11–32 and reread the parable. Then discuss:

⊙ How would you describe how the father treated his younger son?

⊙ How did the elder son think his younger brother deserved to be treated by the father?

⊙ How does the father's love give us a glimpse of God's love?

⊙ What does the elder son's love tell us about human love?

God places no limits on loving us. We are always God's 'beloved children'

OVER TO YOU

⊙ Place yourself in the position of the elder brother. How would you respond to the way you saw your father treating your younger brother on his return home?

⊙ What wisdom for your life do you take away from this parable?

GOD VERSUS 'gods'

Recall what we explored in chapter 2 when we compared the 'Seven Popular Survival Rules in the Greco-Roman World' with the 'Gospel Values for a Thriving World'. Greco-Roman religions professed belief in many realities that they trusted in to be gods. These 'gods' could be whimsical in their dealings with people; and people, as a result, constantly tried to placate and manipulate their gods to keep them 'on their side'.

The **Gospel** and Christianity burst into this culture and preached a radically different God: there is *one* God whose very nature is truth and love and who is *incapable of evil*. God's intentions and desires for people are *always good*. There is no need to question or try to placate and manipulate God. Jesus, the Incarnate Son of God, revealed and assured us of God's love and good will toward us. St. Paul summarized the truth of our faith. He taught:

For I am convinced that neither death, nor life, nor angels, nor rulers, nor things present, nor things to come, nor powers, nor height, nor depth, nor anything else in all creation, will be able to separate us from the love of God in Christ Jesus our Lord.

—Roman 8:38–39

God's love is a totally free and permanent gift. Should we turn our back on God and his love, he waits with open arms for us to come home. True human love gives us but a glimpse into God's love—God places no limits on loving us. We are always God's 'beloved children'. We cannot earn or lose our status as children of God.

WHAT ABOUT YOU PERSONALLY?

⊙ What is your own understanding of God's love?

⊙ How does that understanding reflect Jesus' teaching in Luke 15:11–32 and in St. Paul's teaching in Romans 8:38–39? How is it the same? How is it different?

JOURNAL EXERCISE

⊙ Reflect upon and then write your thoughts on what you might need to change in your understanding about God's love in order to deepen your relationship with God and with family, friends and other people—even those people whom you find it difficult to 'like' or those who find it difficult to like you.

God's love is universal

The Civil Rights Act, passed by Congress and signed by President Lyndon Johnson in 1964, did not end racial tensions in the United States of America. By the late 1960s racial tensions were at a height. The 'Up with People' movement emerged to address the racism at the root of those tensions. The song 'What Color Is God's Skin?' became the movement's hallmark. Hearing and singing those simple words moved many Americans to pause and reflect, and to work toward changing their attitudes and behavior.

OPENING CONVERSATION

Reflect on these words of the chorus of 'What Color Is God's Skin?':

> What color is God's skin?
> What color is God's skin?

I said it's black, brown, it's yellow . . .
it is red,
it is white.
Everyone's the same
in the good Lord's sight.

- ◉ From your own personal experiences, would you conclude that most people think 'Everyone's the same in the good Lord's sight'?
- ◉ Share your thoughts with a partner. Give examples to support your opinion.

OVER TO YOU

- ◉ How do your words and actions show you believe that 'Everyone's the same in the good Lord's sight'? Might you do better? Give specific examples.

Conversion of the Gentile Cornelius

One of the most critical questions facing the early Church was: 'Are Gentiles (non-Jews) the same in God's sight as Jews?' Some Jews who became believers in Jesus answered, 'No.' Gentiles, they argued, must first become Jews before they could be baptized. The resolution of this issue caused much conflict and division within the early Church—even among the Apostles, as we shall see. But first let us look at the conversion and Baptism of Cornelius, the Gentile 'centurion of the Roman Cohort' deployed in Caesarea, and of his household.

PETER IN THE HOUSE OF CORNELIUS | GUSTAVE DORÉ

LET'S PROBE DEEPER

- ⊙ Look up, read and carefully explore the faith story of Cornelius in Acts of the Apostles 10:1—11:18.
- ⊙ Discuss with a partner:
  - What was the significance for Jews of the items on the sheet in Peter's dream?
  - What did the leaders of the early Church, including St. Peter the Apostle, whom Jesus chose to be the 'rock' and leader of the Church, learn from this experience about God's love?

FROM THE WISDOM OF THE CHURCH

God wills that all human beings 'have access to the Father, through Christ, the Word made flesh, in the Holy Spirit, and thus become sharers in the divine nature [Vatican II, *Dogmatic Constitution on Divine Revelation*, no. 2; see also Ephesians 1:9, 2:18; 2 Peter 1:4]' (*Catechism of the Catholic Church* [CCC], no. 51).

GOD'S LOVE EXTENDS TO ALL

Luke tells us that St. Peter first welcomed the two slaves and the soldier whom Cornelius sent to him. Peter then returned with them to Cornelius' house. Luke goes on to report that during Peter's preaching, the Holy Spirit descended on all the members of Cornelius' household and Peter baptized them all. Luke also makes the point that the Jewish believers in Christ who witnessed these events 'were astounded that the gift of the Holy Spirit had been poured out even on the Gentiles' (Acts of the Apostles 10:45).

The Church exists for all people and is the means of salvation for all people. Jesus commissioned St. Peter and the other Apostles to preach and teach that God's love is not limited to Christians and Jews—to specific ethnicities and cultures, to a particular economic or civic status, or age or gender. God's skin is 'every color' and 'no color'. The early Church took time to grasp the full meaning and implications of this truth revealed by Jesus. The Catholic Church continues to open up the meaning of this Revelation and to guide us in applying its meaning to our daily lives.

TALK IT OVER

- ⊙ Why do you think some members of the early Church struggled with including Gentiles fully in the life of the Church without their first becoming Jews?
- ⊙ Have you experienced discrimination against non-Christians by some Christians? If so, share the specifics of your experience.

JOURNAL EXERCISE

- ⊙ Identify and write down at least three ways your faith in God can help improve your ability to respect and honor all people for who they are, 'beloved children of God'.

FROM THE WISDOM OF THE CHURCH

Jesus calls us to conversion. 'This endeavor of conversion is not just a human work. It is the movement of a "contrite heart," drawn and moved by grace to respond to the merciful love of God who loved us first [see Psalm 51:17; John 6:44, 12:32; 1 John 4:10]' (CCC, no. 1428).

CONVERSION TO CHRIST—A LIFELONG JOURNEY

Like St. Peter, we must continually grow to become more Christ-like in our love for 'all'

FAITH WORD

Conversion

Conversion means turning around one's life toward God and trying 'to live holier lives according to the Gospel' [Vatican II, *Decree on Ecumenism*, no. 7]' (CCC, no. 821).

others. We need to cooperate with the graces of the Holy Spirit and grow to be more authentic and clearer signs of God's love for all people— the baptized and the non-baptized. Becoming more and more 'Christ-like' in our love is a lifelong task of **conversion** of soul, heart and mind.

Religious conversion—the conversion of our soul: 'Religious conversion' is another name for conversion of the soul. It means to 'fall more and more in love' with God throughout our life. It is responding to the grace of the divine invitation to live in communion and intimacy with the Holy Trinity, God, who is love.

Moral conversion—the conversion of our heart: 'Moral conversion' is another name for conversion of the heart. A moral life is a 'just' life. The psalmist teaches in Psalm 1 that a moral life is human life lived in right relationship with God, other people, our self and all creation. Moral conversion includes responding to God's grace and growing in our ability to balance our personal needs and interests on behalf of building relationships of love and respect with others because of our love for God.

Intellectual conversion—the conversion of our mind: 'Intellectual conversion' is another

name for conversion of the mind. It is coming to know and believe in God and in all that he has revealed.

This inner conversion of the human person to Christ is the necessary and driving force leading to the conversion of society. It is bringing the Gospel to society 'so as to obtain social changes, . . . so that they conform to the norms of justice and advance the good rather than hinder it [Vatican II, *Dogmatic Constitution on the Church*, no. 36]' (CCC, no. 1888).

THINK, PAIR AND SHARE

⊙ In light of what you have learned so far from studying this chapter, work with a partner and try to arrive at a shared definition of conversion to Christ.
⊙ Then work with the whole class to finish this sentence: 'For a Christian, conversion means . . . .'

JOURNAL EXERCISE

⊙ Reread and reflect on Matthew 22:34–37.
⊙ What would you imagine is your own next step on the way to:
  – conversion of your soul?
  – conversion of your heart?
  – conversion of your mind?
⊙ How and when will you begin to take those steps?

The proclamation of the good news of God's love

OPENING REFLECTION

- Think about a time when you received really 'good news'.
- What was that news? Why was it so good for you?

- What did you 'do' with your good news?
- What do you 'do' with the Good News of Jesus in your life?

St. Paul, Apostle to the Gentiles

The Apostles and other disciples worked night and day spreading the Good News of Jesus. St. Peter and the other Apostles worked so effectively that their fellow Jews became increasingly angry and hostile toward them over their preaching and because of the growing number of Jews who came to believe in Jesus. Saul, a Pharisee from Tarsus, was one of those angry Jews. He was so zealous about protecting Judaism that, having received permission from the elders, he set out for Damascus with one purpose in mind: to seek out, arrest and bring back to Jerusalem the enemies of Judaism for trial and punishment. It was during this journey that Saul was knocked to the ground and blinded—a physical manifestation of his blindness toward Jesus as Messiah. He experienced the risen Lord, who asked, 'Saul, Saul, why do you persecute me?' (Acts of the Apostles 9:4). You know the rest of this well-known conversion story. Saul accepted

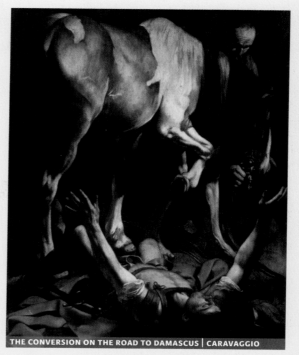

THE CONVERSION ON THE ROAD TO DAMASCUS | CARAVAGGIO

the Lord's call to become his disciple and he preached Jesus so zealously to the Gentiles that he became known as 'the Apostle to the Gentiles'.

LET'S PROBE DEEPER

Now let us take a deeper look at the conversion of Saul.

- Read Acts of the Apostles 9:1–22, 22:4–16, 26:9–18 and Galatians 1:13–17.

- Explore the different points emphasized in each of the passages.
- What is the meaning of Jesus' words to Saul, 'Why are you persecuting me?'

Paul Brings the Gospel to the Gentiles

Christ has sent the Church on a mission to the whole world. After his conversion Saul began to use his Roman name, Paul, and he set out on a series of missionary journeys, first to his fellow Jews and then to Gentiles. Luke describes three of Paul's missionary journeys in Acts of the Apostles 13:1—14:28, 15:36—18:22 and 18:23—21:15. In his missionary work

St. Paul gives witness among his fellow Jews and Gentiles to the truth that Christ 'called together a race made up of Jews and Gentiles which would be one, not according to the flesh, but in the Spirit [Vatican II, *Dogmatic Constitution on the Church*, no. 9; Acts of the Apostles 10:35; 1 Corinthians 11:25]' (CCC, no. 781).

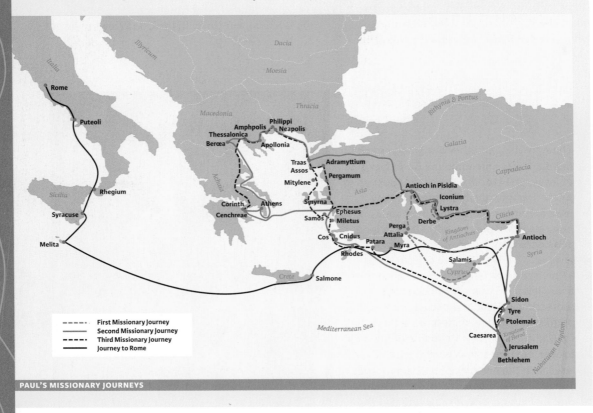

PAUL'S MISSIONARY JOURNEYS

> ## FROM THE WISDOM OF THE CHURCH
> God desires 'that the whole human race may become one People of God, form one Body of Christ, and be built up into one temple of the Holy Spirit' [Pope Paul VI, June 22, 1973; Vatican II, *Decree on the Church's Missionary Activity*, no. 7; *Dogmatic Constitution on the Church*, no. 17).
> —CCC, no. 776

THE MISSIONARY JOURNEYS OF ST. PAUL
First Missionary Journey (Acts of the Apostles 13:1—14:28): Barnabas and John Mark

accompanied St. Paul on his first missionary journey. This journey, which lasted about two years, took Paul and his companions to Cyprus and on to central Asia Minor, modern-day Turkey, to the region of Galatia and Pamphylia, where they proclaimed the Gospel primarily to fellow Jews.

Second Missionary Journey (Acts of the Apostles 15:36—18:22): On his second missionary journey St. Paul revisited some of the local churches he founded during his first missionary journey. He also traveled into

Macedonia, in the northern part of what is Greece today. Paul spent most of his time in the port city of Corinth.

Third Missionary Journey (Acts of the Apostles 18:23—21:15): St. Paul's third missionary journey was centered in Ephesus in Asia Minor. During this journey Paul focused on strengthening the churches he had founded. In addition, he wrote many letters, or epistles, to proclaim Jesus and to clarify his teachings on Jesus and his saving work. The New Testament contains fourteen letters either written by St. Paul or attributed to him.

OVER TO YOU

- What do you think was 'driving' St. Paul to make all these missionary journeys—often in dangerous conditions?
- What might 'drive' you to share the Gospel of Jesus Christ?
- Where and how might you now share the Good News of Jesus? Who could be your 'companion' and join you in spreading the Good News?

JEW OR GENTILE: CONTROVERSY WITHIN THE CHURCH

St. Paul's preaching among the Gentiles was very successful; but it was not without controversy. A major source of the controversy was Paul's teaching the Gentiles in the Diaspora that they did not have to become Jews before being baptized. (The Diaspora was any place outside of Palestine where Jews lived.)

This teaching of Paul was contrary to the teaching and practice of the members of the Church in Jerusalem, who were mostly Jews and who were demanding that Gentile disciples of Jesus first become Jews and comply fully with the Mosaic Law before becoming members of the Church. Paul, of course, did not understand the Gospel in that way and he stood his ground. The 'Apostle to the Gentiles' preached that the Death and Resurrection of Jesus had transformed Jews and Gentiles, men and women, slave and free. All people, both Jews and Gentiles, should be equally welcome.

The *Catechism of the Catholic Church* passes on Paul's understanding of the Gospel and the nature and purpose of the Church:

RUINS WITH ST. PAUL PREACHING | GIOVANNI PAOLO PANNINI

> The Church's first purpose is to be the sacrament of the *inner union of men with God.* Because men's communion with one another is rooted in that union with God, the Church is also the sacrament of the *unity of the human race.* In her, this unity is already begun, since she gathers men 'from every nation, from all tribes and peoples and tongues' [Revelation 7:9]; at the same time, the Church is the 'sign and instrument' of the full realization of the unity yet to come.
>
> —CCC, no. 775

REFLECT AND DISCUSS

- How does the teaching of the Church today reflect Paul's teaching?
- How do you see the Church working for the inner union between God and humanity? The unity of the human race?

JOURNAL EXERCISE

- Read and reflect on Romans 12:1–2 and 2 Corinthians 5:16–17.

ST. PAUL | VATICAN CITY

At the Last Supper Jesus promised:

'I have said these things to you while I am still with you. But the Advocate, the Holy Spirit, whom the Father will send in my name, will teach you everything, and remind you of all that I have said to you.'

—John 14:25–26

The same Holy Spirit who came upon the Apostles at Pentecost continued to be at work in their lives. At the Council in Jerusalem the Apostles and other Church elders, under the guidance of the Holy Spirit, concluded that Gentiles did not have to become Jews before being baptized. This decision meant, in particular, that male Gentiles did not need to be circumcised before they were baptized. St. Peter addressed the Council:

'My brothers, you know that in the early days God made a choice among you, that I should be the one through whom the Gentiles would hear the message of the good news and become believers. And God, who knows the human heart, testified to them by giving them the Holy Spirit, just as he did to us; and in cleansing their hearts by faith he has made no distinction between them and us.'

—Acts of the Apostles 15:7–9

This was the first joint exercise of the divine office that Christ had given to St. Peter and the other Apostles. St. Luke sums up the Council's deliberations:

After they finished speaking, James replied, 'My brothers, listen to me. . . . I have reached the decision that we should not trouble those Gentiles who are turning to God, but we should write to them to abstain only from things polluted by idols and from fornication and from whatever has been strangled and from blood.'

—Acts of the Apostles 15:13, 19–20

OVER TO YOU
⊙ What is the best wisdom for your own life–faith–life journey that you learned from reflecting on this section of the chapter?

⊙ How does your faith in Jesus help you to inform, form and transform your whole outlook on yourself? On life in the world?

COUNCIL AT JERUSALEM: THE EARLY CHURCH DEALS WITH CONTROVERSY
Paul and Barnabas traveled to Jerusalem around AD 48–50 to meet with Peter and James the Elder, who was the leader of the Church in Jerusalem, and other elders of the Church. They gathered to address their differing understandings of the Baptism of Gentiles. This gathering has become known as the Council at Jerusalem. The Council at Jerusalem was a sign of the Holy Spirit at work in the Church.

Passing on the Tradition of the Apostles

People deal with conflict and controversy in many ways. Some confront controversy head on as soon as they become aware of it. Others sit quietly and hope it will just go away. Still others deal with it only when they have to—when there is no alternative. This story describes how the students, administration and staff, and families of South Hadley High School dealt with the conflict and controversy surrounding the bullying of one student.

On January 14, 2010, ninth-grader Phoebe Prince hanged herself in the stairwell of her family's apartment. Phoebe, aged fifteen, took her own life following three months of intensive bullying by fellow students. While many, including school officials and other students, were aware of the bullying, no serious efforts were taken to end the harassment. Upon discovery of Phoebe's suicide the bullying continued, with cruel posts to the victim's social networking webpage. In the final days of March, 2010, nine teenagers were charged in connection with Phoebe's death.

OPENING CONVERSATION

⊙ What wisdom from the Council at Jerusalem would have contributed to dealing more effectively with the bullying of Phoebe Prince?

WHAT ABOUT YOU PERSONALLY?

⊙ Identify ways you see students being treated with disrespect and excluded from full life within your school.

⊙ How might you contribute to building a school community in which all are 'really' welcomed?

Peter and Paul at Antioch

The decision of the Church at the Council at Jerusalem took time to implement fully. St. Paul would not back down; he would not allow Gentiles to be pressured into becoming Jews before becoming fully accepted into the Church. We know from Paul's writings that it took St. Peter some time to fully implement the Council's decision. For example, when Peter and Paul met in Antioch after the Council's decision, St. Peter did sit down and eat with Gentile Christians, but we are also told that he absented himself and ate only with other Jews when James' people arrived. (Read Galatians 2:11–21.)

SAINTS PETER AND PAUL | EL GRECO

⊙ How might you go about changing your own attitudes so as to see, value and accept all people as children of God? Share your thoughts on this with a partner.

APOSTOLIC TRADITION

The Council at Jerusalem is the earliest example of how the Apostles exercised the teaching authority Christ gave them. The community of Apostles has continued in the community of the Pope and the bishops in communion with him. This direct line connection of the Pope and bishops with St. Peter and the other Apostles is called **apostolic succession**.

Since that gathering in Jerusalem the leaders of the Church have gathered in Council on twenty-one other occasions to pass on and teach authentically the faith handed on to the Apostles. These councils are called Ecumenical Councils. An **Ecumenical Council** of the Church is a gathering of all the bishops of the world, in the exercise of their authority over the universal Church. An Ecumenical Council is usually called by the Pope, or at least confirmed and accepted by him. It can be called for a variety of specific reasons, among which is to discern the direction of the life of the Church, clarifying her teachings and mission. The Second Vatican Council (1962–65) was the most recent and last Ecumenical Council.

Today, the Pope and other bishops in union with him work together in unity to continue passing on the **Apostolic Tradition** of the Church. The same Holy Spirit who guided and taught the Apostles and the early Church remains at work in the Church today. Jesus himself assured us that the Holy Spirit, the Spirit of Truth and Love, will always guide the pastors of the Church and the whole Church into a deeper and clearer understanding and living of Revelation until Christ comes again in glory at the end of time.

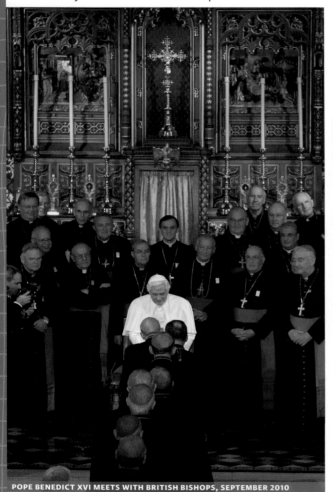

POPE BENEDICT XVI MEETS WITH BRITISH BISHOPS, SEPTEMBER 2010

FROM THE WISDOM OF THE CHURCH

'The Word of God, which is the power of God for salvation to everyone who has faith, is set forth and displays its power in a most wonderful way in the writings of the New Testament' [Vatican II, *Dogmatic Constitution on Divine Revelation*, no. 17; see also Romans 1:16] which hand on the ultimate truth of God's Revelation. Their central object is Jesus Christ, God's incarnate Son: his acts, teachings, Passion and glorification, and his Church's beginnings under the Spirit's guidance [see Vatican II, *Dogmatic Constitution on Divine Revelation*, no. 20].

—CCC, no. 124

FORMATION OF THE NEW TESTAMENT

The Church has also exercised the teaching authority given to her by Christ in writing and approving as authentic the four Gospels and other writings in the New Testament.

God graciously arranged that what he had once revealed for the salvation of all peoples should last for ever in its entirety and be transmitted to all generations. Therefore, Christ the Lord, in whom the entire revelation of the most high God is summed up [see 2 Corinthians 1:20; 3:16—4:6], having fulfilled in his own person and promulgated with his own lips the Gospel promised beforehand by the prophets, commanded the apostles to preach it to everyone as the source of all saving truth and moral law, communicating God's gifts to them. This was faithfully done; it was done by the apostles who handed on, by oral preaching, by their example, by their dispositions, what they themselves had received—whether from the lips of Christ, from his way of life and his works, or by coming to know it through the prompting of the holy Spirit; it was done by those apostles and others associated with them who, under the inspiration of the same holy Spirit, committed the message of salvation to writing.

—Vatican II, *Dogmatic Constitution on Divine Revelation*, no. 7

The writing of the New Testament took place in the second half of the first century AD. The earliest of these writings are the letters of St. Paul, which were written in the fifties. Mark's account of the Gospel, the first to be written, was probably not written until around AD 70. The other accounts of the Gospel and the other writings in the New Testament were completed around the year AD 100 or soon thereafter.

The Gospel is the heart of the New Testament and of all Sacred Scripture. The four written accounts of the Gospel came into being in three stages. These stages were the:

⊙ life and teaching of Jesus;
⊙ preaching of the Apostles and other eyewitnesses of Christ, or **oral tradition**;
⊙ writing of the Gospel message.

As we read and study the four accounts of the Gospel and other New Testament writings it becomes clear that the Death and Resurrection of Jesus were the heart of the apostolic preaching and Apostolic Tradition.

13TH-CENTURY RELIQUARY WITH APOSTLES AND ANGELS

IN THE 9TH-CENTURY BOOK OF KELLS, THE ELABORATE 'CHI RHO' PAGE SEPARATES THE GENEALOGY OF JESUS FROM THE REST OF ST. MATTHEW'S GOSPEL

deeper understanding of the meaning of Jesus' life, Death and Resurrection for all humanity. The building blocks of the written accounts of the Gospel and the other New Testament writings began to take shape.

Sayings and deeds of Jesus: As the early Church grew, the new disciples who did not know Jesus firsthand began pressing the Apostles and other eyewitnesses to share more details about Jesus' life and teachings. Eventually, the key stories that were part of the oral tradition were joined to the account of Jesus' **Passion** (his suffering and Death) and Resurrection.

Genealogies and infancy narratives: The Gospels of Matthew and Luke also added details about Jesus' ancestry and infancy. Both Evangelists included genealogies and the birth of Jesus in their accounts of the Gospel. Matthew, who wrote his Gospel primarily for Jews who became members of the Church, included a genealogy that traces Jesus' ancestry from Abraham to King David to Joseph. (See Matthew 1:1–17.) Luke, on the other hand, who wrote his Gospel primarily for non-Jews, included a genealogy from Joseph to Adam. (See Luke 3:23–38.)

Death and Resurrection of Jesus: Luke, in his Acts of the Apostles, reports that the preaching of the early Church placed particular emphasis on the Death and Resurrection of Jesus Christ. (Read Acts of the Apostles 2:22–36.) As years went by, the Apostles and disciples who witnessed the Death, Resurrection and Ascension of Jesus and the outpouring of the Holy Spirit at Pentecost, continued to pass on by word of mouth (oral tradition) the meaning of these saving events. Gradually and under the guidance and **inspiration** of the Holy Spirit, the Apostles and the early Church grew into a

TALK IT OVER

- Why was it important to commit to writing the details of the faith of the apostolic Church in the life, Death and Resurrection of Jesus and the teachings of Jesus?

JOURNAL EXERCISE

- Identify your favorite passages about Jesus and his teachings.
- What guidance do they give you in living your faith in Christ?
- How can you share those passages with others?

JUDGE AND ACT

**REFLECT ON WHAT YOU HAVE LEARNED
IN THIS CHAPTER**

As you come toward the end of this chapter, pause and reflect on what you have come to understand to be the universality of the love of God for all people. Share the teachings of the Catholic Church on these statements:

- God is truth and love.
- God desires all people to come to knowledge of the truth and be saved.
- Christ established his Church to continue his presence and work in the world until he comes again in glory.

- The Church in this world is the sacrament of salvation, the sign and instrument of the communion of God and humanity.
- Scripture and Tradition pass on the truths of faith that God has revealed for the salvation of all people.
- God's love for all people empowers and moves the Church in every age to accept and fulfill her obligation to proclaim the Gospel and make disciples of all nations.

LEARN BY EXAMPLE

Pope St. John Paul II, a witness to the Church's growth in understanding and living of the Gospel

Pope St. John Paul II served the Church as her 264th pope from October 16, 1978 to his death on April 2, 2005. Pope Francis canonized him on April 27, 2014. Pope St. John Paul II's papacy was the second longest, and he was the first non-Italian pope since 1523. During his ministry as pope, John Paul II showed us how the Church grows in her understanding of Revelation and how she applies this to her teachings and way of life. His many apologies and requests for forgiveness for past wrongs committed by Church leaders and members were among the more significant ways Pope St. John Paul II witnessed to this growth. These included his apologies for the Church's actions during the Inquisition to suppress heresy, including the treatment of Galileo (1564–1642) following his discovery that the Earth revolved around the Sun; the killing of Muslims during the Crusades; the participation of some Christians in the slave trade; and the silence of many Catholics while the Nazis persecuted and murdered more than six million Jews and other peoples during the Holocaust.

One of Pope St. John Paul II's best-known apologies took place in Jerusalem on March 26, 2000. During his visit, he stood by the Wailing (or Western) Wall, placed a hand-written prayer signed by him in a crevice in the wall and, touching the wall, he prayed silently. Explaining the meaning of his actions, he said, 'I assure the Jewish people the Catholic Church . . . is deeply saddened by the hatred, acts of persecution and displays of anti-Semitism directed against the Jews by Christians at any time and in any place.'

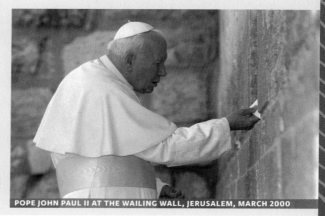

POPE JOHN PAUL II AT THE WAILING WALL, JERUSALEM, MARCH 2000

TALK IT OVER

⊙ In what way were the actions and words of Pope St. John Paul II an expression of the Church's deeper understanding of Jesus and his life and work?

⊙ How did the actions and words of Pope St. John Paul II manifest the work of the Holy Spirit in the Church today?

RESPOND WITH FAMILY AND FRIENDS

St. Paul taught that God reconciled the world in Jesus and entrusted 'the ministry of reconciliation' to us (2 Corinthians 5:19). Look at your own circle of family and friends.

⊙ What conflicts, big or small, could you work at resolving?

⊙ Think about the positive actions you could take to bring about reconciliation in those situations. Perhaps you could encourage others to join you in this endeavor.

JUDGE AND DECIDE

⊙ What dimensions of youth culture, for example, music, games, movies, books, entertainment events, are life-giving and praiseworthy? Why is that?

⊙ What aspects of youth culture are contrary to the values of the Gospel? Be specific.

⊙ How willing are you to stand up and critique the expressions of youth culture that are contrary to the Gospel?

For I am convinced that neither death, nor life, nor angels, nor rulers, nor things present, nor things to come, nor powers, nor height, nor depth, nor anything else in all creation, will be able to separate us from the love of God in Christ Jesus our Lord.

ROMANS 8:38–39

PRAYER REFLECTION

Pray the Sign of the Cross together.

LEADER
Sometimes our words or actions fail to proclaim authentically the good news of God's unconditional love for all people.

Let us take a moment to reflect on the times we may have failed to be living images or signs of God's love for every person.

All reflect on specific instances where your harsh words or mean actions harmed someone, either emotionally or physically.

LEADER
Create in me a clean heart, O God,
and put a new and right spirit within me.
ALL
Create in me a clean heart, O God,
and put a new and right spirit within me.

GROUP 1
Have mercy on me, O God, according to your
   steadfast love. . . .
Wash me thoroughly from my iniquity,
   and cleanse me from my sin.
GROUP 2
For I know my transgressions,
   and my sin is ever before me.
Against you, you alone, have I sinned,
   and done what is evil in your sight. . . .
ALL
Create in me a clean heart, O God,
   and put a new and right spirit within me.

GROUP 1
You desire truth in the inward being;
   therefore teach me wisdom in my secret
      heart.
   Wash me, and I shall be whiter than snow.
GROUP 2
Restore to me the joy of your salvation,
   and sustain in me a willing spirit.

ALL
Create in me a clean heart, O God,
   and put a new and right spirit within me.
                              —From Psalm 51:1–17

All quietly reflect on ways in which your words and actions can be authentic signs of God's unconditional love for all people.

LEADER
Let us pray together:

ALL
Lord Jesus Christ, who said to your Apostles,
Peace I leave you, my peace I give you;
look not on our sins, but on the faith of your
   Church,
and graciously grant her peace and unity
in accordance with your will.
Who live and reign for ever and ever. Amen.

LEADER
Let us share a sign of peace as an expression of our commitment to be a living sign of God's universal and unconditional love for all people.

All share a sign of peace.
Conclude by praying the Sign of the Cross together.

Images of the Church

MYSTICAL BODY
OF CHRIST

PILGRIM
PEOPLE

BRIDE OF
CHRIST

THE
CHURCH

SIGN AND
SACRAMENT OF
THE REIGN OF
GOD

HOLY PEOPLE
OF GOD

SACRAMENT OF
SALVATION

SEED OF THE
KINGDOM

SIGN AND
INSTRUMENT OF
COMMUNION
WITH GOD

THE CHURCH SINCE THE TIME OF THE APOSTLES HAS employed a variety of interrelated images and figures to help us understand the inexhaustible mystery that is the Church. In this chapter we explore key images rooted in the Old Testament and the New Testament. The Old Testament figures and images point to variations within the People of God. The New Testament images center on Christ and his unity with his Church, the new People of God. These images also give us deeper insight into the role that all the baptized have in the ongoing mission of Jesus Christ.

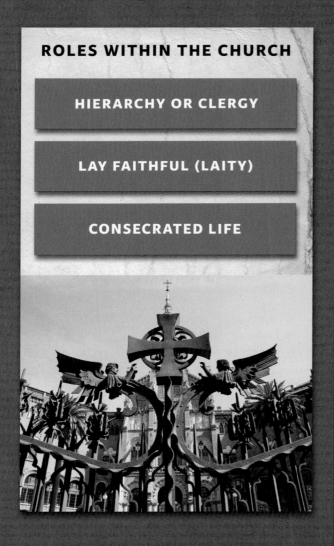

ROLES WITHIN THE CHURCH

HIERARCHY OR CLERGY

LAY FAITHFUL (LAITY)

CONSECRATED LIFE

Faith Focus: The teachings of the Catholic Church that are the primary focus of the doctrinal content presented in this chapter include:

⊙ The Church is a mystery of faith.
⊙ The Church is both visible and spiritual.
⊙ The Church is one, yet formed of two components, human and divine.
⊙ The Church is the sign and sacrament of the reign of God.
⊙ The mystery of the Church is prefigured in the Old Testament.
⊙ Images that are rooted in Scripture and developed in Tradition help us come to an understanding of the mystery of the Church.
⊙ The Christian home is an image of the Holy Trinity; it is the domestic church.

Discipleship Formation: As a result of studying this chapter and discovering the meaning of the faith of the Catholic Church for your life, you should be better able to:

⊙ develop a greater sense of belonging to the Church;
⊙ grow in your understanding of the nature of your relationship with Jesus in and through the Church;
⊙ discern how you can share in the life of the Church;
⊙ grow in your efforts to contribute to the pilgrim journey of the Church;
⊙ appreciate the role of young people in the Church.

Scripture References: These Scripture references are quoted or referred to in this chapter:
OLD TESTAMENT: Genesis 12:2, 15:5–6; **Exodus** 19:5–6; **Deuteronomy** 7:6; **Psalms** 23:1–4; **Isaiah** 2:2–5, 6:13, 7:3, 10:22, 11:1–9, 40:11; **Jeremiah** 23:3; **Hosea** 3:1; **Joel** 3:5; **Obadiah** 17; **Micah** 2:12, 4:1–4
NEW TESTAMENT: Matthew 8:23–27, 22:1–14, 25:1–13; **Mark** 1:14–15, 2:19, 4:35–41; **Luke** 4:16–19, 8:22–25; **John** 10:1–18, 15:1–5 and 8–9, 16:12–13, 17:21; **Romans** 8:19–22, 9:27, 12:4–8; **1 Corinthians** 3:16, 6:15–17 and 19, 12:12–26; **2 Corinthians** 11:2; **Galatians** 4:4–6; **Ephesians** 5:21—6:4; **Colossians** 3:18–21; **1 Peter** 2:5, 3:1–7; **1 John** 4:7, 13, 15–16; **Revelation** 7:9

Faith Glossary: Familiarize yourself with the meaning of these key terms. Definitions are found in the Glossary: **Body of Christ, domestic church, Mystical Body of Christ, People of God**

Faith Word: domestic church
Learn by Heart: John 15:5
Learn by Example: Blessed John Henry Cardinal Newman

Why are there so many images for the Church?

THE GOOD SHEPHERD | 4TH-CENTURY CHRISTIAN IMAGE

Images point to the truth of a reality in a way that words alone cannot capture. For example, to describe a teammate as 'on fire' helps capture the fullness of the teammate's efforts, enthusiasm, dedication and contributions to a team. Jesus and the writers of the New Testament used many images for the Church. You are already familiar with some of these images, for example, 'shepherd and flock', 'vine and branches', 'temple of the Holy Spirit', 'Body of Christ' and 'holy People of God'.

OPENING CONVERSATION

⊙ What other images for the Church do you know?
⊙ Which image is your favorite?
⊙ What does this image help you come to know about the Church? Explain.

STRENGTHS AND LIMITATIONS OF 'IMAGE' LANGUAGE

The Church is an 'inexhaustible mystery' (*Catechism of the Catholic Church* [CCC], no. 753). When it comes to capturing the inner meaning of any mystery of faith, we run into the limitations of language. Images help us overcome those limitations. On the other hand, no single image for the Church captures the fullness of the nature of the Church. If we interpret an image too literally, it can lead us away from discovering its true and full meaning. Let us explore the image of the 'shepherd and the shepherd's flock', which is one of the central images Jesus used for the Church.

LET'S PROBE DEEPER

⊙ Look up and read John 10:1–18.
⊙ What does this image of the Church say to you about Jesus' relationship with the members of the Church?
⊙ What does it say about the relationship of the members of the Church with Jesus?

WHAT ABOUT YOU PERSONALLY?

⊙ How does the image of a good shepherd and flock help you understand your call to live your daily life as a member of the Church?

THE GOOD SHEPHERD AND HIS FLOCK

God's message is clear about his relationship with us. He is a 'good' shepherd. God desires us to come to know him and to live in communion with him, just as a good shepherd and the shepherd's flock know one another and are bonded to one another. The Hebrew people saw their relationship with God in a similar way. The psalmist expresses this faith and trust:

The LORD is my shepherd, I shall not want,
  He makes me lie down in green pastures;
he leads me beside still waters;
  he restores my soul.
He leads me in right paths
  for his name's sake.

Even though I walk through the darkest valley,
  I fear no evil;
for you are with me:
  your rod and your staff—
  they comfort me.

—Psalm 23:1–4

The Church professes the same faith and trust as our ancestors in faith professed. Jesus declared, 'I am the good shepherd.' (Read John 10:1–18.) We belong to the Church, the 'flock' of God, the sheepfold of Jesus the Incarnate Son of God, the Good Shepherd. We bring the wisdom we receive from this image with us to live our life–faith–life journey.

THINK, PAIR AND SHARE
- Compare Psalm 23 with John 10:1–18.
- Talk with a partner about what God is saying to you in both of these passages.
- What challenges do you and other young people face in living as disciples of the Good Shepherd that you cannot meet alone?

- How can being a member of the Church support you? And how can you support other members of the Church?

JOURNAL EXERCISE
- Name one significant challenge to living as a disciple of Jesus that you are currently facing.
- Talk it over in prayer with Jesus, your Good Shepherd.
- Write your prayer in your journal. Revisit your journal entry often during this course of study.

FROM THE WISDOM OF THE CHURCH
'The Church is, accordingly, a sheepfold, the sole and necessary gateway to which is Christ. It is also the flock of which God himself foretold that he would be the shepherd, and whose sheep, even though governed by human shepherds, are unfailingly nourished and led by Christ himself, the Good Shepherd and Prince of Shepherds, who gave his life for his sheep' [Vatican II, *Dogmatic Constitution on the Church*, no. 6; see also Isaiah 40:11; Ezekiel 34:11–31; John 10:1–10, 11–16; 1 Peter 5:4].

—CCC, no. 754

What challenges do you and other young people face in living as disciples of the Good Shepherd that you cannot meet alone?

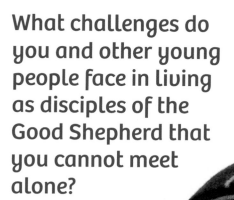

WHY WE NEED THE CHURCH

We often hear the statement, 'I am spiritual, but not religious.' What some people really mean is, 'We do not need religion; we do not really need to be members of the Church.' The truth is, we do. We need a community of faith to support us to live a spiritual life. Human beings are social by nature. We need the encouragement, support and example of others. We need stories and traditions of faith to guide us. We need virtues and values inspired by faith to enable us to live as good people. We need rituals to celebrate our faith and help us express and grow in our relationship with God.

Jesus himself belonged to a community of faith—the descendants of Abraham. No person can be fully 'spiritual'—fully alive—without being connected. 'God desires "that the whole human race may become one People of God, form one Body of Christ, and be built up into one temple of the Holy Spirit [Pope Paul VI]" ' (CCC, no. 776).

Jesus gathered the Twelve Apostles to join with him in the work the Father had sent him to do. 'Twelve' is an image that recalls the twelve tribes of Israel and points to the reality that the Church is the new **People of God**, whom Jesus was calling and gathering. The Church is the community of disciples who are joined inseparably to Christ and to one another in Christ. By its very nature, the Christian life is life in community. One simply cannot be a 'private' Christian. The Church is the way to salvation.

THINK, PAIR AND SHARE

◉ How would you respond to other young people who say, 'Oh, I'm spiritual but not religious. Who needs organized religion? Who needs the Church?'

JOURNAL EXERCISE

◉ In what ways do you need the Church? In what way does the Church need you?
◉ Describe a situation in which your spiritual life is supported by your being a member of the Church, the flock and sheepfold of Christ.

Human beings are social by nature. We need the encouragement, support and example of others

The Church: an inexhaustible mystery

OPENING CONVERSATION
◉ What image would you choose to convey what is particular to your school?
◉ Why would you choose this image?

FROM THE WISDOM OF THE CHURCH
The Church is in history, but at the same time she transcends it. It is only 'with the eyes of faith' [*Roman Catechism*, I, 10, 20] that one can see her in her visible reality and at the same time in her spiritual reality as bearer of divine life.

—CCC, no. 770

IMAGES OLD AND NEW
The Church straddles at all times two basic realities: the visible and the invisible; the human and the divine. The Church is both a visible and a spiritual society. The Church on earth is both a structured organization and a spiritual communion. She both transcends history and is part of history. The Church is always both 'the earthly Church and the Church endowed with heavenly riches' (CCC, no. 771). Images, each in their own way, help us capture part of the reality of who the Church is and the divine purpose and plan for her.

The members of the Church, guided by the Holy Spirit (see John 16:12–13), are always striving to arrive at deeper understandings of the mystery of the Church. In every era since apostolic times, the Church has looked at her present life and the issues she is facing (as the early Church examined her relationship with the Gentiles at the Council at Jerusalem) to discern how best to pass on and teach the faith to this generation. She reads the signs of the times and uses language that will communicate God's word to people in the present.

TALK IT OVER
◉ What are some of the current images you hear or see people use to portray the Church?
◉ What insight do these images give you into the Church?

LET'S PROBE DEEPER
◉ Jesus used the image of a 'vine and branches' to speak to the people living in first-century Palestine, whose landscape was filled with vineyards. Read and reflect prayerfully on John 15:1–5.
◉ Discuss with a partner how the image of a 'vine and branches' helps us understand partially the mystery of the Church.
◉ Think of a contemporary image for the Church that communicates the same meaning. How does it do so?

JOURNAL EXERCISE
◉ Using the 'vine and branches' image, describe in words or illustrate how your belonging to the Church influences your daily life.

The Church is both visible and spiritual, a hierarchical society and the Mystical Body of Christ. She is one, yet formed of two components, human and divine . . . which only faith can accept.

—CCC, no. 779

The Instrumental Church: Sign and Sacrament of the Reign of God

The Church is the sign and instrument of the communion of people with God the Holy Trinity and with one another. She is the sacrament of salvation and of God's reign in the world. This means that the Church is a concrete visible instrument through which God invites and makes people sharers in the invisible saving grace of God. There are many images that seek to convey this dimension of the mystery of the Church. These images suggest something that can be seen, touched and heard as the Church moves through history; for example, the Church as the 'seed and beginning of the kingdom'; the 'sheepfold or flock' whose nurturing shepherd is Jesus; a 'cultivated field that Jesus tills, plants, waters, grows and harvests'.

The Church is also an *ark*. The ark of Noah, providing protection amidst the storms of the world, prefigured the Church. Recall the appearance of Jesus calming the turbulent waters of the Sea (or Lake) of Galilee (see Matthew 8:23–27; Mark 4:35–41; Luke 8:22–25). The Church is also the *remnant*—the faithful among the People of God of the Old Covenant (see Isaiah 6:13, 7:3, 10:22; Jeremiah 23:3; Joel 3:5; Obadiah 17; Micah 2:12), through whom God will assure the future of his people and the covenant. Through the remnant of ancient Israel, who prefigured the Church (see Romans 9:27), God will bring forth the new creation and Kingdom of God foretold by the prophets.

The New Testament also uses the image of a *temple* for the Church. The destruction of the Temple in Jerusalem in AD 70 had a devastating impact on Jews who became believers in Christ, as it did on all Jews. Slowly they began to see the Church as the new temple of God. They saw that Jesus was the new and eternal High Priest, and the new Moses promulgating a new Torah (Law). Other New Testament writings teach that the Church is the temple of the Holy Spirit. Her members are 'living stones' (1 Peter 2:5) and temples of the living God (see 1 Corinthians 3:16, 6:19).

THE SEE OF GALILEE | AFTER ALEXANDRE BIDA

TALK IT OVER

⊙ Which of these images for the Church appeals most to you?

⊙ Share what this image might mean for your life, and what it means for the lives of all Christians.

HOSPITAL DE SANT PAU I DE LA SANTA CREU, BARCELONA, SPAIN, BUILT IN THE 15TH CENTURY

REFLECT AND DISCUSS

- When you think of the Church as something you can see, what comes to mind?
- What structures and institutions within the Catholic Church can you name; for example, parishes?
- What roles within the Church make these structures and institutions function well?

ROLES AND RESPONSIBILITIES WITHIN THE CHURCH

The Church is the Body of Christ. (Read 1 Corinthians 12:12–26 and Romans 12:4–5.) We will explore the roles and responsibilities of the members of the Church in greater detail later in this text. But now let us recall and take a brief look at some of the visible, concrete roles within the Church that help make her an effective, visible instrument of God's grace. The baptized serve the Church as members of these three 'states of life': (1) hierarchy or clergy; (2) lay faithful, or laity; and (3) consecrated life. The structures of the Church include the Vatican and the Curia; archdioceses and dioceses and their many offices; parishes and monasteries and convents; and pastoral service organizations such as hospitals and schools, Catholic Relief Services and Catholic Charities.

At the heart of the Church's function as the 'sacrament' of God's reign is her celebration of the Seven Sacraments. The sacraments make present the mystery of salvation in Christ by the power of the Holy Spirit. In the Seven Sacraments the faithful encounter Christ in a unique manner. Through the sacraments that Christ himself gave to her, the Church initiates and sustains Christians as disciples of Jesus (Baptism, Confirmation and Eucharist), heals (Penance and Reconciliation, and Anointing of the Sick), and calls some of the baptized to serve the communion of the whole Church (Holy Orders and Marriage).

THINK, PAIR AND SHARE

- Work with a partner. Come up with a concrete contemporary image for the Church that portrays her as a visible society that brings God's saving grace to the world. Try to think of an image that might speak particularly to young people.
- Create the image using words (story, song lyrics, verse) or a graphic.
- Share the image with the class.

JOURNAL EXERCISE

- How can you be a clearer image of God's saving grace at work in the world? Be specific.

The Church: a communion of love

OPENING REFLECTION

⦿ Place yourself in the presence of the Lord. See Jesus looking you straight in the eye. Listen to him as he speaks directly to you:

I am the true vine and my Father is the vine grower. . . . Abide in me as I abide in you. Just as the branch cannot bear fruit by itself unless it abides in the vine, neither can you unless you abide in me. I am the vine, you are the branches. . . . My Father is glorified by this, that you bear much fruit and become my disciples. As the Father has loved me, so I have loved you; abide in my love.

—John 15:1, 4–5, 8–9

⦿ Share your reflections with a partner:
  – What is Jesus saying about your relationship with him? His relationship with you?
  – Which of your activities mirror your life as a disciple of Jesus? Your being a member of his Church?

⦿ What are you doing to bear much fruit? In your family? Among your friends?

FROM THE WISDOM OF THE CHURCH

The Church's first purpose is to be the sacrament of the *inner union of men with God*. Because men's communion with one another is rooted in that union with God, the Church is also the sacrament of the *unity of the human race*. In her, this unity is already begun, since she gathers men 'from every nation, from all tribes and peoples and tongues' [Revelations 7:9]; at the same time, the Church is the 'sign and instrument' of the full realization of the unity yet to come.

—CCC, no. 775

THE CHURCH AS AN INTERPERSONAL COMMUNION OF LOVE: SIGN AND INSTRUMENT OF LIFE-GIVING COMMUNION WITH GOD

The Church is not only a visible society; she is also a spiritual communion, the **Mystical Body of Christ**. By God's will and purpose the Church is 'interpersonal'. She is the sign and instrument of the life-giving communion uniting God, his Church and all humanity. Joined to Christ in Baptism, we are reborn as adopted children of God the Father and temples of the Holy Spirit. St. Paul teaches:

But when the fullness of time had come, God sent his Son, born of a woman, born under the law, in order to redeem those who were under the law, so that we might receive adoption as children. And because you are children, God has sent the Spirit of his Son into our hearts, crying, 'Abba! Father!'

—Galatians 4:4–6

IMAGES FROM SACRED SCRIPTURE

In the Old Testament we see the Church as 'communion' prefigured and prepared for in God's calling of Abraham and the election and gathering of his descendants, the Israelites, to enter into covenant with him and form his own people (Genesis 12:2 and 15:5–6). 'Israel is to be the sign of the future gathering of all nations [see Exodus 19:5–6; Deuteronomy 7:6; Isaiah 2:2–5; and Micah 4:1–4]' (CCC, no. 762). The prophet Hosea describes God's relationship with his people to be similar to the intimate love binding spouses (Hosea 3:1). In chapters 3 and 4 of Song of Songs, God reveals the depth of his love for and relationship with his people.

The New Testament continues to teach this Revelation. The Fourth Gospel passes on the account of Jesus praying at the Last Supper for his disciples, the Church: 'As you, Father, are in me and I am in you, may they also be in us' (John 17:21). Jesus also uses the image of 'bridegroom' for himself, to teach his disciples of the depth of his relationship with the Church (Mark 2:19). St. Paul, building on that image, describes the Church as the Bride of Christ, 'as a bride "betrothed" to Christ the Lord so as to become but one spirit with him [see Matthew 22:1–14; 25:1–13; 1 Corinthians 6:15–17; 2 Corinthians 11:2]' (CCC, no. 796).

All of these images point to the Church as a 'people', the new 'People of God' (CCC, no. 762) that one enters through Baptism and faith. The community of Jesus' disciples is one people, the one family of the children of God, bonded and made one in God, who is love.

> Beloved, let us love one another, because love is from God. . . . By this we know that we abide in him and he in us, because he has given us of his Spirit. . . . God abides in those who confess that Jesus is the Son of God, and they abide in God. So we have known and believe the love that God has for us. God is love, and those who abide in love abide in God, and God abides in them.
>
> —1 John 4:7, 13, 15–16

Joined to Christ, the Incarnate Son of God, in Baptism, we are made sharers in the very life of the Holy Trinity. Through our encounter with Christ in the other sacraments we are nourished to live in communion with God by the graces of the sacraments.

THINK, PAIR AND SHARE

- What does the image of the 'bridegroom' say about Jesus' relationship with his Church?
- What do you think the words 'abide in him and he in us' say about the relationship between Christ and his Church?
- What does this mean for you? For young people today?

FROM THE WISDOM OF THE CHURCH

The risen Christ unites his faithful people to himself in an intimate way by means of the Holy Spirit. . . . They form one body, the Church, whose unity is experienced in the diversity of its members and its functions.

—*Compendium of the Catechism of the Catholic Church, no. 156*

THE LAST SUPPER | WINTERHALDER WORKSHOP

We, who are many, are one body in Christ, and individually we are members one of another.

ROMANS 12:5

THE ONE BODY OF CHRIST

The Church is the **Body of Christ**. This is perhaps the best known and most used image that helps us understand the communion of love uniting Christ and his Church and the members of the Church with one another. Let us briefly review Paul's use of this image. Between AD 52 and 57, a time when the Church in Corinth was experiencing divisions among her members, St. Paul wrote to the Church in Corinth:

For just as the body is one and has many members, and all the members of the body, though many, are one body, so it is with Christ. For in the one Spirit we were all baptized into one body—Jews or Greeks, slaves or free—and we were all made to drink of one Spirit.

—1 Corinthians 12:12–13

And sometime during AD 57–58, while he was in Corinth, Paul reminded the Church in Rome:

For as in one body we have many members, and not all the members have the same function, so we, who are many, are one body in Christ, and individually we are members one of another. We have gifts that differ according to the grace given to us: prophecy, in proportion to faith; ministry, in ministering; the teacher, in teaching; the exhorter, in exhortation; the giver, in generosity; the leader, in diligence; the compassionate, in cheerfulness.

—Romans 12:4–8

'Christ "is the head of the body, the church" [Colossians 1:18]. The Church lives from him, in him and for him. Christ and the Church make up the "whole Christ" [St. Augustine]; "Head and members form, as it were, one and the same mystical person" [St. Thomas Aquinas]' (*Compendium of the Catechism of the Catholic Church*, no. 157).

WHAT ABOUT YOU PERSONALLY?

⊙ Which of the images for the Church explored in this section of the chapter helps you best understand the Church as a 'communion of love'?

⊙ How does the image 'Body of Christ' help you take part in the life of the Church?

THE CHURCH: THE FAMILY OF GOD

'Family' also has a powerful place among the images of God the Holy Trinity and of the Church. In the Acts of the Apostles and in Paul's letters, we hear early believers identify themselves as brothers and sisters in the Lord. We hear God addressed as Father, Christ as brother, and believers in general addressed as children of God. Ideally, there is no greater familiarity or closer bonds than between family members. The Church is the community of adopted sons and daughters of God, of siblings of Jesus and one another.

'The Christian family is a communion of persons, a sign and image of the communion of the Father and the Son in the Holy Spirit' (CCC, no. 2205). The Christian family is the domestic church, the church of the home—it is 'a specific revelation and realization of ecclesial communion, and for this reason it can and should be called a *domestic church*. It is a community of faith, hope, and charity; it assumes singular importance in the Church, as is evident in the New Testament [see Ephesians 5:21—6:4; Colossians 3:18–21; 1 Peter 3:1–7]' (CCC, no. 2204).

Each member of the domestic church participates in the evangelizing and missionary work of the Church given to her by Christ. At the Baptism of a child the Church prays for the parents that they 'will be the first teachers of their child in the ways of faith . . . and also the best of teachers, bearing witness to the faith by what they say and do' (*Rite of Baptism of One Child*, 70).

OVER TO YOU

⊙ How has your family nurtured you in living your faith in Christ? For example, what faith traditions does your family celebrate?

⊙ How can you contribute to your family being an image of the Holy Trinity by living as a domestic church?

FAITH WORD

Domestic Church

The Christian home is the place where children receive the first proclamation of the faith. For this reason the family home is rightly called 'the domestic church', a community of grace and prayer, a school of human virtues and of Christian charity.

—CCC, no. 1666

The Church: the seed of the Kingdom

her identity and mission, of who the Church is and of how she is to live in the world. The images of the growth of a seed and people on a journey (pilgrim people) help us explore this dimension of the mystery of the Church.

THE SEED OF THE KINGDOM

The Church is always and forever the sign and instrument of the coming of the Kingdom. The Kingdom of God is the final stage of the divine plan of salvation. The Greek word *eschaton* means 'final age'. The Church is at work bringing about the new creation, the fulfillment of the divine plan of salvation. She is preparing the way for the coming of the reign of God, when Christ will come again in glory.

When you look around, you quickly realize that humanity and the world fall far short of being the fullness of God's reign of love and freedom, peace and justice that the prophet Isaiah described in Isaiah 11:1–9 and that Jesus inaugurated (see Mark 1:14–15; Luke 4:16–19). God's saving work in the world continues to unfold. The Church is both the seed and sign of that eschatological hope (see Mark 4:26–29). She is always and forever urging humanity to 'do God's will on earth as it is in heaven'.

Already the final age of the world is with us (see 1 Corinthians 10:11) and the renewal of the world is irrevocably under way; it is even now anticipated in a certain real way, for the church on earth is endowed already with a sanctity that is true though imperfect. However, until the

OPENING REFLECTION

⊙ What do you remember about when you were a toddler? A kindergartener? An elementary, middle school or junior high student? What can you do now that you could not do when you were younger?

⊙ As you look to the next few years and beyond, what are your dreams for yourself? What do you want to achieve?

The Eschatological Church: the Seed of the Kingdom and Pilgrim People

The Holy Spirit has guided the Church, since her beginning, in growing in the understanding of

arrival of the new heavens and the new earth in which justice dwells (see 2 Peter 3:13) the pilgrim church, in its sacraments and institutions, which belong to this present age, carries the mark of this world which will pass, and it takes its place among the creatures which groan and until now suffer the pains of childbirth and await the revelation of the children of God (see Romans 8:19–22).

—Vatican II, *Dogmatic Constitution on the Church*, no. 48

THE PEOPLE OF GOD: A PILGRIM PEOPLE

The image of the Church as a 'pilgrim people', a people always on a journey, is rooted in the Old Testament. The Church, the new People of God, is prefigured in the Exodus journey of the Hebrews from slavery in Egypt through the wilderness toward the land God promised them. The Church is the sign and sacrament of the journey of both the People of God and the entire human family from slavery to sin to new life in Christ. She is both the means and the goal of God's plan for humanity.

The Church, the new Pilgrim People of God, is the way of salvation. Christ founded the Church with a divine purpose and mission. She has the divine purpose and mission to work to bring about the reign of God and unite all humanity in Christ to form the one family and People of God, 'a people made one by the unity of the Father, the Son and the holy Spirit' (Vatican II, *Dogmatic Constitution on the Church*, no. 4, citing St. Cyprian of Carthage, *On the Lord's Prayer*, 23). She is to work to achieve this purpose not by ignoring the world but by digging in and working with all people 'for the establishment of a more human world' (Vatican II, *Dogmatic Constitution on the Church in the Modern World*, no. 57).

TALK IT OVER

⊙ How would you respond to someone who says, 'Isn't the Church being hypocritical in telling other people to be holy and to avoid sin when many Catholics, including the clergy, are guilty of sin?'

WHAT ABOUT YOU PERSONALLY?

⊙ What do the images for Church 'seed of the Kingdom' and 'pilgrim people' say to you about your life as a disciple of Jesus Christ?
⊙ What do these images challenge and motivate you to do?

PILGRIM ON THE ROAD TO SANTIAGO DE COMPOSTELA, SPAIN

JUDGE AND ACT

REFLECT ON WHAT YOU HAVE LEARNED IN THIS CHAPTER

As you come toward the end of this chapter, pause and reflect on what you have come to understand about why the Church uses images to help us grasp the mystery of the Church. Share the teachings of the Catholic Church on these statements:

- ◉ The Church is a mystery of faith.
- ◉ The Church is the sign and sacrament of the reign of God.
- ◉ The Church is both visible and spiritual, a hierarchical society and the Mystical Body of Christ.
- ◉ The mystery of the Church is prefigured in the Old Testament.
- ◉ Images that are rooted in Scripture and developed in Tradition help us come to an understanding of the mystery of the Church.
- ◉ The Church is the seed of the Kingdom of God.
- ◉ The Church is a pilgrim people, the new People of God.
- ◉ The Christian home is an image of the Holy Trinity; it is the domestic church, or church of the home.

OVER TO YOU

- ◉ What have you learned from this chapter that moves you to a deeper understanding of the mystery of the Church?
- ◉ What wisdom have you learned for living as a more faithful disciple of Jesus Christ?

VATICAN COUNCIL II: RESPONDING TO THE SIGNS OF THE TIMES

Pope St. John XXIII, who was named a saint of the Church by Pope Francis on April 27, 2014, served the Church as pope from October 28, 1958 to June 3, 1963. He responded to the reality that the Church is the seed and the beginning of the Kingdom of God. John XXIII believed that the Church always needs to read and respond to the 'signs of the times' and interpret the Gospel in light of them. Only when the Church is truly in touch with the world can she be a clear sign and instrument of salvation to the people of the world in which she exists. This was one of the main reasons Pope St. John XXIII announced on January 25, 1959 that he would convoke the Second Vatican Council. The Pope opened the Council on October 11, 1962, and his successor, Pope Paul VI, closed it on December 8, 1965.

The Council issued sixteen documents. The *Dogmatic Constitution on the Church* (*Lumen Gentium*) emphasized that the work of the Church is the work of all the baptized and is not limited to the hierarchy. The Church is first and foremost a 'people', the new People of God. In the *Pastoral Constitution on the Church in the Modern World* (*Gaudium et Spes*), the Council spoke about the meaning of the Church's work in the world and taught that all the baptized are to join with humanity in building a more human world.

Among his final words Pope St. John XXIII is reported to have repeated his vision for the Church:

COUNCIL FATHERS ATTENDING THE SECOND VATICAN COUNCIL

Today, more than ever . . . we are called to serve man as such, and not merely Catholics; to defend above all and everywhere the rights of the human person, and not merely those of the Catholic Church. . . . [T]he needs [of the world], made plain in the last fifty years and a deeper understanding of doctrine, have brought a new situation. . . . It is not that the Gospel has changed, it is that we have begun to understand it better. Those who have lived as long as I have . . . were enabled to compare different cultures and traditions, and know that the moment has come to discern the signs of the times, to seize the opportunity and to look far beyond.

—Pope St. John XXIII, May 24, 1963

REFLECT AND DISCUSS

⊙ How did the Second Vatican Council give witness to what you learned about the Church in this chapter?

⊙ What meaning do the work and words of Pope St. John XXIII have for your life of faith?

LEARN BY EXAMPLE

Blessed John Henry Cardinal Newman (1801–90), philosopher, theologian and seeker of the truth

John Henry Newman was ordained a priest in the Anglican Communion and was received into the Catholic Church in 1845. Pope Leo XIII named Newman, a priest, a Cardinal of the Church—an honor ordinarily bestowed only on bishops. In an address to the Bishops of England and Wales, Pope Benedict XVI described the life and work of Cardinal Newman, saying, '[He] left us an outstanding example of faithfulness to revealed truth by following that "kindly light" wherever it led him, even at considerable personal cost. Great writers and communicators of his stature and integrity are needed in the Church today, and it is my hope that devotion to him will inspire many to follow in his footstep.' And on September 8, 2010 he named Cardinal Newman a Blessed of the Church.

In his own day and time Newman challenged the Church to understand and appreciate more deeply the role of the laity in the Church. When asked about the laity's role, he responded, 'Well, it would be rather empty without them.' In 1859 Newman published *On Consulting the Faithful in Matters of Doctrine*, in which he argued that the lived and professed faith of the faithful plays a vital role in the development of the doctrine of the Church.

Newman referred to the laity's steadfast adherence to the authentic Tradition of the Church as the *consensus fidelium*, or the consent of the faithful. By this Newman meant that the Holy Spirit communicates the truth about faith and morals to all baptized people and not just to bishops and theologians. Vatican II, one hundred years later, affirmed:

The whole body of the faithful who have received an anointing which comes from the holy one (see 1 John 2:20 and 27) cannot be mistaken in belief. It shows this characteristic through the entire people's supernatural sense of the faith, when 'from the bishops to the last of the faithful,' it manifests a universal consensus in matters of faith and morals.

—*Dogmatic Constitution on the Church*, no. 12

Cardinal Newman believed, as the Catholic Church teaches, that the whole Church is guided by the Holy Spirit and works together to grow in understanding of the Word of God. The Magisterium does not fulfill its responsibility in isolation; the Magisterium listens to the voice of the whole Church to interpret Revelation authentically.

TALK IT OVER

John Henry Cardinal Newman, as Pope St. John XXIII did, gave witness to the reality that the Church is always growing in her understanding of the truth.

- ⊙ What wisdom does Cardinal Newman's teaching provide for young people in the Church today?
- ⊙ What can you learn for your own life from the life and teachings of Cardinal Newman?

RESPOND WITH FAMILY AND FRIENDS

- ⊙ Discuss and decide how you might be clearer signs of God at work in your neighborhood.
- ⊙ Choose one of your ideas and put it into action together.

WHAT WILL YOU DO NOW?

- ⊙ What can and will you do to help bring about the kingdom of justice, peace and love that Jesus inaugurated and that the Church continues to build?
- ⊙ Write your reflections in your journal. Revisit them often, and act upon them.

LEARN BY HEART

'I am the vine, you are the branches.
Those who abide in me and I in them
bear much fruit,
because apart from me you can do nothing.'

JOHN 15:5

Pray the Sign of the Cross together. Then quietly reflect on the Church and her mission to be the sacrament of God's saving work in the world.

LEADER

Let us look at the images on this page, one at a time, and ask ourselves:

- ⊙ What does this image say to me about the Church?
- ⊙ What does this image say to me about who I am as a member of the Church?

All pair up, reflect quietly on the images, and share reflections.

LEADER

Blessed John Henry Cardinal Newman left us a treasury of hymns and prayers that includes this 'Daily Prayer'. Let us pray it together.

ALL

May he support us all the day long,
till the shades lengthen and the evening comes,
and the busy world is hushed,
and the fever of life is over,
and our work is done.
Then in his mercy may he give us a safe lodging,
and a holy rest and peace at the last. Amen.

All conclude by dipping the fingers of their right hand in holy water, recalling their Baptism, and blessing themselves as they pray the Sign of the Cross together.

CHAPTER 5

The Church's Unity in Christ

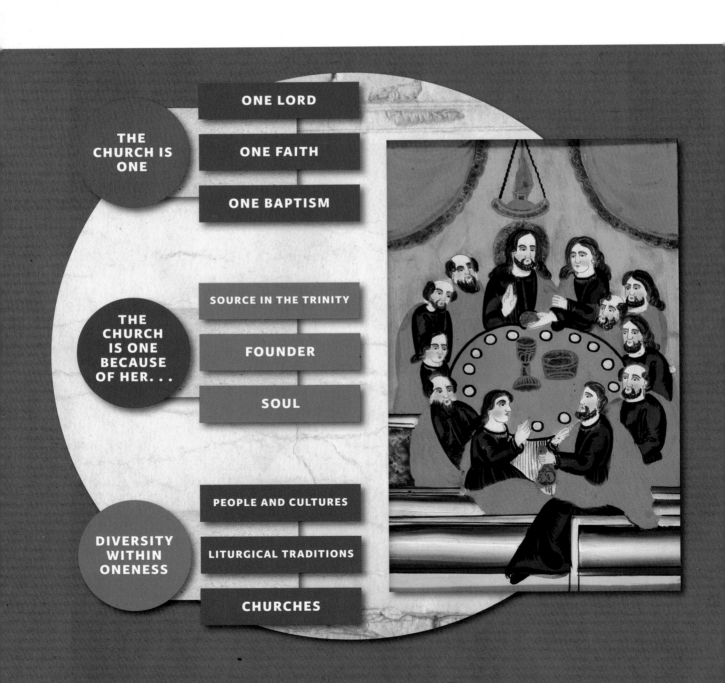

THE CHURCH IS ONE
- ONE LORD
- ONE FAITH
- ONE BAPTISM

THE CHURCH IS ONE BECAUSE OF HER. . .
- SOURCE IN THE TRINITY
- FOUNDER
- SOUL

DIVERSITY WITHIN ONENESS
- PEOPLE AND CULTURES
- LITURGICAL TRADITIONS
- CHURCHES

IN THE NICENE CREED WE PROFESS WITH THE CHURCH, 'I believe in one, holy, catholic and apostolic Church.' One, holy, catholic and apostolic are the four Marks, or essential characteristics, of the Church. 'The sole Church of Christ which . . . we profess to be one, holy, catholic, and apostolic . . . subsists in the Catholic Church' (*Catechism of the Catholic Church*, no. 870). In this chapter we begin our study of the Marks of the Church. This chapter explores the first Mark, *one*. In chapters 6 and 7 we will study the teaching of the Catholic Church on the remaining three Marks, 'holy', 'catholic' and 'apostolic'.

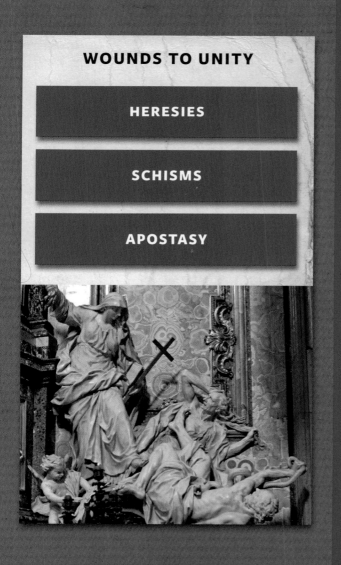

WOUNDS TO UNITY

HERESIES

SCHISMS

APOSTASY

Faith Focus: The teachings of the Catholic Church that are the primary focus of the doctrinal content presented in this chapter include:
- ⊙ The four Marks of the Church are one, holy, catholic and apostolic.
- ⊙ The Church is one; the Church's unity is founded in Jesus Christ through the Holy Spirit.
- ⊙ The Church is united in charity (love), in the profession of faith, in the common celebration of the sacraments and in apostolic succession.
- ⊙ The multiplicity and diversity of peoples, cultures and liturgical traditions within the Church enrich the unity of the Church.
- ⊙ Heresy, schism and apostasy wound the unity of the Church.
- ⊙ The Holy Spirit guides the Church to work to bring about Christ's will for the unity of his followers.

Discipleship Formation: As a result of studying this chapter and discovering the meaning of the faith of the Catholic Church for your life, you should be better able to:
- ⊙ deepen your trust in Jesus Christ, the Head and source of unity within the Church;
- ⊙ appreciate the importance of stating the faith of the Catholic Church precisely and accurately;
- ⊙ recognize diversity as a positive force that deepens the unity of the Church;
- ⊙ identify ways Catholics and other Christians can support one another in living as disciples of Jesus;
- ⊙ identify and decide on ways in which you can promote such unity.

Scripture References: These Scripture references are quoted or referred to in this chapter:
OLD TESTAMENT: Genesis 2:18–24, 9:9–13
NEW TESTAMENT: Matthew 16:13–19, 26:20–25, 47–50; **Mark** 2:13–17, 9:33–37; **Luke** 9:46–48, 22:24–27, 23:49; **John** 14:6, 17:20–23, 20:1–10, 21:15–19; **Acts of the Apostles** 2:14; **1 Corinthians** 10:17, 12:12–13, 21, 27; **Ephesians** 4:3–5

Faith Glossary: Familiarize yourself with the meaning of these key terms. Definitions are found in the Glossary: **apostasy, apostolic succession, Apostolic Tradition, atonement, Deposit of Faith, ecclesial communities, ecumenism, evangelization, heresy, hierarchy, hypostatic union, Incarnation, inculturation, Liturgy, Magisterium, sacrament, salvation, schism, the Twelve**

Faith Words: apostasy; apostolic succession; schism
Learn by Heart: John 17:21
Learn by Example: Franciscan Friars and Sisters of the Atonement

Why strive for unity?

The Mann Gulch Disaster

Smokejumpers make up an elite group of the men and women who dedicate their lives to working together fighting wildfires. They parachute into areas ahead of the fire to suppress its advance. On August 5, 1949 a crew of sixteen smokejumpers under the leadership of their foreman, Wagner Dodge, was dispatched from Missoula, Montana on a C-47 transport plane and headed to contain a raging wildfire in Mann Gulch in the Helena National Forest in Montana. Most of the crew members were relatively inexperienced smokejumpers.

During their training season, Dodge had spent little time helping the crew learn fire-fighting techniques; instead, he had focused on base maintenance. The crew did not come to know Dodge or one another well. This led to a lack of confidence in Dodge's leadership and in their trust in one another's abilities.

For more than sixty years, the Mann Gulch incident has been studied as a case study in group dynamics as an example of 'a recipe for disaster'. Tragically, that is how the Mann Gulch mission ended. Thirteen of the sixteen smokejumpers lost their lives in the fire.

INVESTIGATING THE MANN GULCH FIRE

OPENING CONVERSATION

⊙ What wisdom might you learn from this incident about people working together? About leadership?

⊙ Share with a partner an example of a group of people whom you know who work well together. What is the basis of the group's unity and effectiveness?

⊙ Share also an example of a group of people who did not or do not work well together. Identify the causes and the consequences of their disunity.

⊙ Discuss how diversity might contribute to unity and effectiveness or disunity and ineffectiveness.

THE COMMUNITY OF JESUS' DISCIPLES

Jesus gathered a very diverse group of people to follow him and become his first community of disciples. He called together people who were accepted and also people who were not accepted within Judaism. He welcomed those whom Jews ignored, cast aside and excluded from participating in the daily life of society.

The Twelve, the original Apostles, whom Jesus gathered around him to be his closest circle of disciples, included the outspoken Simon Peter and the reflective John. There was also Andrew who believed immediately, and Thomas who still doubted after spending three years with Jesus. Then there was Nathaniel who was a devout

Jesus gathered a very diverse group of people to follow him and become his first community of disciples

Jew, and Levi (Matthew) the tax-collector who, following Roman law, charged people more than was legally owed in taxes. Mark reports that after he welcomed Levi into the Twelve, Jesus went to Levi's house and ate dinner 'with many tax collectors and sinners'— people normally shunned by 'devout' Jews who followed the Mosaic law. (Read Mark 2:13–17.)

The four accounts of the Gospel report that Jesus also chose women to be among a larger inner circle of his disciples. For example, the three Synoptic Gospels record that the women at the foot of the Cross on Calvary were with Jesus from the beginning of his public life and ministry. Luke specifically reports that they 'had followed him from Galilee' (Luke 23:49). This was also contrary to the social norms of Jesus' time and certainly would have been neither a common nor an acceptable practice among rabbis and other Jewish leaders.

ORDER WITHIN THE DIVERSITY AMONG THE DISCIPLES

The four Gospels and other New Testament writings clearly tell us that there was both harmony and divisiveness among the Twelve. The disciples argued between themselves about who was the most important among them. (Read Mark 9:33–37, 10:35–37; Luke 9:46–48, 22:24–27). Judas betrayed Jesus and separated himself from the group. (Read Matthew 26:20–25, 47–50.) They struggled and sometimes disagreed about their understanding of who Jesus was, the nature of his mission and the meaning of his teachings. These same struggles continued after the Resurrection and Ascension and Pentecost. For example, recall the Gentile controversy and the Council at Jerusalem. Through it all, the early Church found and maintained its unity and faith in Jesus Christ and the work of the Holy Spirit among them.

Jesus is the Savior of all people; he gathered together Jew and Gentile, 'saints' and 'sinners', men and women into one community to become the one People of God. He fully intended them to work together as 'one' to continue his saving mission to the world after he returned to his Father.

REFLECT AND DISCUSS

⊙ What does the diversity within the original group of disciples say to you about Jesus' mission? About the work of the Church?

JESUS PRESENTING ST. PETER WITH THE KEYS | ST. PETERS, VATICAN CITY

⊙ How do you see that same diversity at work in the Church today? In your parish and in your school community?

JESUS CHOOSES AND APPOINTS A LEADER AMONG THE TWELVE

Jesus, while preaching in Caesarea Philippi, asked his disciples, 'Who do people say that the Son of Man is?' (Matthew 16:13). The dialogue went back and forth until Peter made his well-known confession of faith, 'You are the Messiah, the Son of the living God' (Matthew 16:16). Matthew continues:

And Jesus answered him, 'Blessed are you, Simon son of Jonah! For flesh and blood has not revealed this to you, but my Father in heaven. And I tell you, you are Peter, and on this rock I will build my church, and the gates of Hades will not prevail against it. I will give you the keys of the kingdom of heaven, and whatever you bind on earth will be bound in heaven, and whatever you loose on earth will be loosed in heaven.'
—Matthew 16:17–19

After the Resurrection, the risen Christ would reaffirm the leadership role he was giving to Peter. (Reread John 21:15–19.) The other disciples recognized and accepted Peter's leadership. For example, Mary Magdalene first reported the Resurrection to Peter. When Mary, along with the disciple whom Jesus loved, and Peter returned to the empty tomb, they all waited for Peter to enter the tomb. (Read John 20:1–10.) After the Holy Spirit came upon the disciples at Pentecost, they all left the house together. But it was Peter, 'standing with the eleven', who first proclaimed Jesus Christ in the marketplace in Jerusalem. (Read Acts of the Apostles 2:14.) And at the Council of Jerusalem, you will recall, Peter asserted the leadership role the Lord had given to him.

LEADERSHIP OF THE CHURCH TODAY

Christ endowed his Church with a structure until the Kingdom is fully achieved. The Pope, the Vicar of Christ and the successor of St. Peter, and the other bishops, the successors of the other Apostles, have continued this ministry and apostolic leadership within the Church since the days of the early Church. The Church gives the name **apostolic succession** to this passing on of the ministry of Peter and the Apostles 'from the Apostles to bishops, and from them to other bishops down each generation, by means of ordination' (*United States Catholic Catechism for Adults* [USCCA], 504).

The Pope and the other bishops in communion with him are members of the **hierarchy** of the Church. The word 'hierarchy' comes from the Greek *hier-arche*, which translates as 'holy (*hier*) order (*arche*)'. Jesus gave the Apostles and their successors the responsibility to order the Church in her work and mission. Holy Orders, or Ordination, is the 'Sacrament in which a bishop ordains a man to be conformed to Jesus Christ by grace, to service and leadership in the Church' (USCCA, 514–15). The ordination of bishops and their co-workers, priests, comes down in an unbroken line from the Apostles and maintains 'the fraternal concord of God's family' (CCC, no. 815). The leadership function of the Pope, bishops and priests is to serve the communion, or unity, of the whole Church.

Under the leadership of the Pope and the bishops in communion with him, each of the baptized has a specific and vital role to play in forging the unity of the Church and of the human race in Christ. (In chapters 7 and 12 of this text we will explore the threefold office, or role, of the hierarchy in more depth.)

TALK IT OVER

⊙ Discuss your knowledge and understanding of the leadership of the Church.

Draw from what you have learned not only in theology classes but also from your study of the history of the Church.

⊙ How do you see the leaders of the Church today promoting unity within the Church? Within our society? Within the global community?

WHAT ABOUT YOU PERSONALLY?

⊙ How can you work for unity in your family? Among your friends, both Catholic and non-Catholic?

FAITH WORD

Apostolic Succession

The passing on of the office of bishop from the Apostles to bishops, and from them to other bishops down each generation, by means of ordination. This office includes the sanctifying, teaching, and governing roles within the Church.
—USCCA, 504

POPE FRANCIS' FIRST PUBLIC APPEARANCE, MARCH 13, 2013

Diversity within oneness

Father, are in me and I am in you, may they also be in us, so that the world may believe that you have sent me. The glory that you have given me I have given them, so that they may be one, as we are one, I in them and you in me, that they may become completely one, so that the world may know that you have sent me and have loved them even as you have loved me.'

—John 17:20–23

The Church's 'oneness' is a visible unity and a credible sign to the world that Jesus was indeed God's own Son, 'the way, and the truth, and the life' (John 14:6). A lack of unity and peace within the Church will be a countersign to the Gospel and an obstacle to the Church's fulfilling the work Jesus commissioned and shares with her.

OPENING REFLECTION
⊙ Think of a time or times when you have worked successfully with others in your family, school or parish to achieve a common goal.
⊙ What disposed the group to work together successfully?

MAY THEY ALL BE ONE
Unity and oneness is the essence of the Church. '[The] Church is one because of her source: "the highest exemplar and source of this mystery is the unity, in the Trinity of Persons, of one God, the Father and the Son in the Holy Spirit" ' (CCC, no. 813). In his prayer for his disciples at the Last Supper, Jesus described and expressed his desire for unity among his followers. He prayed:

'I ask not only on behalf of these, but also on behalf of those who will believe in me through their word, that they may all be one. As you,

FROM THE WISDOM OF THE CHURCH
The Church is the Body of Christ. . . . In the unity of this Body, there is a diversity of members and functions. . . . [The Church] lives from him, in him, and for him; he lives with her and in her.

—CCC, nos. 805, 806, 807

ONE IN JESUS
One in her founder: 'The Church is one *because of her founder*: for "the Word made flesh, the prince of peace, reconciled all men to God by the cross . . . restoring the unity of all in one people and one body" ' (CCC, no. 813). As you have already explored in this course of study, St. Paul used the image of the 'Body of Christ' (see 1 Corinthians 12:12–13) to teach that the Church is one in Christ Jesus. To make his point he compared the Church to the functionality of the human body. 'The

Church is this Body of which Christ is the head: she lives from him, in him, and for him; he lives with her and in her' (CCC, no. 807).

Every part of the body is needed if the body is to function well. 'The eye cannot say to the hand, "I have no need of you", nor again the head to the feet, "I have no need of you" ' (1 Corinthians 12:21). The same is true of the Church. Building up the unity of the Church and, indeed, peace and unity in the world, is a sign of the work of the Holy Spirit living with the Church and in every Christian. For in the one and the same Spirit we were all baptized into the one Body of Christ. We are 'the body of Christ and individually members of it' (1 Corinthians 12:27).

One in her soul: 'The Church is one *because of her "soul"* ' (CCC, no. 813). 'The Spirit is the soul . . . of the Mystical Body, the source of its life, of its unity in diversity, and the riches of its gifts and charisms' (CCC, no. 809). We have explored that the Church is the temple of the Holy Spirit, who builds, animates and sanctifies the Church. 'It is the Holy Spirit, dwelling in those who believe and pervading and ruling over the entire Church, who brings about that wonderful communion of the faithful and joins them together so intimately in Christ that he is the principle of the Church's unity' (CCC, no. 813).

OVER TO YOU
- ⊙ Think of a situation in your parish or school where an individual or group worked effectively to bring about unity when there was disunity.
- ⊙ What gifts did they use?
- ⊙ What can you learn about the work of the Church from this experience?

> FROM THE WISDOM OF THE CHURCH
> The Church is one: she acknowledges one Lord, confesses one faith, is born of one Baptism, forms only one Body, is given life by the one Spirit, for the sake of one hope (see Ephesians 4:3–5), at whose fulfillment all divisions will be overcome.
>
> —CCC, no. 866

Christ Has No Body Now, but Yours

Christ has no body now, but yours.
No hands, no feet on earth but yours.
Yours are the eyes through which
he looks with compassion on the world.
Yours are the feet
with which he walks to do good.
Yours are the hands
with which he blesses the world.

—St. Teresa of Ávila (1515–82)

ST. TERESA OF ÁVILA | ST. PETER'S BASILICA, VATICAN CITY

BASILICA OF MONTSERRAT, CATALONIA, SPAIN

The Church is united in the common celebration of the sacraments

ONE LORD, ONE FAITH, ONE BAPTISM
The Church is united in charity, in the profession of one faith, in the common celebration of the sacraments and in apostolic succession. You have explored how living the Great Commandment of love and apostolic succession expresses and builds up the unity of the Church. We will now look at how the Church's profession of one faith and celebration of the Seven Sacraments express and build up that unity.

Profession of one faith: 'There is . . . one Lord, one faith . . .' (Ephesians 4:4–5). The one **Deposit of Faith**, contained in Sacred Scripture and Sacred Tradition, is taught and passed on authentically by the **Magisterium** of the Church. Wherever we live, in whatever corner of the world, we profess this one faith of the Church. The Apostles' Creed and the Nicene Creed are summaries of this faith.

Celebration of worship and the sacraments: The Seven Sacraments are celebrations of our life in Christ and of the faith of the Church. Joined to Christ in Baptism, we become members of his Church. The baptized person's initiation into the Church is completed in Confirmation and the Eucharist. St. Paul taught that we are bonded in unity by our reception of the same body of

Christ in the Eucharist. 'Because there is one bread, we who are many are one body, for we all partake of the one bread' (1 Corinthians 10:17). Reconciliation and Anointing of the Sick heal us in moments of weakness. Holy Orders and Matrimony give some members of the Church the mission to serve the unity of the whole Church.

JOURNAL EXERCISE
- Read and reflect on the meaning of Ephesians 4:4–5 for your life right here, right now.
- Create a poster that depicts the Church's call to be a united community.

DIVERSITY: THE BEAUTY OF THE CHURCH
The waters of the flood point to the waters of Baptism; in Baptism we die to sin and rise to new life in Christ. Jesus is the new and everlasting covenant, in which all creation is to be reborn. Diversity within her unity has been a hallmark of the Church since apostolic times. 'From the beginning, this one Church has been marked by a great *diversity* which comes from both the variety of God's gifts and the diversity of those who receive them' (CCC, no. 814). This diversity is expressed in the multiplicity of peoples, cultures and liturgical traditions within one Church. The unity within the Church

is prefigured in God's covenant with Noah, humanity and all creation:

'As for me, I am establishing my covenant with you and your descendants after you, and with every living creature. . . . This is the sign of the covenant that I make between me and you and every living creature that is with you, for all future generations: I have set my bow in the clouds, and it shall be a sign of covenant between me and the earth.'
—Genesis 9:9–13

OVER TO YOU

⊙ Why might the 'bow in the clouds', which many interpret to be a rainbow, be a strong image of the beauty of the Church?

Diversity of people and cultures: 'It is with and through their own human culture, assumed and transfigured by Christ, that the multitude of God's children has access to the Father, in order to glorify him in the one Spirit' (CCC, no. 1204). The Catholic Church is truly 'catholic'. She evangelizes, or brings the Gospel to all peoples in all lands and all cultures. This dimension of the Church's mission of **evangelization** is called the 'inculturation of the Gospel'. This statement from the United States Conference of Catholic Bishops captures the heart of the process of **inculturation**:

True inculturation occurs when the gospel penetrates the heart of cultural experience and shows how Christ gives new meaning to authentic human values. However, the Church must never allow herself to be absorbed by any culture, since not all cultural expressions are in conformity with the gospel.
—*To the Ends of the Earth: A Pastoral Statement on World Mission*, no. 44

The Catholic Church in the United States of America is a reflection of the universal Church. We are a Church of many cultural families, including (1) European, (2) Hispanic, (3) African American, (4) Native American, (5) Asian-Pacific, and (6) migrant cultural families. Each cultural family within the Church contributes to the richness and beauty of the Church in the United States. Each gives a unique and distinctive cultural expression

The waters of the flood point to the waters of Baptism

We are a Church of many cultural families and each contributes to the richness and beauty of the Church

of the Catholic faith. 'The great richness of such diversity is not opposed to the Church's unity' (CCC, no. 814). It is part of the genius and mission of the Church to 'make herself at home' in every culture. Unity through uniformity would be like a straightjacket. Unity through diversity is a great grace from God.

Diversity of liturgical traditions: The 'catholic' mission of the Church is the source of the diverse liturgical traditions within the Church. 'The diverse liturgical traditions have arisen by the very reason of the Church's mission' (CCC, no. 1202). At her **Liturgy** the members of the Body of Christ join with Christ the Head to give praise and glory to the Father through the power of the Holy Spirit. The major liturgical traditions, or rites, celebrated by the Church include the Latin rite (which includes the Roman rite and other rites such as the Ambrosian rite and those of religious orders,) and the Byzantine, Alexandrian or Coptic, Syriac, Armenian, Maronite and Chaldean rites. Each of these rites in its own way contributes to the Church's celebration of her life in Christ. Similar to the images of the Church, no one rite or liturgical tradition fully expresses the mystery of our life in Christ.

All the liturgical traditions and rites that the Church recognizes as faithful 'to **apostolic Tradition**, that is, the communion in the faith and the sacraments received from the apostles, a communion that is both signified and guaranteed by apostolic succession' (CCC, no. 1209) 'signify and communicate the same mystery of Christ' (CCC, no. 1208).

Diversity of Churches: The diversity within the oneness of the Catholic Church is also expressed in the communion of the twenty-one Eastern Catholic Churches and the Western (sometimes called Latin) Church. The Eastern Catholic Churches originate in Eastern Europe, Asia or Africa and have their own liturgical and legal systems. There are about 17 million Eastern Catholics worldwide. The Byzantine Catholic Church, the Chaldean Catholic Church, the Coptic Catholic Church, the Maronite Catholic Church, the Melkite Catholic Church and the Ukrainian Catholic Church are the best known of the Eastern Churches. Each of these Churches has its own distinctive languages, ways of celebrating the sacraments, structures of governance and other traditions.

THINK, PAIR AND SHARE

⊙ Talk with a partner about some of the distinctive traditions of the Church, and ways your family and parish might celebrate those traditions.

⊙ Discuss what you can learn from one another about unity in faith through diversity of expression and celebration of the one faith of the Church.

Words, the source of both unity and division

OPENING CONVERSATION

- ⊙ What do you think? Do words matter? Do they have a power or are they neutral?
- ⊙ Recall a situation from one of the accounts of the Gospel when the 'power' of Jesus' words impacted his listeners. Share your example.

OVER TO YOU

- ⊙ Recall a time when you have experienced the power of positive words and of negative words spoken to you.
- ⊙ Now recall a time when your words affected others positively and negatively.
- ⊙ What did you learn about the power of the spoken word?

In the beginning was the Word...

WOUNDS TO UNITY

Words have been a source of both unity and division within the Church. The word 'orthodoxy' captures the importance of stating the faith of the Church precisely and accurately. The word 'orthodoxy' comes from the Greek word *orthodoxa*, which means 'right (*ortho*) words (*doxa*)'. Using the right words to state the faith of the Church is necessary for both our understanding of the faith and our living the faith.

The use of the 'wrong words' can lead to **heresy**, **schism** and even **apostasy**. A heresy is 'a religious teaching that denies or contradicts truths revealed by God' (USCCA, 514). Sometimes members of the Church believe in a heresy so obstinately that they break away from the Church. This is called a schism. A schism is 'the refusal to submit to the pope's authority as head of the Church' (USCCA, 342). Sometimes a member of the Church may choose to abandon the Christian faith completely. This is called apostasy. Apostasy is the 'total repudiation of the Christian faith' (CCC, no. 2089 and Glossary).

Here are some of the major divisions that have occurred within the Church when groups separated themselves from the Church:

- – First century: Jews and Jewish Christians separated over Jesus as Messiah.
- – Fifth century: Following the Council of Ephesus in 431, the followers of Nestorius formed the Assyrian Church, but later returned to union with Rome.
- – Fifth century: Following the Council of Chalcedon in 451, those who followed the Monophysite heresy formed the Oriental Orthodox Churches and separated themselves from the Church.

- Ninth century: In 1054 the Pope in Rome and the bishop of Constantinople excommunicated each other. This led to the breach between the Roman Catholic Church and the Eastern Orthodox Church.

- Sixteenth century: Martin Luther and other Protestant reformers separated themselves and their followers from the authority of the Pope and the Roman Catholic Church.

RELIGION OVERTHROWING HERESY AND HATRED | PIERRE LEGROS THE YOUNGER

HERESIES WITHIN THE EARLY CHURCH

We will look briefly at the heresies of Gnosticism, Arianism, Nestorianism, Monophysitism and Apollinarianism to explore the importance of stating the Church's faith in Jesus Christ accurately if we are to share that faith with others. The words these heresies used resulted in their denial of the apostolic teaching on the **Incarnation**. 'By the Incarnation, the Second Person of the Holy Trinity assumed our human nature, taking flesh in the womb of the Virgin Mary. There is one Person in Jesus and that is the divine Person of the Son of God. Jesus has two natures, a human one and a divine one' (USCCA, 515).

Each of these heresies in its own way denied that Jesus was either fully divine or fully human—that Jesus was true God and true man. This denial of the divinity or the humanity of Christ also had consequences for the meaning of **salvation**. If Jesus was not a true man—truly and fully human in all ways except sin—there would be no true **atonement** for the sins of humanity, no salvation. If Jesus was not fully divine, his sacrifice on the Cross would not truly be the work of God.

Now, let us take a brief look at these five key heresies of the early Church.

Gnosticism: Gnostics taught that the human body is corrupt. Because of that belief they taught that Jesus did not really have a human body. Jesus was not a true man; he only *appeared* to be 'man'. Gnostics also claimed that salvation comes from secret knowledge (*gnosis*) that Jesus told his Apostles. Salvation was not for everyone, but just for a select few who accepted the secret teachings of Jesus and became 'enlightened'.

Arianism: In the fourth century, Arianism taught that Jesus was not truly God. This heresy is an example of how the choice between two words can make a huge difference in authentically stating the faith of the Catholic Church. The two words are *homoousios* and *homoiousios*. Notice the letter 'i' in *homoiousios*. The letter 'i' made a world of difference. Arianism taught that Jesus was of a similar substance (*homoiousios*), but not of the same substance, as God. The First Council of Constantinople in 381 rejected this heresy and taught that Jesus was '*of the same substance*' (*homoousios*) as God, or the same nature as God. In other words, Jesus was fully God. Jesus our Savior was truly divine and truly human.

Apollinarianism: In the fourth century, Apollinarius (310–90), Bishop of Laodicea, and his followers falsely taught that Jesus was not fully human. They believed that Jesus has only one nature, the divine nature. For if Jesus had a human nature and, therefore, a human will, he could not be without sin. Because of this teaching, Apollinarianism leads to a view of salvation that is contrary to the Church's teaching. If Jesus were not fully human, he could not save humanity. The First Council of Constantinople (381) also condemned this heresy.

Nestorianism: In the fifth century, Nestorius (d. c. 451), Patriarch of Constantinople, thought he could solve the mystery of Jesus by proposing that Jesus was two separate persons, a human person joined to the divine Person of the Son of God. The Church, at the Council of Ephesus in 431, reaffirmed the faith of the Church that Jesus is one divine Person in whom the divine nature and a human nature are united. This teaching of the Church is called the '**hypostatic union**'.

JESUS CALLS PETER AND ANDREW | ST. PETER'S, VATICAN CITY

Jesus, the Savior of the world, is inseparably true God and true man who is one divine Person, who freely sacrificed his life on the Cross.

Monophysitism: In the sixth–seventh century, Monophysitism falsely taught that Jesus had only one nature, a divine nature. The human nature of Jesus ceased to exist as such in Christ when the Son of God assumed it. Without the Son of God taking on flesh and becoming truly man, there can be no salvation. The Council of Chalcedon (451) condemned this heresy.

POPE ST. PIUS X IN THE LATE NINETEENTH CENTURY

Society of St. Pius X

Wounds to the Church's unity are not limited to the past. For example, the refusal of Archbishop Marcel Lefebvre (1905–91), who had served as a missionary bishop in Africa, to accept the authority of the Church has led to the formation of the Society of St. Pius X (SSPX) and their separation of themselves from the Pope and the Catholic Church. As did his predecessors John Paul II and Benedict XVI, Pope Francis is in dialogue with the leadership of the Society of St. Pius X to heal those wounds.

CULTS AND SECTS

Groups of Christians today, as has happened from the days of the early Church, have formed into 'cults' and 'sects'. These groups' interpretation of the Gospel is contrary to both the fundamental teachings of Christianity and the teachings of the Catholic Church; for example, the doctrines of the Holy Trinity and the divinity of Christ. In addition, cults and sects exert great psychological pressure, authority and control over their members.

Among the sects or cults today are: The Church of Scientology, The Unification Church (The Holy Spirit Association for the Unification of World Christianity), The Watchtower Bible and Tract Society, The Church of Bible Understanding, Movement for the Restoration of the Ten Commandments of God, The International Churches of Christ (Boston Movement), The Family (Children of God) and Christian Identity Movement (Aryan Nations, Christian Identity Church).

REFLECT AND DISCUSS

⊙ Why is it important for Christians to believe in the Holy Trinity and in the full divinity and the full humanity of Jesus?

WHAT ABOUT YOU PERSONALLY?

⊙ How would you answer Jesus' question to Peter, 'Who do you say I am?'

No one is an island

OPENING CONVERSATION

Some four hundred years ago, the English poet and Anglican priest John Donne (1572–1631) penned these immortal lines to begin his poem 'No Man Is an Island':

No man is an island entire of itself; every man is a piece of the continent, a part of the main.

⊙ What meaning do Donne's words have for you?

⊙ Recall the account about the creation of the human person in Genesis 2:18–24. How do Donne's words reflect this Revelation?

The First Great Schism: Eastern Schism of 1054

PATRIARCH KIRILL I   POPE FRANCIS

Recall Jesus' words to Peter, 'I tell you, you are Peter, and on this rock I will build my church' (Matthew 16:18). 'The Lord made St. Peter the visible foundation of his Church. He entrusted the keys of the Church to him' (CCC, no. 936). The Pope is the successor of St. Peter and 'the Vicar of Christ and pastor of the universal Church on earth' (CCC, no. 936). The schism of 1054 was the result of the Patriarch of the Church in the East not fully accepting this declaration of Christ.

Over the centuries the Roman Empire divided into East and West, with their centers of government in Constantinople and Rome, respectively. Both capitals became equal centers of Catholic faith. Political tensions and often wars emerged between the two parts of the Empire, and religious tensions emerged as well. The tensions eventually led to a division, or schism, between the Church in the East and the Church in the West.

The reasons for the schism are many and cannot be captured in this brief overview. Essentially, Eastern and Western Christianity remained united in their profession of the apostolic faith, sharing the same creeds and sacraments. However, there was disagreements between the Pope, the bishop of Rome, and the Patriarch of Constantinople as to who should have universal jurisdiction in matters of Church governance. This tension was heightened by other disputes, for example, about the kind of bread to be used for the Eucharist (leavened or unleavened), and whether priests and bishops must have beards.

The final breach of union within the Church is usually dated from 1054. In that year, legates sent by Pope Leo IX had an intense dispute with Patriarch Michael Cerularius, and they mutually excommunicated each other. Thereafter, the Church split into the Roman Catholic Church and the Eastern Orthodox Church. This breach continues today. While separated from each other in many ways, the Roman Catholic Church and the Orthodox Church share in a rich Tradition, which they express in a diversity of traditions. This reality has been expressed over and over again in recent years at the meetings between the popes and the patriarchs of the Orthodox Church.

LET'S PROBE DEEPER

◉ Work in groups or with a partner and research one of the following:
- Eastern Orthodox Churches;
- Eastern Catholic Churches that are in communion with the Pope.

◉ Present your findings to the class at the conclusion of your study of this chapter or course of study.

The Protestant Reformation

History books mark the beginning of the Protestant Reformation on October 31, 1517, when Martin Luther, an Augustinian monk, nailed 'Ninety-Five Theses' to the door of the Castle Church in Wittenberg, Germany. In his 'Theses' Luther called for a variety of reforms within both the teachings and practices of the Roman Catholic Church. The Protestant Reformation resulted in many reformers and their followers separating themselves from the Roman Catholic Church. Today, there are more than 33,000 Protestant denominations worldwide.

Luther wanted to give priority to Scripture in the life of the Church. This eventually led to Luther's teaching of *sola scriptura* (Scripture alone); in other words, the Bible alone is the measure of the faith. This, in turn, led to the denial of Apostolic Tradition as a true source of faith and of the Magisterium as the teacher of the faith.

Luther also called for reform to correct erroneous pastoral practices of the clergy. This led to Luther's teachings of *sola gratia* (grace alone) and *sola fidei* (faith alone); in other words, a person is saved by grace and faith alone and not by any human effort. Luther could not resolve his disagreements with the Church, and Pope Leo X excommunicated him on January 3, 1521.

The call for reformation grew wider and other reformers soon followed Luther's lead.

MARTIN LUTHER | LUCAS CRANACH THE ELDER

Ulrich Zwingli (1484–1531) in Switzerland, John Calvin (1509–64) in France, and John Knox (c. 1505–72) in Scotland were among these Protestant reformers. In England King Henry VIII challenged the Pope's authority over his right to divorce and remarry. After protracted debate King Henry, by a decree of Parliament, declared himself to be the head of the Church in England.

The Catholic Church responded with her own efforts at reforming the Church. These efforts are known as the Catholic Reformation. The Council of Trent (1545–63) became the center of the Catholic Reformation.

All validly baptized Christians are bonded members of the Body of Christ in the world

TALK IT OVER

- What are some obvious things that distinguish Catholics and other Christians? What are some of the things they share in common?
- Describe your own attitude toward people of other Christian faith communities. How did you come to have this attitude?

BROTHERS AND SISTERS IN THE LORD

Today there are more than 270 non-Catholic Christian denominations, or **ecclesial communities**, in the United States. How are we to understand the relationship between the numerous ecclesial communities and the Catholic Church? The Second Vatican Council teaches three points we need to keep in mind. First, 'the unique Church of Christ' as founded by Jesus 'subsists in the Catholic Church, which is governed by the successor of Peter and by the bishops in communion with him' (*Dogmatic Constitution on the Church*, no. 8). Second, people on both sides—Catholic and Protestant—'were to blame' for the fragmentation that came with the Reformation (*Decree on Ecumenism*, no. 3). Third, all who are 'brought up in the faith of Christ . . . are accepted as sisters and brothers in the Lord by the children of the Catholic Church' (*Decree on Ecumenism*, no. 3).

Echoing Vatican II, the *Catechism* states that '[M]any elements of sanctification and of truth are found outside the visible confines of the Catholic Church' (CCC, no. 819). Clearly, all validly baptized Christians are made brothers and sisters in Christ; all are bonded members of the Body of Christ in the world.

- The Church at Vatican II taught that all Christians must be ready to learn from one another. What can other Christians learn from Catholics? Catholics learn from other Christians?
- The Catholic Church teaches that all Christians should support one another in living as disciples of Jesus. What are some ways the Catholic Church might put this teaching into practice?

THE SPIRIT OF CHRIST, THE SPIRIT OF UNITY

Clearly, if Christians are to fulfill the prayer of Jesus at the Last Supper 'that all [my disciples] may be one', then we still have a lot of work to do. The Second Vatican Council called all Christians to take part in this work. This work of the Church is called '**ecumenism**'. Ecumenism involves 'the efforts among all Christians to bring about the fulfillment of Christ's will for the unity of his followers' (USCCA, 511). The first principle of ecumenism is fostering a change of heart and a renewal of our minds that leads us all to ask forgiveness from God and from our separated brothers and sisters for our part in the fragmentation of the one Church of Jesus Christ. Ecumenical dialogues with Orthodox Churches and other ecclesial and faith communities emphasize the common Baptism of all Christians and common service to love even to the point of joint martyrdom.

REFLECT AND DECIDE

- How can Catholic high school students contribute to promoting reconciliation and unity among all Christians?

JOURNAL EXERCISE

- Create an image that depicts the Church to be.
- How does that image mirror or not mirror Jesus' desire for his Church?
- What more might you do to work for the unity among his followers that Jesus prayed for at the Last Supper?

EASTERN ORTHODOX CHRISTIANS ON THE VIA DOLOROSA IN JERUSALEM, GOOD FRIDAY 2012

REFLECT ON WHAT YOU HAVE LEARNED IN THIS CHAPTER

As you come toward the end of this chapter, pause and reflect on what you have come to understand about the Catholic Church's teaching on the first Mark of the Church, 'one'. Share the teachings of the Catholic Church on these statements:

- ⊙ The Church's unity is founded in Jesus Christ through the Holy Spirit.
- ⊙ The Church is united in charity (love), in the profession of faith, in the common celebration of the sacraments and in apostolic succession.
- ⊙ The multiplicity and diversity of peoples, cultures and liturgical traditions within the Church enrich the unity of the Church.
- ⊙ Heresy, schism and apostasy wound the unity of the Church.
- ⊙ The Holy Spirit guides the Church to work to bring about Christ's will for the unity of his followers.

LEARN BY EXAMPLE

The Franciscan Friars and Sisters of the Atonement, and the Church's work of ecumenism

The Franciscan Friars of the Atonement are a Roman Catholic religious society founded by Fr. Paul (previously Lewis) Wattson in 1898 in Graymoor, New York. The mission of the Friars, also known as the Graymoor Franciscans, is to work for reconciliation and unity among all peoples—with God and with one another. The Friars' mission statement includes the words: 'Pain can be healed, hatred turned to love, division turned to unity. The Church can and will become one.' The Friars work at achieving their mission through social, ecumenical and pastoral ministries in the United States, Canada, England, Italy and Japan.

FRIARS OF THE ATONEMENT AT GRAYMOOR, 1946

The origin of the Franciscan Friars of the Atonement is rooted in the desire of Episcopalian Sr. Laura White and Episcopalian Reverend Lewis Wattson. Both wished to found a movement based on the way of St. Francis. In 1898 they established the Society of the Atonement. The Society consisted of the Franciscan Sisters of the Atonement and the Franciscan Friars of the Atonement. Both branches of the Society petitioned Rome for acceptance into the Catholic Church. In October 1909, Rome accepted both the Franciscan Sisters and the Franciscan Friars into the Church.

Earlier in 1908 Reverend Wattson and Reverend Spencer Jones, another Episcopalian priest, inaugurated a week-long Prayer for Christian Unity. This week of prayer is known today as the Week of Prayer for Christian Unity and is celebrated each year from January 18 through January 25.

TALK IT OVER

⊙ How does your parish celebrate the Week of Prayer for Christian Unity?

⊙ How can all the members of your school work together to build up the unity of the members of the Church? Of all people?

RESPOND WITH FAMILY AND FRIENDS

⊙ Research a local project that is reconciling people and building harmony within your parish or neighborhood. Join with family members and friends and take part in that work.

DECIDE AND ACT

⊙ Reflect on the diversity of people within your school and parish.

⊙ How well are you contributing to the 'uniqueness' of both your cultural heritage and your gifts for building up unity within your parish and school?

⊙ How are your efforts contributing to the unity of the Church throughout the world?

⊙ Draw up a list of ways you might take part more actively in that work of the Church.

'[T]hat they may all be one. As you, Father, are in me and I am in you, may they also be [one] in us, so that the world may believe that you have sent me.'

JOHN 17:21

Pray the Sign of the Cross together.

LEADER
Today's prayer reflection follows the *lectio divina* prayer format. We will read and listen to the Word of God and choose ways to make living God's word part of our life.

Read

LEADER
Recall that we live in the presence of one God, who is Father, Son and Holy Spirit. (*Pause*) Open your Bible to the seventeenth chapter of John's Gospel. Prayerfully and slowly read John 17:20–23. Notice what word stands out for you, what resonates for you in Jesus' words to his disciples.

All read the passage in silence and pause for reflection (and perhaps some sharing of thoughts on what was read).

Meditate

LEADER
Reread the passage. This time as you read, place yourself at the Last Supper as an observer.

All read the passage and pause. Talk to God quietly about what you are seeing and hearing.

Contemplate

LEADER
Read the passage again. Now listen to what God may be saying to you. It may help to focus on a particular word or image that seems most significant.

All read the passage. Focus on a particular word or image that seems most significant. Rest in the presence of God.

Pray

LEADER
Slowly come out of contemplation. Look into your heart for the personal prayer the Spirit of God is teaching and inviting you to pray.

All raise your hearts in prayer.

Act

LEADER
Ask yourself, 'What decision is God inviting me to make to live in union with him and others?' (*Pause*)

All share decisions or overall responses to the prayer experience.

LEADER
Let us glorify God by our efforts to live in communion with him and all people.

Conclude by praying the Sign of the Cross together.

THE LAST SUPPER | 19TH-CENTURY GERMAN GLASS PAINTING

CHAPTER 6

A Holy Nation, God's Own People

THE CHURCH IS HOLY

THE CHURCH IS THE **COMMUNITY** OF GOD'S HOLY PEOPLE

ALL WHO BELONG TO THE CHURCH ARE CALLED TO **HOLINESS OF LIFE**

WE MUST COOPERATE WITH **THE GRACE OF GOD** TO GROW IN HOLINESS

THE HOLY SPIRIT TEACHES AND STRENGTHENS US TO LIVE **THE WAY OF JESUS**

WE ALWAYS NEED PURIFICATION, PENANCE, CONVERSION AND RENEWAL

JESUS, THE WAY TO HOLINESS AND FULLNESS OF LIFE

THE CHURCH, THE MYSTICAL BODY OF CHRIST, IS holy. 'Christ, the Son of God, who with the Father and the Spirit is hailed as "alone holy", loved the Church' (*Catechism of the Catholic Church*, no. 823). In this chapter we explore the second Mark of the Church, *holy*. The Church is the community of God's holy people who lives in communion with the Holy Trinity. All who belong to God through the Church are called to live in holiness of life. Holiness is a gift, a grace, from the all-holy God.

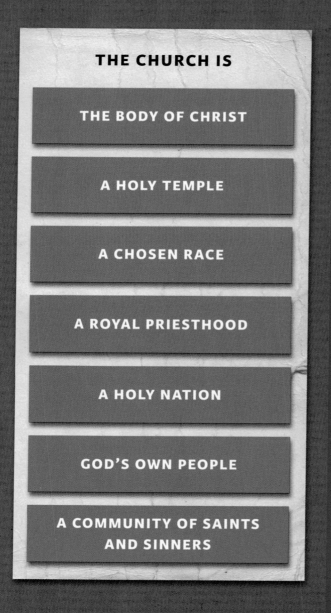

THE CHURCH IS

- THE BODY OF CHRIST
- A HOLY TEMPLE
- A CHOSEN RACE
- A ROYAL PRIESTHOOD
- A HOLY NATION
- GOD'S OWN PEOPLE
- A COMMUNITY OF SAINTS AND SINNERS

Faith Focus: The teachings of the Catholic Church that are the primary focus of the doctrinal content presented in this chapter include:

⊙ The Church is holy; she is the Communion of Saints, the Holy People of God, both living and dead.
⊙ All human beings are called to live in holiness.
⊙ Christ sanctifies the Church through the Holy Spirit and grants the means of holiness to the Church.
⊙ The members of the Church must cooperate with God's grace.
⊙ While her members sin, the Church herself is sinless.
⊙ Mary is the Mother of the Church; she is our model of what it means to be a member of the Church.
⊙ The members of the Church are always in need of purification, penance, conversion and renewal.

Discipleship Formation: As a result of studying this chapter and discovering the meaning of the faith of the Catholic Church for your life, you should be better able to:

⊙ value yourself and your life as 'holy';
⊙ deepen your trust in Jesus Christ, the Head of the Church, and strive to live a life of holiness;
⊙ accept and utilize the gifts of the Holy Spirit in your journey to holiness;
⊙ be aware of the relationship you have with the Communion of Saints, with all the faithful, those living on earth and those who have died;
⊙ be inspired by the Blessed Virgin Mary as a model of holiness;
⊙ realize that ordinary people can be and are saints;
⊙ recognize the connection between your call to holiness and your call to justice.

Scripture References: These Scripture references are quoted or referred to in this chapter:
OLD TESTAMENT: **Leviticus** 11:44–45; **Isaiah** 1:17; **Amos** 5:24
NEW TESTAMENT: **Matthew** 5:4–8; **Mark** 1:24; **Luke** 1:26–38, 48, 6:43–45, 9:23; **John** 2:1–12, 10:10, 14:9, 19:26–27; **Acts of the Apostles** 9:2 and 13; **Romans** 5:20; **1 Corinthians** 6:1, 11:17–34, 12:27, 16:1; **2 Corinthians** 5:21, 6:16; **Ephesians** 1:3–6, 2:21; **2 Timothy** 4:6–8; **Hebrews** 2:17, 7:26, 12:1; **1 Peter** 1:15–16, 2:9

Faith Glossary: Familiarize yourself with the meaning of these key terms. Definitions are found in the Glossary: **actual graces, Annunciation, Assumption, canonization, charism, Communion of the Saints, conversion, eternal life, gifts of the Holy Spirit, grace, holiness, holy day of obligation, Immaculate Conception, Liturgy of the Hours, miracle, Original Sin, perpetual virginity of Mary, piety, purgatory, sacrament, sacramental grace(s), sanctifying grace, sin, temptation,** *Theotokos,* **virtue, vocation**

Faith Word: Communion of the Saints; canonization
Learn by Heart: John 10:10
Learn by Example: St. Teresa de los Andes

How can we be holy?

CALLED TO BE SAINTS

The members of the Church 'are called "saints" [Acts of the Apostles 9:13; 1 Corinthians 6:1, 16:1]' (*Catechism of the Catholic Church* [CCC], no. 823). St. Paul gives the name 'saint' to the members of the Church. We are all called to be saints. Every person is called to strive for **holiness** of life. Belonging to the Church does not automatically make a person holy. We must cooperate with the **grace** of God to live and grow in holiness. Grace is the 'help God gives us to respond to our vocation to become his adopted sons and daughters. The divine initiative of grace precedes, prepares, and elicits our free response in faith and commitment' (*United States Catholic Catechism for Adults* [USCCA], 514).

St. Irenaeus (c. 125–c. 200), Bishop of Lyons and Father of the Church, had a unique way to describe a holy person. He wrote, 'The glory of God is the human person fully alive; and to be fully alive is to behold the vision of God.' Saints, both here on earth and in heaven, are 'fully alive' and give glory to God.

Beholding the Vision of God

St. Irenaeus' phrase 'to behold the vision of God' suggests that God's best hope, or vision, for all people is that we become fully alive. We become fully alive by focusing on God, making God the center of our life and trying to bring a God-awareness to every situation in our life. By so doing, we make our faith permeate every nook and cranny of our life.

We can behold the vision of God in the human face of God in Jesus Christ. Remember the conversation between Jesus and Philip the Apostle, in which Jesus said to Philip, 'whoever has seen me, has seen the Father' (John 14:9). To behold the vision of God means to fix our eyes on Jesus, the firstborn of humanity (see Ephesians 1:3–6) and the 'Holy One of God' (Mark 1:24), as the fullness of the Revelation of God. Jesus, the Holy One

of God, is the way to holiness and fullness of life—life with God. All holiness comes from God, who created us to share in his holiness. God restored humanity to sharing in that holiness through the saving work of Jesus Christ.

WHAT ABOUT YOU PERSONALLY?

- How does your faith in God color your vision of life, or give shape to your outlook on life?
- What does your faith in God help you to 'see' about your life that you might not 'see' otherwise?

THE GIFT OF FULLNESS OF LIFE

God desires that we embrace the gift of life and live it to the full. Jesus taught, 'I came that [you] may have life, and have it abundantly' (John 10:10). We strive to live our life abundantly, and we glorify God when we care for both our physical and spiritual life. We see the importance of doing this reflected in nature. For example, a potted plant with drooping leaves that has been left on a sunny window sill for too long may be alive, but it is signaling that it is far from fully alive. The writer of the Psalms was clearly aware of the insights into human life—including our life with God—found in creation. To breathe, to have a heartbeat and brain activity means that a person is alive. But in order to be 'fully alive' we need the nourishment of the grace of God that is freely and abundantly given in Jesus Christ.

OVER TO YOU

- Name some ways in which your family and your parish and school community support you in living your faith.

- How does maintaining a 'God-vision' add to your fullness of life and the joy of living your life?

THE GIFT OF LIFE

God the Creator, the Holy Trinity, gives us more than physical life; God gives us the great gift of sharing in the very life of God. Jesus and the Father have sent the Holy Spirit, the giver of life, who dwells within us. In Baptism we are reborn into the abundant life of God in Christ. In the Eucharist and other **sacraments**, we receive the graces to embrace the gift of our life and become more and more fully alive. At Mass we are sent forth to 'Go in peace, glorifying the Lord by your life'.

Life, both physical and spiritual, is God's gift to us, and it is not given just for one's own self. Life is given to be shared with others, as God shares his life with us. Jesus Christ lived and gave his life for the world; he is the model and the way of how we are to live our life and live it to the full.

JOURNAL EXERCISE

- Describe some of the challenges to living your life in Christ to the full.
- How might accepting and meeting those challenges help you discover the abundance of life Jesus wishes you to experience and enjoy?

Holiness of life and fullness of life

OPENING REFLECTION

'Pious' is a word we often associate with holiness or use to describe a person whom we think is holy.

⊙ What images come to mind when you hear someone described as 'pious'?

⊙ What might be your reaction if your friends described you as 'pious'?

HOLINESS AS WHOLENESS

We sometimes associate holiness of life with a false understanding of being 'pious'; for example, an understanding of **piety** as being nice to everyone, saying many prayers, going to church a lot, talking about Jesus all the time, wearing medals or putting stickers on the back of our car, and so on. A person who is truly 'pious' is one who is putting into practice the gift and **virtue** of piety. Piety, or Reverence, is one of the seven **gifts of the Holy Spirit**. The graces of this gift of the Holy Spirit help us express our love and respect for God and for everything connected with God.

At Baptism we first receive the gift of **sanctifying grace** and the sevenfold gift of the Holy Spirit. We receive the gift of new life in Christ, which is far greater than what was lost by **Original Sin**. 'The victory that Christ won over sin has given us greater blessings than those which sin had taken from us: "where sin increased, grace abounded all the more" [Romans 5:20]' (CCC, no. 420).

The gift and virtue of piety urges and enables us to strive to live a life of holiness as God desires and gives us his grace to do. Holiness is a 'state of goodness in which a person—with the help of God's grace, the action of the Holy Spirit, and a life of prayer—is freed from sin and evil' (USCCA, 514). The words 'holy' and 'whole' have the same root words, namely, *hool* (Middle English) and *hal* (Old English), meaning 'healthy, unhurt, entire'. Striving for holiness of life is getting your life together and cooperating with God's grace to heal its brokenness and restore it to 'wholeness', to holiness.

OVER TO YOU

⊙ Think about one thing in your life right now that is making you feel that the parts of your life are not 'in sync'.

⊙ How might you 'get it together'?

⊙ How will your faith in Jesus help?

HOLINESS OF LIFE—THE WAY OF JESUS

Luke describes the first Christians as people 'who belonged to the Way' (Acts of the Apostles 9:2). This is the 'way' of Jesus, the holy One of God. Sometimes Catholics mistakenly think that only priests and members of religious orders have the **vocation** to strive for holiness of life. This, of course, is not the case. All Christians by Baptism received the gift of sanctifying grace and have been made sharers in the holiness of God. The word 'sanctifying' comes from a Latin verb that means 'to make holy'. The Second Vatican Council taught:

> The Lord Jesus, divine teacher and model of all perfection, preached holiness of life, which he both initiates and brings to perfection, to each and every one of his disciples no matter what their condition of life: 'You, therefore, must be perfect, as your heavenly Father is perfect' (Matthew 5:4–8). . . . It is therefore quite clear that all Christians in whatever state or walk in life are called to the fullness of the Christian life and to the perfection of charity, and this holiness is conducive to a more human way of living even in society here on earth.
>
> —Vatican II, *Dogmatic Constitution on the Church*, no. 40

We, as Jesus the Holy One of God was, are to be compassionate to people in need. We are to be honest and truthful in all our personal dealings. We are to work for justice and freedom for all. We are to care not only for our personal well-being but also for the well-being of others—without placing any limitation on whom we identify to be our neighbor.

We cannot live this 'way' on our own. Jesus gave us the Church. Christ sanctifies the Church through the Holy Spirit and grants the means of holiness to the Church. The Holy Spirit, whom we receive at Baptism, teaches and strengthens us to live the way of Jesus. The Holy Spirit is the 'soul of the Church' and the purveyor of God's abundant grace. The Holy Spirit is the sanctifier and sustainer. The Holy Spirit is the source of holiness and wholeness of life. Welcoming and cooperating with his gifts, his graces, is the only way to live the way of Christ, to live a holy life. When we do, our lives will bear 'fruit'. (Check out Luke 6:43–45.)

THINK, PAIR AND SHARE
- Review the gifts and fruits of the Holy Spirit on page 262 of this text.

⊙ Discuss with a partner where you see evidence of the gifts of the Holy Spirit at work in your life and in the lives of people in your neighborhood.

MARY, THE MOTHER OF THE CHURCH AND MODEL OF FAITH

Mary is *panagia*, all-holy. She is full of grace and is blessed among all women. God has favored, or blessed, Mary with unique graces that manifest her singular sharing in the holiness of God. These graces flow from Mary's 'connection' with her Son. Mary is the Virgin Mother of Jesus, the Son of God, who became incarnate in her womb by the power of the Holy Spirit. Mary is indeed the Mother of God. She is **Theotokos**, 'God-bearer'.

God blessed Mary with the singular grace of freedom from all sin from the first moment of her conception in the womb of her mother and during her entire life on earth. The Church names this grace the **Immaculate Conception**. By the singular grace of God and by the merits of Jesus Christ, Mary was preserved immune from Original Sin and remained free from all personal sin throughout her life, from the first moment of her conception.

God also blessed Mary with the singular grace of **perpetual virginity**. Mary was a virgin before the conception of Jesus, during his conception and birth, and she remained a virgin throughout her entire life. Likewise, God blessed Mary with the unique grace of the **Assumption**. When her 'earthly life was finished, because she was sinless, she was kept from corruption and taken soul and body into heavenly glory' (USCCA, 505).

Mary's yes to God at the **Annunciation** models for us the life of faith and holiness. (Read Luke 1:26–38.) Her whole life on earth, from its beginning to its end, models for us living 'the way' of holiness of life—living in communion with God the Father, Son and Holy Spirit. Truly all generations call and honor Mary as blessed (see Luke 1:48).

The Catholic Church honors Mary with many images and titles that express our love and devotion for her. First, Mary is the Mother of the Church. Jesus gave us his mother to be our mother, too. (Read John 19:26–27.) Mary is the 'New Eve and the Mother of the Church', the new People of God. In the Litany of the Blessed Virgin Mary, we honor her and express our faith in her role in the divine plan of salvation when we pray to her as 'Mother of divine grace', 'Mother of good counsel', 'Mirror of justice', 'Throne of wisdom', 'Shrine of the Spirit', 'Ark of the Covenant', 'Health of the sick', 'Refuge of sinners', 'Comfort of the troubled' and 'Queen of peace', 'Mother of Christ', 'Mother of the Church' and 'Help of Christians'.

So we reach out to her in prayer. We trust and are confident that Mary 'continues in heaven to exercise her maternal role on behalf of the members of Christ' (Pope Paul VI, *Creed of the People of God*, quoted in CCC, no. 975).

LET'S PROBE DEEPER

- Read Luke 1:26–38 and discuss it with a partner.

JOURNAL EXERCISE

- What did you learn from Mary for your own holiness of life?
- What is your favorite title for Mary? Why?
- See if you can come up with a new title for Mary that expresses your devotion to Mary.

THE ANNUNCIATION | JAMES TISSOT

Mary's yes to God at the Annunciation models for us the life of faith and holiness

A holy Church of saints and sinners

C.S. Lewis (1898–1963) is one of the many Christian writers who have used fiction to express their faith in Christ. Edmund Pevensie is one of the most compelling characters in C.S. Lewis' series of novels *The Chronicles of Narnia*. *The Lion, the Witch and the Wardrobe* tells the story of Edmund's worst mistake—he gives in to the **temptation** of the evil White Witch and betrays his siblings as well as his loyalty to Aslan, the Great Lion. Edmund joins the Witch, who promises him great power and an endless supply of sweet Turkish delight. He runs away to her palace, where the Witch shows her true colors and imprisons him upon his arrival. Suffering in the dungeon of the White Witch, Edmund realizes his mistake and regrets it very much. The Witch decides to execute Edmund as a traitor, but Aslan offers his life as a ransom for Edmund, setting him free. After the glorious return of Aslan, Edmund is forgiven and becomes one of the great kings of Narnia.

TILDA SWINTON AND SKANDAR KEYNES IN 'THE LION, THE WITCH AND THE WARDROBE'

OPENING REFLECTION

 Think of a time when someone you know, read about or heard about might have acted as Edmund did.

> ## FROM THE WISDOM OF THE CHURCH
> The Church is holy: the Most Holy God is her author; Christ, her bridegroom, gave himself up to make her holy; the Spirit of holiness gives her life.
> —CCC, no. 867

THE CHURCH IS HOLY

The story of the Church on earth is a story of successes and failures, of faithfulness and infidelity. Sometimes members of the Church are not successful in their struggle to live the Gospel, and they **sin**. Our inclination toward sin is one of the effects of Original Sin; and the sinful choices we make result from our freely and knowingly giving in to that inclination. So, what is our hope of growing in holiness? God's grace (sanctifying grace) restores us to holiness lost by sin. God's grace helps us live our lives according to his will (**actual graces**); and God's grace enables us to live out our Christian vocation according to our state in life (**sacramental graces** and **charisms**).

The Church is the Body of Christ; she is both visible and invisible. 'She is one, yet formed of two components, human and divine. That is her mystery, which only faith can accept' (CCC, no 779). While the members of the Church may sin, the Church is always holy; she is still the Body of Christ (recall 1 Corinthians 12:27), the Holy One of God, who is her Head. The Church is 'the temple of the living God' (2 Corinthians 6:16)—'a holy temple in the Lord' (Ephesians 2:21), 'a chosen race, a royal priesthood, a holy nation, God's own people [1 Peter 2:9]' (CCC, no. 803).

The members of the Church are always in need of God's grace to be successful in our struggle to live in right and loving relationship with God, ourselves, and others

The Church's holiness flows from the abiding gift of the Holy Spirit, who guarantees both her holiness and her ability to sustain her members' efforts to grow in holiness. The Holy Spirit, the Spirit of holiness, 'whom Christ the head pours out on his members, builds, animates and sanctifies the Church. She is the sacrament of the Holy Trinity's communion with men' (CCC, no. 747).

OVER TO YOU

⊙ How does knowing that the Holy Spirit, the Spirit of Jesus, remains with the Church even during times of the infidelity of her members help you in your personal struggle to strive for holiness of life?

REPENT AND BELIEVE THE GOOD NEWS

The Church on earth and in **purgatory** is 'at once holy and always in need of purification' (CCC, no. 827). This purification requires a *conversion of heart* as the faithful "try to live holier lives according to the Gospel" [Vatican II, *Decree on Ecumenism*, no. 7]' (CCC, no. 821). Our purification comes about by our responding to God, who constantly welcomes us into his loving embrace.

God's grace invites and empowers our continued purification and **conversion**. Because human nature has been weakened by Original Sin, the members of the Church on earth are always in need of God's grace to be successful in our struggle to live in right and loving relationship with God, ourselves, and others—to live holy and just lives. The Church gives us this profile of a life of conversion:

Conversion is accomplished in daily life by gestures of reconciliation, concern for the poor, the exercise and defense of justice and right [see Amos 5:24, Isaiah 1:17] by the admission of faults to one's brethren, fraternal correction, revision of life, examination of conscience, spiritual direction, acceptance of suffering, endurance of persecution for the sake of righteousness. Taking up one's cross each day and following Jesus is the surest way of penance [see Luke 9:23].

—CCC, no. 1435

JOURNAL EXERCISE

⊙ Think of ways in which you are striving for holiness of life. Where in your life might you need a fresh start? What things are standing in the way of your living your life as a disciple of Jesus to the fullest? Write your thoughts.

A CHURCH OF SAINTS AND SINNERS

St. Paul often addressed the members of the early Church as 'saints'. This does not mean that Paul was praising the members of the early Church for being perfect and beyond admonishment and sin. Paul was both acknowledging and encouraging those to whom he was writing, who were striving and struggling to live holy lives. The members of the early Church, just as you, were going about doing their best every day to live the 'way' of Jesus, worshiping together, caring for the needy, working for justice, and learning and living the faith. The New Testament letters, in fact, reveal that there were many problems, conflicts, power struggles and life choices among Christians that were clearly contrary to what it means to be a disciple of Christ. For example, read 1 Corinthians 11:17–34.

Even when St. Paul was about to admonish them, he still addressed them as saints. Growing in holiness of life includes cooperating with the grace of God as we strive to overcome temptation and to repent when we have sinned.

[The Church] endeavours to serve Christ, who, 'holy, innocent, and undefiled' (see Hebrews 7:26), knew nothing of sin (see 2 Corinthians 5:21), but came only to expiate the sins of the people (see Hebrews 2:17). The church, however, clasping sinners to its bosom, at once holy and always in need of purification, follows constantly the path of penance and renewal.
—*Dogmatic Constitution on the Church*, no. 8

TALK IT OVER

St. Paul would address you as 'saints' if he were writing a letter to your school or parish.

- How might this shape your understanding of your school or parish?
- How might this shape your interaction with those around you?
- What one thing could you do today to live up to this title?

WHAT ABOUT YOU PERSONALLY?

- Do you consider yourself a 'saint'? Why or why not?
- Who might you address as a 'saint'? Why?

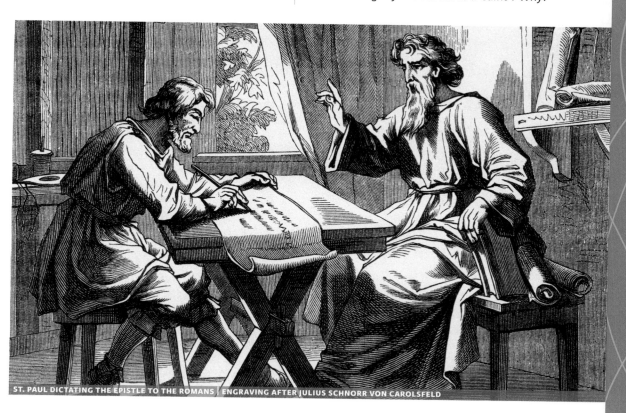

ST. PAUL DICTATING THE EPISTLE TO THE ROMANS | ENGRAVING AFTER JULIUS SCHNORR VON CAROLSFELD

The Communion of Saints

ST. PIO OF PIETRELCINA, CASTELLAMMARE DEL GOLFO, ITALY

death. Just as we can ask a living person to pray for us, we can ask a saint to pray for us, and we can pray for the souls in purgatory.

This practice of the Catholic Church gives witness to the Church's belief that the Church is a Communion of Saints. She is a communion of holy people and holy things, 'above all the Eucharist, by which "the unity of believers, who form one body in Christ, is both represented and brought about" [Vatican II, *Dogmatic Constitution on the Church*, no. 3]' (CCC, no. 960). The term **Communion of the Saints** refers both to those 'now in the Church and those members who have already gone before us and are either in Purgatory or heaven' (USCCA, 507).

Strictly speaking, Catholics do not 'pray to' the saints. We ask the saints to pray for us, to pray with us, and to bring our own prayers into the presence of God. First and foremost among the saints is the Blessed Mother, the Mother of the Church. We are confident that just as Jesus listened to her when she petitioned him at the wedding feast of Cana (read John 2:1–12), Mary hears and listens to our prayers. In addition to the saints named by the Church, we can also talk 'privately' with a deceased parent, sibling, grandparent, other family member or friend. Just as they could pray for us when they were living, so they can still pray for us now.

OPENING REFLECTION
⊙ Who have you known who has died and whom you believe is living in the presence of God?
⊙ What can you learn from their example for your own life now?

THE SAINTS PRAY FOR US
The Church celebrates All Saints' Day on November 1. On this **holy day of obligation** the Church honors and remembers all the 'saints' who have lived among us. Through Baptism we have a bond with the faithful, both living and dead, that can never be broken, not even by

THINK, PAIR AND SHARE
⊙ What role does praying to Mary and the saints have in your school? Your family? Your own life?

JOURNAL EXERCISE
⊙ Write down the names of your relatives or friends who have died and whom you trust are now living eternally with all the angels and saints in God's presence.

Communion of the Saints

This refers to members of the Church through all time—those now in the Church and those members who have already gone before us and are either in Purgatory or heaven.

—USCCA, 507

Canonization

The name for the solemn declaration by the pope that a deceased member of the faithful may be proposed as a model and intercessor to the Christian faithful and venerated as a saint, on the basis of the fact that the person lived a life of heroic virtue or remained faithful to God through martyrdom.

—USCCA, 506

- ⊙ What would you like to say to a deceased relative or friend? Share your thoughts.
- ⊙ What wisdom can you learn from remembering their lives? Journal your thoughts.

FROM THE WISDOM OF THE CHURCH

By *canonizing* some of the faithful, [that is,] by solemnly proclaiming that they practiced heroic virtue and lived in fidelity to God's grace, the Church recognizes the power of the Spirit of holiness within her and sustains the hope of believers by proposing the saints to them as models and intercessors [see Vatican II, *Dogmatic Constitution on the Church*, nos. 40, 48–51].

—CCC, no. 828

CANONIZATION: THE CHURCH NAMES SAINTS

The Catholic Church has a long tradition of canonizing, or officially naming, members of the Church to be saints in heaven. The Church canonizes a member of the Church only after a very careful scrutiny of the person's life and teachings. Here is a summary of the **canonization** process:

- ⊙ The canonization process begins with people who knew the candidate best, those closest to him or her, who were inspired by the person's holiness of life. They propose the person for review to the local bishop, who makes an investigation into the person's life.

- ⊙ If there is sound evidence of a holy life, the bishop sends the results of the investigation on to Rome for further review by the Congregation for the Cause of Saints. If the Congregation approves, the person is declared 'Venerable' and his or her cause for canonization continues.
- ⊙ The next step in the process is the verification of at least one **miracle**, the restoration of someone to good health attributed to a person's intercession before God. The Church carefully investigates the claims of the miraculous cure to verify that it is authentic— truly a miracle that is medically unexplainable.
- ⊙ The Church next declares the person 'Blessed' and proposes them for veneration and prayers of intercession within their local area. During this step in the process, another miracle attributed to the intercession of the 'Blessed' is identified and authenticated.
- ⊙ Finally, the Pope formally 'raises the person to the altar' and declares her or him to be a saint. The Church proposes the person for veneration and imitation by the whole Church.

THINK, PAIR AND SHARE

- ⊙ Talk about your favorite saint or saints and why they are your favorite.
- ⊙ Discuss the wisdom you have learned from the life of your favorite saints that can

PROCESSION OF HOLY MARTYRS | BASILICA OF SANT'APOLLINARE NUOVO, RAVENNA, ITALY

All who belong to God in Jesus Christ are on the same 'way' to sainthood, albeit at different points along the way

inspire young people to live as disciples of Jesus.

⊙ Join with the class and create a chart titled 'Wisdom from the Saints for Young People'. Include a phrase describing how each saint on the chart is a model of holiness and justice.

OVER TO YOU

⊙ If you are not named after a saint, consider choosing your favorite saint to be your patron saint.

ETERNAL LIFE AMONG THE SAINTS

We can think about our call to strive for holiness of life in many ways. St. Paul used the image of running a race. Paul imagined living his life in Jesus Christ as a race. Near the end of his life, as he awaited execution in prison, he wrote to his friend and companion Timothy:

As for me, I am already being poured out as a libation, and the time of my departure has come. I have fought the good fight, I have finished the race, I have kept the faith. From now on there is reserved for me the crown of righteousness, which the Lord, the righteous judge, will give to me on that day, and not only to me but also to all who have longed for his appearing.

—2 Timothy 4:6–8

All of us who belong to God in Jesus Christ are running a similar race in life. Some of us are at the start, preparing for Baptism or having just been baptized into the Body of Christ. Many of us are running along the course, dealing with its hills and straight ways. Some are near death and reaching the finish line as Paul was, hoping for the crown of living in God's eternal presence in heaven. There are those faithful who have finished the race. They are the saints in heaven, and they are standing in the bleachers, cheering us on. The writer of the Letter to the Hebrews tells us:

Therefore, since we are surrounded by so great a cloud of witnesses, let us also lay aside every weight and the sin that clings so closely, and let us run with perseverance the race that is set before us, looking to Jesus the pioneer and perfecter of our faith, who for the sake of the joy that was set before him endured the cross, disregarding its shame, and has taken his seat at the right hand of the throne of God.

—Hebrews 12:1

WHAT ABOUT YOU PERSONALLY?

⊙ All who belong to God in Jesus Christ are on the same 'way' to sainthood, albeit at different points along the way. Where are you on that 'way'?

⊙ Consider also those who are in the bleachers, cheering you on.
  – How have they encouraged and supported you in your life of faith?
  – Thank them.

REFLECT ON WHAT YOU HAVE LEARNED IN THIS CHAPTER

As you come toward the end of this chapter, pause and reflect on what you have come to understand about the Catholic Church's teaching on the holiness of the Church. Share the teachings of the Catholic Church on these statements:

◉ All human beings are called to live in holiness.
◉ The Church is 'a holy nation, God's own people'.
◉ Christ sanctifies the Church through the Holy Spirit and grants the means of holiness to the Church.
◉ The Holy Spirit is the source of holiness and wholeness of life.
◉ The members of the Church must cooperate with God's grace.
◉ While her members sin, the Church herself is sinless.
◉ The Church is a Communion of Saints.
◉ Mary is the Mother of the Church; she is our model of what it means to be a member of the Church.
◉ The members of the Church are always in need of purification, penance, conversion and renewal.

OVER TO YOU

◉ Identify one good decision that you can make to live your vocation to strive for holiness of life. Then make and keep it.

MAKE A GOOD START EACH MORNING

At the beginning of this chapter we learned that 'beholding God's vision' is a key to living Jesus' way of holiness of life. One way you can behold God's vision is to pause each morning, remember your call to holiness of life, and let a sense of belonging to God permeate the whole day. Traditionally, we have called this first pause for prayer the 'Morning Offering'. Praying in the morning can help orient everything you experience during the day in the right direction. Your morning prayer can be as simple as praying, 'Thank you for the gift of this day. Help me live it as a disciple of Jesus.' Or you might pray a traditional form of the Morning Offering, or pray the Morning Prayer from the **Liturgy of the Hours**, or you might begin each day by praying the Lord's Prayer.

OVER TO YOU

◉ What wisdom do you see in beginning your day with prayer?

LEARN BY EXAMPLE

St. Teresa de Los Andes (1900–20), doing little things well and with love

St. Teresa of Los Andes was the first native of Chile to be canonized. Born Juanita Fernandez Solar, she was a strong swimmer, played the piano very well and was a practical joker. During her high school years she read *Story of a Soul*, the autobiography of St. Thérèse of Lisieux, who lived her life by this simple spirituality: strive to live in holiness by doing the 'little things' well and with love.

Attracted to this simple way of living, Juanita, at the age of nineteen, joined the Carmelite community in Los Andes and took the name Teresa to honor her patron

saint, St. Thérèse. Three months before her twentieth birthday Teresa contracted typhus and died. Pope St. John Paul II canonized Teresa on March 21, 1993. In his homily the Pope summarized the meaning of her life. He said:

> In a secularized society which turns its back on God, this Chilean Carmelite whom to my great joy I present as a model of the perennial youth of the Gospel, gives the shining witness of a life which proclaims to the men and women of our day that it is in loving, adoring and serving God that the human creature finds greatness and joy, freedom and fulfillment.

St. Teresa's life on earth was short—she was barely older than a high school senior today. Yet in that short life she loved God passionately, and people took notice.

TALK IT OVER
- ◉ What are you passionate about—those heartfelt interests that engage you to use your gifts and talent?
- ◉ How can these desires lead you and those around you to a fuller life in God?

RESPOND WITH FAMILY AND FRIENDS
- ◉ Discuss with your family and friends the passions that motivate you.
- ◉ Reflect together on how you can be a source of hope, good example and encouragement to those around you to strive for justice and holiness of life.
- ◉ Choose one thing and practice it with passion; live life to the fullest!

WHAT WILL YOU DO NOW?
- ◉ Reflect on the connection between your call to holiness and your call to justice.
- ◉ What is the most effective work of justice that you can do now?

LEARN BY HEART

'I came that they may have life, and have it abundantly.'

JOHN 10:10

Pray the Sign of the Cross together.

Opening Prayer

LEADER

God is the source of all holiness,
the holiness of the Church and our personal
holiness.
Take a few moments to reflect on your call to
strive for holiness of life. (*Pause*)
Let us now express our repentance and sorrow
for our failure to respond faithfully to our call to
holiness:

ALL

I confess to almighty God
and to you, my brothers and sisters,
that I have greatly sinned,
in my thoughts and in my words,
in what I have done
and in what I have failed to do,
through my fault, through my fault,
through my most grievous fault;
therefore I ask blessed Mary ever-Virgin,
all the Angels and Saints,
and you, my brothers and sisters,
to pray for me to the Lord our God.

The Word of God

READER

A reading from the Book of Leviticus.
I am the LORD your God;
sanctify yourselves therefore and be holy,
for I am holy. . . .
For I am the LORD who brought you up from the
land of Egypt, to be your God;
you shall be holy, for I am holy.

—Leviticus 11:44–45

The word of the Lord.

ALL

Thanks be to God.
Pause and reflect on the Word of God.

READER

A reading from
the First Letter of
Peter.
[A]s he who called
you is holy,
be holy
yourselves in all
your conduct;
for it is written,
'You shall be holy,
for I am holy.'
—1 Peter 1:15–16

The word of the
Lord.

ALL

Thanks be to God.

*Pause and reflect
on the Word of
God.*

ST. AUGUSTINE OF HIPPO | SIMONE MARTINI

Concluding Prayer

LEADER

We are temples of the Holy Spirit. Let us raise up
our hearts and minds in prayer to the Holy Spirit.

ALL

Breathe in me, O Holy Spirit, that my thoughts
    may all be holy.
Act in me, O Holy Spirit, that my work, too, may
    be holy.
Draw my heart, O Holy Spirit, that I love only
    what is holy.
Strengthen me, O Holy Spirit, to defend all that
    is holy.
Guard me so, O Holy Spirit, that I may always be
    holy.
Amen.
    —Prayer attributed to St. Augustine of Hippo

Pray the Sign of the Cross together.

CHAPTER 7

The Church: Catholic and Apostolic

GOD'S INFINITE LOVE IS FOR ALL PEOPLE

THE CHURCH IS BOTH THE MEANS AND THE GOAL OF GOD'S PLAN OF SALVATION

CHRIST FOUNDED THE CHURCH ON THE APOSTLES

THE CATHOLIC CHURCH HAS NO BORDERS

WE UNDERTAKE OUR 'MISSION' OF EVANGELIZATION IN THE SPIRIT OF THE APOSTLES

THE RISEN JESUS IS WITH THE CHURCH 'UNTIL THE END OF THE AGE'

EVERY CHRISTIAN IS CALLED TO TAKE PART IN THE **WORK OF EVANGELIZATION**

THIS CHAPTER FOCUSES ON THE THIRD AND fourth Marks of the Church, *catholic* and *apostolic*. We explore in more detail the meaning of Jesus' commissioning of the Apostles to 'make disciples of all nations . . . teaching them to obey everything that I have commanded you' (Matthew 28:19). This work of the Church is called evangelization.

'PREACH THE GOSPEL AT ALL TIMES AND WHEN NECESSARY USE WORDS.' —ST. FRANCIS OF ASSISI

Faith Focus: The teachings of the Catholic Church that are the primary focus of the doctrinal content presented in this chapter include:

⊙ The Church has been sent by Christ on a mission to the whole world and she exists worldwide.
⊙ The Church exists for all people and is the means of salvation for all people, even for non-members.
⊙ Christ founded the Church on the Twelve, with Peter the leader among the Apostles.
⊙ The Church is guided by the successors of the Twelve, the Pope and the other bishops in communion with him.
⊙ The Magisterium has the responsibility of authentically interpreting Revelation, namely, Scripture and Tradition.
⊙ God calls all members of the Church to share the Gospel with others.

Discipleship Formation: As a result of studying this chapter and discovering the meaning of the faith of the Catholic Church for your life, you should be better able to:

⊙ value the common dignity of all people;
⊙ become more 'catholic' in your attitude and daily behavior toward other people;
⊙ see more clearly the role and responsibilities you have as a member of the Church in the fulfillment of her mission;
⊙ take part in the 'new evangelization' efforts of the Church;
⊙ grow in your understanding of the Gospel as 'salvific';
⊙ make the connection between being 'catholic and apostolic' and the social teachings of the Catholic Church.

Scripture References: These Scripture references are quoted or referred to in this chapter:
OLD TESTAMENT: **Genesis** 3:15, 4:1–16, 11:1–9
NEW TESTAMENT: **Matthew** 3:11, 4:18–22, 7:12, 10:1–4 and 40, 16:13–20, 23, 20:17, 25:31–46, 28:19; **Mark** 3:13–14, 16:15; **Luke** 6:31, 10:1–12, 16 and 17–31, 18:31; **John** 1:22–23, 29–34 and 35–51, 13:20, 17:18, 20:21, 21:15–17; **2 Corinthians** 5:14; **1 Timothy** 2:4; **Revelation** 21:14

Faith Glossary: Familiarize yourself with the meaning of these key terms. Definitions are found in the Glossary: **Apostle, apostolic exhortation, catholic, college of bishops, creed, Eleven (the), evangelization, new evangelization, sacred chrism, social teaching of the Catholic Church, Twelve (the)**

Faith Words: apostle; catholic; creed; evangelization
Learn by Heart: Saying attributed to St. Francis of Assisi
Learn by Example: Maryknoll Lay Missioners

What does it mean to be 'catholic'?

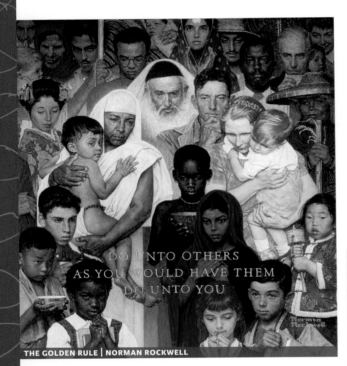

THE GOLDEN RULE | NORMAN ROCKWELL

St. Matthew and St. Luke both include the Golden Rule among Jesus' teachings on discipleship. (Read Matthew 7:12 and Luke 6:31.)

OPENING CONVERSATION
- What is the ethnic profile of your class? How diverse are the cultural backgrounds? Make a list!
- What are some of the things that unite your class in its diversity?
- How can living the Golden Rule unite and form a diverse people into a community?
- What other teachings of Sacred Scripture are at the heart of the Golden Rule?

FROM THE WISDOM OF THE CHURCH
[The Church is] the assembly of those whom God's Word 'convokes', [that is], gathers together to form the People of God. . . . The Church is both the means and the goal of God's plan.
—*Catechism of the Catholic Church* (CCC), nos. 777 and 778

There are nearly seven billion people in the world today. They live in 195 countries, speak about seven thousand different languages, and belong to countless ethnic and cultural groups. People look, speak, think, act and relate differently from one place to another. With so much diversity, we might wonder what unites the human race. Is there anything that could possibly hold us all together? Is there anything that could be said of all people everywhere?

A mosaic that adorns the United Nations' headquarters in New York City offers one suggestion. It is a reproduction of Norman Rockwell's *The Golden Rule* (1961). Beneath the many different faces on this mosaic, you read the words, 'Do Unto Others As You Would Have Them Do Unto You.' More than twenty religions in the world proclaim some version of this Golden Rule.

THE GLOBAL FAMILY—GOD'S FAMILY
The term 'global family' is widely used today. Our global family is made up of many peoples, all of whom are descendants of our first parents, Adam and Eve. The Book of Genesis in chapters 1 through 10 reveals that both unity and diversity are hallmarks of the 'human family'. Reflecting on these truths revealed in the Book of Genesis gives us some insight into what it means to be 'human' and also what it means to bear the name 'Christian'—to be a disciple of Jesus Christ, the Savior of the world, and a member of the Church that he founded, which is '**catholic**'.

First, God creates every person in his image; we are to value and respect every person without exception as sacred, as an image of God. Second, God does not create us to live as isolated individuals, living only for ourselves and our self-interest. God creates us to live in communion with God, among ourselves and with all creation. Third, we are stewards of God's household, his creation, and we are to work to restore the unity and harmony of God's family that was broken by Original Sin. (Read the stories of Cain and Abel in Genesis 4:1–16 and the Tower of Babel in Genesis 11:1–9.)

God desires and promised to restore the unity of the entire human family. He expressed that desire and promised that one day he would save the world. (Read Genesis 3:15.) God fulfilled that promise in Jesus Christ, the Incarnate Word of God. Jesus is the Savior of the world. The Church is a sign and instrument of God's offer of salvation. Through his Church the unity among all peoples is to be restored. We, the disciples of Christ, are to work with the Holy Spirit to bring about the healing of our global family, to form the one family and one People of God. We are to heal the divisiveness and brokenness that are the consequences of Original Sin. The Catholic Church teaches:

[A]ny kind of social or cultural discrimination in basic personal rights on the grounds of sex, race, color, social conditions, language or religion, must be curbed and eradicated as incompatible with God's design.
—Vatican II, *Pastoral Constitution on the Church in the Modern World*, no. 29

JOURNAL EXERCISE
- ◉ List as many things as you can identify that you may have in common with all people.
- ◉ What do those things reveal about the global family, the one family of God?
- ◉ What are you doing or can you do better to work for unity in your family or among your friends?

FROM THE WISDOM OF THE CHURCH
The Church is catholic: she proclaims the fullness of the faith. She bears in herself and administers the totality of the means of salvation. She is sent out to all peoples. She speaks to all men. She encompasses all times. She is 'missionary of her very nature' [Vatican II, *Decree on the Church's Missionary Activity*, no. 2].
—CCC, no. 868

FAITH WORD

Catholic

One of the four marks or notes of the Church, taken from the Nicene Creed. The Church is catholic or universal both because she possesses the fullness of Christ's presence and the means of salvation, and because she has been sent out by Christ on a mission to the whole of the human race.
—CCC, Glossary

THE FIRST COUNCIL OF NICAEA | ST. SOPHIA CATHEDRAL, KYIV, UKRAINE

GO INTO THE *WHOLE* WORLD

Jesus is the Savior of the World—of the *whole* world. '[A]ll salvation comes from Christ the Head, through the Church which is his Body' (CCC, no. 846). In both his words and deeds Jesus revealed, over and over, that God's love is catholic. God's love knows no borders. God offers his saving love to all people without exception. The Church is catholic because Christ is always present in her. She is catholic because Christ has given the Church a share in his mission with the command to '[g]o into all the world and proclaim the good news to the whole creation' (Mark 16:15). Salvation comes from the Church even to non-believers.

It is from God's love for all men that the Church in every age receives both the obligation and the vigor of her missionary dynamism, 'for the love of Christ urges us on [2 Corinthians 5:14]'. Indeed, God 'desires all men to be saved and to come to the knowledge of the truth [1 Timothy 2:4]'; . . . God wills the salvation of everyone through the knowledge of the truth.

—CCC, no. 851

'To proclaim the faith and to plant his reign, Christ sends his apostles and his successors. He gives them a share in his own mission. From him they receive the power to act in his person' (CCC, no. 935). The Church uses the word **evangelization**, which has the same Latin root as 'gospel', to name this mission.

The Church is a 'Church without borders'. ' "All men are called to belong to the new People of God", so that, in Christ, "men may form one family and one People of God" ' (Vatican II, *Dogmatic Constitution on the Church*, no. 13, quoted in CCC, no. 804). Every Christian has the vocation and the responsibility to take part in the Church's work of evangelization. Evangelization begins 'at home' by witnessing to and sharing the good news of God's saving love with the people closest to us—and then beyond to all people to 'form the one People of God'. Those who through no fault of their own do not know Christ or the Catholic Church are not excluded from salvation; in a way known to God, all people are offered the possibility of salvation in Christ. The Church's work of evangelization is the work of the whole Church for the whole world. (We will explore the Church's work of evangelization in more detail in the next section of this chapter.)

THINK, PAIR AND SHARE

⊙ Work with a partner to identify examples from Jesus' life of how he revealed God's unconditional love for all people.

⊙ Discuss where you see people excluded in today's world because some judge them to be unlovable.

⊙ Share experiences of someone excluding you because of your Catholic faith.

OVER TO YOU

⊙ Look at your life right now. Choose some person or people who need to hear the good news of God's love.

⊙ How can you be an evangelist, one who proclaims the Gospel, to them?

The work of a 'new evangelization'

St. Francis of Assisi, while kneeling before the cross in the chapel of San Damiano in Assisi, heard the command, 'Rebuild my Church.' This command became the inspiration and driving force that gave direction to the life and mission of Francis. At first Francis thought the crucified Jesus was giving him a simple task, namely, to rebuild the chapel of San Damiano, which had fallen into physical ruin. Later Francis understood that Christ was calling him to rebuild the Church beyond the town of Assisi. Christ was calling Francis to the work of evangelization.

OPENING CONVERSATION

The statement 'Preach the Gospel at all times and when necessary use words' is attributed to St. Francis.

⊙ What do you think this statement means?
⊙ From what you know of the life of St. Francis, how well does the statement summarize his life?
⊙ Name some ways in which you see people preaching the Gospel without using words. Give specific examples.

OVER TO YOU

⊙ Create a visual presentation of St. Francis' statement.
⊙ Display it at home where it will remind you that Jesus calls you to take part in his Church's work of evangelization.
⊙ Take part in the Church's work of evangelization and share your presentation digitally with your friends.

A 'NEW EVANGELIZATION'

On December 8, 1975, Pope Paul VI promulgated the apostolic exhortation *Evangelii Nuntiandi*, or 'On Evangelization in the Modern World'. An **apostolic exhortation** is a document written by the Pope to the Church encouraging its people to take some particular action. In *Evangelii Nuntiandi* Pope Paul VI reiterated that 'the Church exists in order to evangelize' (no. 14) and proposed a deeper understanding of the missionary mandate the Church received from Jesus. For a long time, many Christians thought that the work of evangelization was the work of sending missionaries to faraway places to preach the Gospel to people who had never heard of Jesus and the Gospel.

Pope Paul VI proposed a **'new evangelization'**. The Pope's teaching on evangelization is 'new' in the sense that the Church is not just to announce the Gospel to non-Christians, but to all people, including the baptized. The faith life of every Christian, the Pope admonished, can become

ST. FRANCIS OF ASSISI | EL GRECO

FAITH WORD

Evangelization

This is the ministry and mission of proclaiming and witnessing Christ and his Gospel with the intention of deepening the faith of believers and inviting others to be baptized and initiated into the Church.

—*United States Catholic Catechism for Adults* [USCCA], 512

routine, taken for granted, lukewarm—much like the faith life of the Church was when Francis received the command, 'Rebuild my Church.' The United States Conference of Catholic Bishops (USCCB) in their *Strategic Plan for the New Evangelization* named three specific goals to guide the Catholic Church in the United States in this work. They wrote:

> The *New Evangelization* as a journey of faith, worship and witness, presents three opportunities or audiences for the transmission of the Christian faith:
> • To engage more intently those who are faithful and need to be renewed with increased catechesis;
> • To reach out to those who have never heard the gospel proclaimed; and

• To re-engage those who are baptized but have lost a living sense of the faith in their daily lives.

The Gospel is the leaven that permeates people's personal lives *and* society and culture. Wherever the baptized bring the Gospel, we bring the leaven of what Pope Paul VI called 'liberating salvation'. This includes working for the full human development, both spiritual and physical, of people. The Church brings the message and grace of the Gospel and the teachings of Christ into society in her *words and deeds*. Whether or not people are open to accept that message and accompanying graces, the Church proclaims boldly the truth that God calls and invites all people to live in communion with him, to 'form one family and one People of God' (CCC, no. 804). Our whole life should preach that God offers his healing, or saving, grace to all people to live a just and holy life.

REFLECT AND SHARE
⊙ What is the call to a 'new evangelization'? What does it mean for the lives of high-school-age Christians?
⊙ How might it apply to life within your school?

WHAT ABOUT YOU PERSONALLY?
⊙ What message are you preaching among your friends? At home?

- What does the call to a 'new evangelization' say to you about the values you put into practice among your friends?

THE PROPHETIC MISSION OF THE BAPTIZED

In the Rite of Baptism, the newly baptized are anointed with the consecrated oil of **sacred chrism**. This anointing is a sign that the newly baptized have been made sharers in Christ's prophetic work.

'Christ . . . fulfills this prophetic office, not only by the hierarchy . . . but also by the laity [*Dogmatic Constitution on the Church*, no. 35]'. Lay people . . . fulfill their prophetic mission by evangelization, 'that is, the proclamation of Christ by word and the testimony of life'. For lay people, 'this evangelization . . . acquires a specific property and peculiar efficacy because it is accomplished in the ordinary circumstances of the world [*Dogmatic Constitution on the Church*, no. 35]'.

—CCC, nos. 904 and 905

Caritas International and Catholic Relief Services are Catholic organizations. Members of Caritas International and Catholic Relief Services give living witness to the 'new evangelization' proposed by Pope Paul VI. Both organizations model ways in which the hierarchy, religious and lay people join together to announce the Gospel of Jesus Christ.

Caritas International: Caritas International is a coalition of 164 Catholic social agencies set up by conferences of Catholic bishops from some 165 countries throughout the world. Caritas works in over two hundred countries and territories to bring relief during famines and natural disasters, to promote development of self-help programs among local peoples, and to serve people in a wide variety of ways. For example, Caritas volunteers responded to the devastating 2011 earthquake that hit Japan and the tsunami that flooded large regions along its coast.

Catholic Relief Services: In 1943 the Catholic Bishops formed Catholic Relief Services (CRS),

which is a member of Caritas International. The mission of Catholic Relief Services as stated on its website is:

Catholic Relief Services carries out the commitment of the Bishops of the United States to assist the poor and vulnerable overseas. We are motivated by the Gospel of Jesus Christ to cherish, preserve and uphold the sacredness and dignity of all human life, foster charity and justice, and embody Catholic social and moral teaching. . . . As part of the universal mission of the Catholic Church, we work with local, national and international Catholic institutions and structures, as well as other organizations, to assist people on the basis of need, not creed, race or nationality.

Each year Catholics in the United States are invited to take part in this work. Your parish has an annual collection to support the mission and work of Catholic Relief Services. For example, when the terrible earthquake hit Haiti on January 12, 2010, the Catholic Bishops in the United States called for a general collection throughout all the parishes in the United States.

OVER TO YOU
- What situations or people are you aware of who would benefit from hearing the Gospel of liberating salvation?
- How can you respond to one of those situations?

CARITAS INERNATIONAL DELIVERS AID TO LIBERIA'S DISPLACED PEOPLE

In the spirit of the Apostles

THE BAPTISM OF JESUS | JAMES TISSOT

in the wilderness, "Make straight the way of the Lord" ' (John 1:22–23). Matthew's account adds:

'I baptize you with water for repentance, but one who is more powerful than I is coming after me; I am not worthy to carry his sandals. He will baptize you with the Holy Spirit and fire.'
—Matthew 3:11

The Fourth Gospel adds this detail:

The next day he saw Jesus coming toward him and declared, 'Here is the Lamb of God who takes away the sin of the world! This is he of whom I said, "After me comes a man who ranks ahead of me because he was before me." I myself did not know him; but I came baptizing with water for this reason, that he might be revealed to Israel.' And John testified, 'I saw the Spirit descending from heaven like a dove, and it remained on him. I myself did not know him, but the one who sent me to baptize with water said to me, "He on whom you see the Spirit descend and remain is the one who baptizes with the Holy Spirit." And I myself have seen and have testified that this is the Son of God.'
—John 1:29–34

John the Baptist was the last of the Old Testament prophets and the first evangelist of the good news of salvation in Christ. Central to John the Baptist's mission was his role to announce Jesus to be the 'promised one' of God, the Son of God and the Savior of the world.

Jesus was about thirty years of age when John the Baptist, the son of Elizabeth and Zechariah, was proclaiming that the reign of God 'is near', calling people to repent of their sins and baptizing them in the waters of the Jordan River. When priests and Levites asked John, 'Who are you? Let us have an answer for those who sent us. What do you say about yourself?', John replied by quoting the prophet Isaiah, 'I am the voice of one crying out

OPENING REFLECTION

◉ What do these Gospel stories about John the Baptist tell you about the Church's and your work of evangelization?
◉ What do you tell others about Jesus?

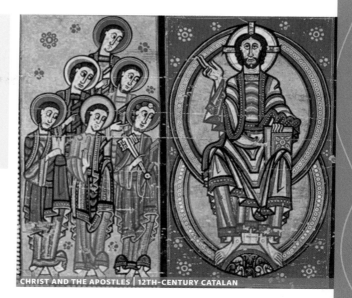

CHRIST AND THE APOSTLES | 12TH-CENTURY CATALAN

JESUS CHOOSES THE 'TWELVE'

John's and Matthew's accounts of the Gospel tell us that after his baptism by John the Baptist, Jesus called and gathered disciples. 'Jesus associated his disciples with his own life, revealed the mystery of the Kingdom to the disciples and gave them a share in his mission, his joy, and his sufferings' (CCC, Glossary; see also CCC, nos. 767, 787).

In Matthew's account Jesus says to the fishermen Peter and his brother Andrew, 'Follow me, and I will make you fish for people' (Matthew 4:19). (Read John 1:35–51 and Matthew 4:18–22.) These first disciples would be numbered among his closest disciples and become known as the **Twelve**. Matthew gives us the names of the Twelve:

Jesus summoned his twelve disciples and gave them authority over unclean spirits, to cast them out, and to cure every disease and every sickness. These are the names of the twelve apostles: first, Simon, also known as Peter, and his brother Andrew; James son of Zebedee, and his brother John; Philip and Bartholomew; Thomas and Matthew the tax collector; James son of Alphaeus, and Thaddeus; Simon the Cananaean, and Judas Iscariot, the one who betrayed him.

—Matthew 10:1–4

TALK IT OVER

⊙ What do you think it was about Jesus' invitation that led Peter and Andrew and John and James to leave what they were doing 'immediately' and follow Jesus?

Many other men and women, whole families and people of all ages and from all walks of life came to believe in Jesus and became his disciples. In Luke's account of the Gospel we read of Jesus appointing and sending seventy other disciples in pairs with the mission to prepare people's hearts to receive the Good News. (Read Luke 10:1–12.)

THE CHURCH IS APOSTOLIC

The Church is apostolic. 'She is built on a lasting foundation: "the twelve apostles of the Lamb" [Revelation 21:14]' (CCC, no. 869). Jesus took the Twelve aside and prepared them to be the leaders among his disciples. He instructed them and sent them forth to share the Good News through their words and deeds. (Read Matthew 20:17 and Luke 18:31.) The risen Christ would entrust these **Apostles** to continue his mission after his Ascension. 'The apostolic office is permanent in the Church, in order to ensure that the divine mission entrusted to the Apostles will continue to the end of time' ('Apostle', in CCC, Glossary).

In [the Twelve], Christ continues his own mission: 'As the Father has sent me, even so I send you' [John 20:21; see also John 13:20; 17:18]. The apostles' ministry is the continuation of his mission; Jesus said to the Twelve: 'he who receives you receives me' [Matthew 10:40; see also Luke 10:16].

—CCC, no. 858

'I AM WITH YOU UNTIL THE END OF THE AGE'
The risen Jesus did not abandon his work on earth when he ascended to heaven. He is still present with his Church and will be present with her on earth 'until the end of the age'—until his work is completed at the end of time. This promise of the risen Lord reveals that the Church 'is both visible and spiritual . . . formed of two components, human and divine. That is her mystery, which only faith can accept' (CCC, no. 779).

The Apostles showed us the human side of the Church. The Twelve often struggled to 'get it'.

They often missed the point of Jesus' teaching. They vied for power and recognition. Thomas doubted Jesus; Peter denied him; and Judas betrayed him with a kiss.

After the Ascension Matthias, Barnabas and Paul would be chosen to be Apostles. And the power of the Holy Spirit would transform them and the Eleven into 'bold' evangelizers. All, with the exception of John, would lead the Church with a faith that would result in their martyrdom. This transformation is a testimony to the power of God, the divine component, at work in the Church. It reveals that the grace of God can transform even the least among us.

THINK, PAIR AND SHARE
⊙ Work with a partner. You are one of the 'pairs' of disciples Jesus is sending out on mission. Read over Luke 10:1–12, 17–20. Pay close attention to the precise instructions that Jesus gives you. Discuss:
– What good news do you have to share?
– What may be some of the challenges that lie ahead for you?
– Why will you come back with so much joy?
⊙ Share your dialogue with the class.

WHAT ABOUT YOU PERSONALLY?
⊙ When have you felt yourself 'sent' to share your faith in Jesus?
⊙ How did you respond?

THE PRIMACY OF PETER, 'THE ROCK'
In chapter 5 of this text you learned that Jesus chose Simon, whom he renamed Peter, to be the 'rock', the visible foundation, on whom he would build his Church. The name Peter, or Cephas in Greek, means 'rock'. (Reread Matthew 16:13–20.) After the Resurrection, the risen Christ appeared to Peter and the other disciples who were fishing in the waters of the Lake of Galilee. After eating breakfast with them, he asked Peter:

'Simon son of John, do you love me more than these?' He said to him, 'Yes, Lord; you know that I love you.' Jesus said to him, 'Feed my lambs.' A second time he said to him, 'Simon son of John, do you love me?' He said to him, 'Yes, Lord; you know that I love you.' Jesus said to him, 'Tend

FAITH WORD

Apostle

The title traditionally given to those specially chosen by Jesus to preach the Gospel and to whom he entrusted responsibility for guiding the early Church.

—USCCA, 504

ST. PETER | PETER PAUL RUBENS

my sheep.' He said to him the third time, 'Simon son of John, do you love me?' Peter felt hurt because he said to him the third time, 'Do you love me?' And he said to him, 'Lord, you know everything; you know that I love you.' Jesus said to him, 'Feed my sheep.'

—John 21:15–17

The Pope, the bishop of Rome, continues the work of St. Peter. Christ governs the Church 'through Peter and the other apostles, who are present in their successors, the Pope and the **college of bishops**' (CCC, no. 869). Working in union with the Pope, the bishops lead and guide the Church with the grace of the Holy Spirit. '[A]ll the bishops of the Church with the Pope at their head form a single "college", which succeeds in every generation the "college" of the Twelve Apostles, with Peter at their head, which Christ instituted as the foundation of the Church. This college of bishops together with, but never without, the Pope has supreme and full authority over the universal Church' (CCC, Glossary; see also CCC, nos. 861, 880, 883). You will recall from chapter 5 that this unbroken line of succession between St. Peter and the Pope and between the other Apostles and the bishops of the Church in communion with the Pope is called apostolic succession.

TALK IT OVER
- Who is the present Pope? Share what you know about him.
- Who is your bishop? Share what you know about him.
- What is the name of your pastor and parish priests?

WHAT ABOUT YOU PERSONALLY?
All of us who belong to the Church share in the mission to proclaim the Gospel. In our own way, Christ sends each of us on 'mission'.
- Where are you being sent?
- What good news will you bring there?

ST. PETER RECEIVES THE KEYS | PIETRO PERUGINO

Sharing the message of salvation

BILL PAXTON, KEVIN BACON AND TOM HANKS IN *APOLLO 13*

How do you get your news? Online? iPhone? YouTube? Twitter? Television? Conversation in the school cafeteria? Parish youth group? Film is also a source that helps us remember news, both good news and bad news. The docudrama *Apollo 13* (1995) chronicles NASA's 1970 moon mission, which turned into a battle for survival. During the descent the crew lost communication with the Houston Control Center, and four long minutes went by without a word. Then, the microphone crackled and Captain Jim Lovell's voice finally came through, 'Hello, Houston! This is Odyssey. It's good to see you again.' Cheering erupted as everyone celebrated.

OPENING REFLECTION
⊙ What is the best good news you have ever heard?
⊙ Did you share that good news or keep it to yourself? Why is that?

THE APOSTLES' CREED
From her very beginning the Church has shared and celebrated the good news of salvation. The word 'gospel', you will recall, means 'good news'. The members of the early Church gathered together to support one another (fellowship), to celebrate Eucharist, and to hear and live by the teachings of the Apostles. The Church has shared the essentials of the Apostles' teachings in many ways; one of these ways is through the Apostles' Creed and the other **creeds** of the Church.

The Apostles' Creed is a brief and 'faithful summary of the apostles' faith' (CCC, no. 194). Today, people who are to be baptized profess that faith of the Church in question-and-answer format. At Mass on Easter Sunday, the baptized, using the same question-and-answer form, renew their baptismal profession of faith. Praying the Apostles' Creed unites us to the Apostles and proclaims to the world the good news of our salvation in Jesus Christ.

REFLECT AND SHARE
⊙ How does your faith in Christ and his Church shape who you are as a person?
⊙ How do you share that faith with others?

FAITH WORD

Creed
A brief, normative summary statement or profession of Christian faith, e.g. the Apostles' Creed, the Nicene Creed. The word 'Creed' comes from the Latin *Credo*, meaning 'I believe', with which the Creed begins. Creeds are also called Symbols of Faith.

—CCC, Glossary

Martyrdom was the common death for the Apostles, many members of the early Church and generations of Christians since then

CRUCIFIXION OF ST. PETER | HEILSBRONN MONASTERY, GERMANY

THE TEACHINGS OF THE APOSTLES TODAY

The Spirit of Truth, promised by Jesus and sent by the Father and the Son, set St. Peter and the other Apostles on fire to proclaim the Gospel boldly. That same Spirit is with the successors of St. Peter and the other Apostles today. Guided by the Holy Spirit, the Pope and the bishops in communion with him have authoritatively and authentically interpreted Sacred Scripture and Sacred Tradition down through the ages and they continue to fulfill that office today. The Holy Spirit is always leading the Church in her understanding of and living of the Good News. That same Spirit of Truth and Love will be guiding the Church into a deeper and clearer understanding of Revelation until Christ comes again in glory at the end of time.

THINK, PAIR AND SHARE

⊙ Reflect on what you have learned about who Jesus Christ is, what he taught, and what he accomplished when he lived among us. Pair up and discuss: What is the best news in the Gospel?

⊙ How do you see the Catholic Church working with other Christians to share that good news?

⊙ How are your diocese and parish and Catholic school community sharing that good news? How are young people taking part in that work?

OVER TO YOU

⊙ How do you share the good news of salvation in Jesus? With whom do you share that news?

⊙ What more could you do to share and live the Gospel in your home?

NO EASY TASK

Jesus clearly told his disciples that proclaiming the Gospel would be no easy task. It would cost them. It even might cost them their lives—as he told them it would cost him. Recall Jesus' words to the seventy disciples as he sent them forth ahead of him to prepare people for his coming: 'Go on your way. See, I am sending you out like lambs into the midst of wolves' (Luke 10:3).

When Jesus made it known that he would suffer and die in order to do the work he was sent to do, the Apostles, led by Peter, objected. Jesus replied to Peter, 'Get behind me, Satan! You are a stumbling block to me; for you are setting your mind not on divine things but on human things' (Matthew 16:23). In other words, there is and will be a cost for being a faithful disciple of Jesus.

The world is not always ready or willing to hear, accept and live the Gospel. As Jesus' fulfilling his mission as Savior led him to the Cross, we must be open to accept whatever it costs us to live as his faithful disciples. As we explored in chapter 2, Christians have always been willing to pay that price. Martyrdom was the common death for the Apostles, many members of the early Church and generations of Christian since then. The blood of martyrs was and continues to be the 'seed of the Church'.

TALK IT OVER

⊙ What price is the Church paying for proclaiming the Gospel in our country today? In other parts of the world? Give specific examples.

WHAT ABOUT YOU PERSONALLY?

⊙ What cost have you paid for sharing your faith in Jesus and the Gospel of salvation?
⊙ What price are you willing to pay to make your life 'good news', a 'living Gospel' for others?

REFLECT ON WHAT YOU HAVE LEARNED IN THIS CHAPTER

As you come toward the end of this chapter, pause and reflect on what you have learned about the Church from exploring the two Marks of the Church, *catholic* and *apostolic*. Share the teachings of the Catholic Church on these statements:

⊙ The Church founded by Jesus is catholic and has been sent by him on a mission to the whole world.

⊙ The Church is the means of salvation for all people, even for non-believers.

⊙ The Church founded by Jesus is apostolic; she is built on the foundation of the Twelve Apostles.

⊙ Jesus gave the primacy of leadership among the Apostles to St. Peter.

⊙ The Church today is guided by the successors of the Twelve: the Pope and the other bishops in communion with him.

⊙ The Pope, the bishop of Rome, and other bishops in communion with him have the office and responsibility of authentically interpreting Revelation, namely, Scripture and Tradition.

⊙ The Pope and bishops work as a 'college of bishops'.

⊙ God calls all members of the Church to share the Gospel with others.

TALK IT OVER

⊙ Share with a partner the most valuable wisdom you have learned in this chapter.

⊙ Join up with another pair of students and share ideas on what putting this wisdom into practice might mean for young Catholics today.

BEING CATHOLIC AND APOSTOLIC: LIVING THE SOCIAL TEACHING OF THE CATHOLIC CHURCH

The words 'Preach the Gospel at all times and when necessary use words', which are attributed to St. Francis of Assisi, sum up his life. The **social teachings of the Catholic Church** guide us in preaching the Gospel by our deeds. 'The Church's social teaching is a rich treasure of wisdom about building a just society and living lives of holiness amidst the challenges of a modern society' (USCCA, 421). This social doctrine of the Catholic Church is built on the Church's response

POPE FRANCIS ON THE BALCONY OF ST PETER'S, VATICAN CITY, MARCH 2013

to the biblical mandate to reach out to orphans, widows, aliens and other people in need. The *preferential option for the poor and the vulnerable* is one of the central principles of that doctrine. The bishops of the Church in the United States teach:

A basic moral test is how our most vulnerable members are faring. In a society marred by deepening divisions between rich and poor, our tradition recalls the story of the Last Judgment (Matthew 25:31–46) and instructs us to put the needs of the poor and vulnerable first.

—USCCA, 423

People suffering from poverty in any of its many forms are often, if not routinely, forgotten and excluded by others. Things, perhaps, are no different today than they were in Jesus' time. (Recall Jesus' teaching in the parable of the Rich Man and Lazarus in Luke 16:19–31.) People living in economic poverty are often 'not seen' and ignored both by individuals and by the very structures and laws of a society.

People can also be treated unfairly and unjustly by the very structures of society because of their gender, race, beliefs, and even their age and their body size and shape. This is also sometimes done in subtle ways by individuals;° for example, by students isolating a less popular student in the cafeteria, or by a student or group of students bullying another student. Excluding others unfairly betrays the Gospel and the command to proclaim the Gospel to all people.

REFLECT AND DECIDE

⊙ From your study of the Catholic Church, who have you come to know who has put into practice the Church's teaching on 'the preferential option for the poor and the vulnerable'?
⊙ How is your school community taking part in that work?
⊙ How can you take part in that work?

LEARN BY EXAMPLE

Maryknoll Lay Missioners, living the Gospel of salvation

Christ has sent his Church 'to the nations that she might be "the universal sacrament of salvation" [Vatican II, *Decree on the Missionary Activity of the Church*, no. 1]' (CCC, no. 849). From her beginning the Church has sent forth missionaries to proclaim Christ to the nations. Today, Maryknoll Lay Missioners continue this work. Maryknoll Lay Missioners is a Catholic organization whose members live and work with poor communities in Africa, Asia and the Americas. Inspired by the mission of Jesus, they work to instruct and help people to meet their basic human needs and to create a more just and compassionate world. Maryknoll Lay Missioners describe their vocation:

We are inspired by the rich tradition of Catholic Social Teaching, and we are grounded in the history and spirit of our Maryknoll mission family. We strive together for justice, peace and fullness of life. Our ministries are offered in response to the needs of the people with whom we live and work, and with respect for the integrity of all creation. We challenge unjust structures and systems, seeking transformation of the very powers that create and benefit from the marginalization of communities. Even amidst sin and suffering, we celebrate the holiness of everyday life and we proclaim the hope of resurrection.

Maryknoll Lay Missioners currently live the Gospel of salvation and serve people in six countries worldwide: Asia–Cambodia, Africa–Kenya, Tanzania, Latin America–Brazil, El Salvador and Bolivia.

OVER TO YOU

- ◉ When have you ever heard a call that challenged you to share the Gospel? Share your story.
- ◉ Has your sharing the Good News ever inspired someone else to do the same? Explain.

SHARING FAITH WITH FAMILY AND FRIENDS

- ◉ What can you do with your family and friends to grow together in your understanding of the faith and mission of the Catholic Church?

WHAT WILL YOU DO NOW?

- ◉ Who might you ask to join with you in sharing the Gospel?
- ◉ How will you share the Good News?
- ◉ Whatever you do, remember the words of St. Francis, 'Preach the Gospel at all times and when necessary use words.'

LEARN BY HEART

'Preach the Gospel at all times and when necessary use words.'

ATTRIBUTED TO ST. FRANCIS OF ASSISI

PRAYER REFLECTION

Pray the Sign of the Cross together.

LEADER
God of Life,
    we praise you and give you thanks for calling
    us to proclaim the Gospel of your Son,
    Jesus Christ.
Send us your Spirit
    to guide us in growing in understanding, in
    wisdom and in faithfulness to our catholic and
    apostolic faith.

ALL
Amen.

LEADER
Let us now pray and reflect on the meaning of the
Apostles' Creed for our life. (*Pause*)

READER
I believe in God, the Father almighty,
Creator of heaven and earth, . . .

LEADER
Let us each reflect on ways in which God, the
Holy Trinity, has blessed us lately.

All pray silently or offer a word or phrase out loud.

READER
and in Jesus Christ, his only Son, our Lord, . . .

LEADER
Let us each reflect on the good news that Jesus
has brought to our life.

All pray silently or offer a word or phrase out loud.

READER
who was conceived by the power of the Holy
Spirit, born of the Virgin Mary, . . .

LEADER
Let us each reflect on the many blessings that
the Holy Spirit has given us. What could we
accomplish by the power of the Holy Spirit and
through the intercession of Mary?

All pray silently or offer a word or phrase out loud.

READER
suffered under Pontius Pilate,
was crucified, died, and was buried; . . .

LEADER
Let us each reflect on the suffering that is part of
our life or the lives of those around us. Where do
we need Christ's healing love?

All pray silently or offer a word or phrase out loud.

READER
and descended into hell;
on the third day he rose again from the dead; . . .

LEADER
Let us each reflect on the dead ends in our life.
How might Christ lead us out of these to live our
life more fully?

All pray silently or offer a word or phrase out loud.

READER
he ascended into heaven,
and is seated at the right hand of God the Father
almighty, . . .

LEADER
Let us each reflect on how we can trust more
fully in Jesus' love for us. Do we really believe he
is ultimately in charge?

All pray silently or offer a word or phrase out loud.

READER
from there he will come again to judge the living
and the dead.

LEADER
Let us each reflect on how we can stand up for
God's justice.

All pray silently or offer a word or phrase out loud.

READER

I believe in the Holy Spirit, . . .

LEADER

Let us each reflect on how the Spirit is moving in our life right now. How can we be more open to where the Spirit leads us?

All pray silently or offer a word or phrase out loud.

READER

the holy catholic Church,
the communion of saints, . . .

LEADER

Let us each reflect on how the community of believers has helped and is helping us to grow in our faith. What can we do to participate more fully in the life of the Church?

All pray silently or offer a word or phrase out loud.

READER

the forgiveness of sins, . . .

LEADER

Let us each reflect on what stands in the way of our relationship with God and others?

All pray silently or offer a word or phrase out loud.

READER

the resurrection of the body, . . .

LEADER

Let us each reflect on how we can accept the gift of life, and the strength, health, vitality and creativity that God has given us.

All pray silently or offer a word or phrase out loud.

READER

and life everlasting.

LEADER

Let us each reflect on how we can live our life more fully now, with the hope of eternal life.

All pray silently or offer a word or phrase out loud.

LEADER

Loving God of all, thank you for your gift of faith.
Strengthen our belief and help our unbelief,
    in times of trouble, uncertainty and doubt.
Inspire our faith by the work of your Holy Spirit,
    who guides us in living faithfully in the path of
        your Son Jesus.
We ask this in Jesus' name.

ALL

Amen.

Conclude by praying the Sign of the Cross together.

CHAPTER 8

One Family of God

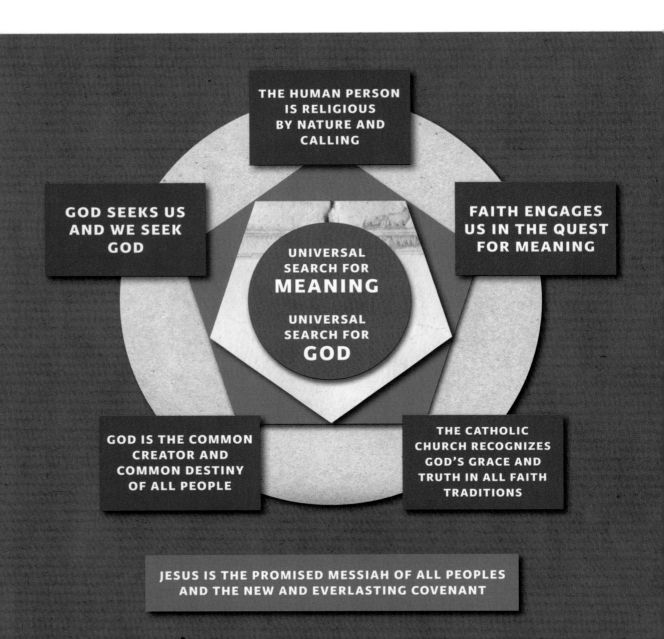

THE HUMAN PERSON IS RELIGIOUS BY NATURE AND CALLING

GOD SEEKS US AND WE SEEK GOD

FAITH ENGAGES US IN THE QUEST FOR MEANING

UNIVERSAL SEARCH FOR **MEANING**

UNIVERSAL SEARCH FOR **GOD**

GOD IS THE COMMON CREATOR AND COMMON DESTINY OF ALL PEOPLE

THE CATHOLIC CHURCH RECOGNIZES GOD'S GRACE AND TRUTH IN ALL FAITH TRADITIONS

JESUS IS THE PROMISED MESSIAH OF ALL PEOPLES AND THE NEW AND EVERLASTING COVENANT

THE HUMAN PERSON IS RELIGIOUS BY NATURE and by calling. In this chapter we explore the relationship between Catholics, non-Catholic Christians and people of other religions who do not believe in Jesus Christ. Catholics share the common bond of Baptism with all Christians. Divisions have occurred within the Church throughout her history. Today, Christians are working together to heal those divisions and to restore her unity—the 'oneness' Christ prayed for at the Last Supper. God desires all people to form one family, the one People of God.

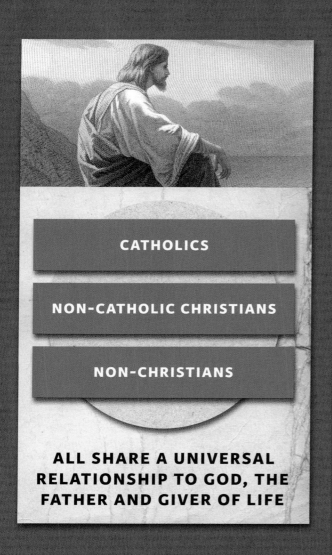

CATHOLICS

NON-CATHOLIC CHRISTIANS

NON-CHRISTIANS

ALL SHARE A UNIVERSAL RELATIONSHIP TO GOD, THE FATHER AND GIVER OF LIFE

Faith Focus: The teachings of the Catholic Church that are the primary focus of the doctrinal content presented in this chapter include:

⊙ The Church founded by Jesus Christ is one.
⊙ The Church is both the means and the goal of God's plan for humanity and the place where humanity must rediscover its unity and salvation.
⊙ The Church knows that she is joined in many ways to the baptized who are honored by the name of Christian, but do not profess the Catholic faith in its entirety or have not preserved unity or communion under the Pope, the successor of St. Peter.
⊙ All nations form but one community because God is the creator and the savior and the final destiny of all people.
⊙ The Catholic Church recognizes all the goodness and truth found in other religions as preparation for the Gospel.

Discipleship Formation: As a result of studying this chapter and discovering the meaning of the faith of the Catholic Church for your life, you should be better able to:

⊙ appreciate that faith is fundamental in the universal quest for the meaning of your life;
⊙ recognize and foster the special relationship that exists between the Catholic Church and other Christian faith traditions;
⊙ respect and recognize God's grace and truth in non-Christian faith traditions;
⊙ esteem the Jewish faith in its special relationship with Catholicism;
⊙ engage in authentic dialogue with those of the same and different faith traditions in the spirit of ecumenism;
⊙ stand up against bigotry and prejudice toward Judaism or other religions;
⊙ engage in authentic and sincere interreligious dialogue and promote religious tolerance, peace and harmony.

Scripture References: These Scripture references are quoted or referred to in this chapter:
NEW TESTAMENT: John 14:6, 17:21; **Romans** 11:17–24; **1 Corinthians** 12:1–31; **2 Corinthians** 5:17–18; **Galatians** 3:26–28; **Ephesians** 4:1–6

Faith Glossary: Familiarize yourself with the meaning of these key terms. Definitions are found in the Glossary: **Body of Christ, covenant, ecclesial communities, ecumenism, hope, Orthodox Churches, People of God, divine Revelation, schism**

Faith Words: ecumenism; communion
Learn by Heart: 2 Corinthians 5:17–18
Learn by Example: Avery Cardinal Dulles, S.J.

What does it all mean?

Life sometimes presents great and unforgettable moments. These moments are often extraordinary and radically different from our day-to-day experiences. Such moments can stop us in our tracks and make us pause and reflect on the greater meaning of life. Births and deaths, new encounters and partings, changes and transitions are often the context of such moments.

OPENING CONVERSATION

⊙ When have you experienced an unforgettable moment? Where were you? Who was with you?

⊙ How do such experiences help you encounter God?

⊙ What was the best wisdom you learned from these experiences?

⊙ How might this wisdom continue to impact your life?

THE UNIVERSAL SEARCH FOR MEANING: THE UNIVERSAL SEARCH FOR GOD

Consider the following:

On September 11, 2001 the French filmmaker Jules Naudet was filming inside one of the towers of the World Trade Center in New York City when the tower was struck by a highjacked airliner; but he managed to escape from the collapsing building. This experience prompted Naudet, an unbeliever by his own account, to face the profound questions about faith and the meaning of life and to create a new film project, *In God's Name* (2007). The experience of producing and filming *In God's Name*, in which twelve of the world's most prominent religious leaders give answers to the fundamental questions of life, gave Naudet 'an amazing outlook and hope for the future'. He explained, 'What we found in all these people in these regions and these faiths—we saw tolerance; we saw love; we saw compassion. And time and again that was always there.'

Jules Naudet is not alone in turning to faith in God after such a life-changing experience as surviving the devastation of September 11, 2001. The human person is religious by nature and calling. Faith in God offers us the ability to contemplate and to find hope in the deeper meaning of such experiences.

When profound moments impact life, faith engages us in the quest for greater meaning. God seeks us and we seek God. Different faith traditions share in this quest in different, yet remarkably similar, ways.

Humanity forms but one community. This is so because all stem from the one stock which God created to people the entire earth, and also because all share a common destiny, namely God.

—Vatican II, *Declaration on the Relation of the Church to Non-Christian Religions*, no. 1

The Catholic Church joins with people of other faith traditions in search of this common destiny. All humanity has a common origin and a common end. 'To reunite all his children, scattered and led astray by sin, the Father willed to call the whole of humanity together into his Son's Church' (*Catechism of the Catholic Church* [CCC], no. 845). The Church is in the world as a light to lead all people in this search to achieve that destiny. She 'enlightens all men and women' and 'proclaims . . . Christ who is the way, the truth, and the life [John 14:6]. In him, in whom God reconciled all things to himself [see 2 Corinthians 5:18–19], people find the fullness of their religious life' (Vatican II, *Declaration on the Relation of the Church to Non-Christian Religions*, no. 2). In Christ's Church the fullness of Revelation and the means of salvation—the means of attaining that destiny—is found.

REFLECT AND DISCUSS

- Why do people turn to faith and religion for insight into the meaning of the most profoundly human experiences?

FROM THE WISDOM OF THE CHURCH
The Catholic Church recognizes in other religions that search, among shadows and images, for the God who is unknown yet near since he gives life and breath and all things, and wants all men to be saved. Thus, the Church considers all goodness and truth found in these religions as 'a preparation for the Gospel, and given by him who enlightens all men that they may at length have life' [Vatican II, *Dogmatic Constitution on the Church*, no. 16].

—CCC, no. 843

DIALOGUE AMONG FAITH TRADITIONS

The Catholic Church through Baptism lives in a special relationship with **Orthodox Churches** and Protestant **ecclesial communities**. Together we seek to find the meaning of human life and the answers to life's deepest questions in the Incarnate Word of God, Jesus Christ.

Non-Catholic Christians 'who believe in Christ and have been properly baptized are put in a certain, although imperfect, communion with the Catholic Church' (CCC, no. 838). The Catholic Church respects and recognizes God's grace and truth in all faith traditions, Christian and non-Christian. Among these non-Christian traditions, Judaism and Islam are closest to Christianity in our shared belief in one God.

TALK IT OVER

- Share what you know about the faith beliefs and practices of your friends who celebrate their faith in religious traditions other than the Catholic Church.

ENGRAVING AFTER ALEXANDRE BIDA

SECOND ECUMENICAL KIRCHENTAG HELD IN MUNICH, GERMANY IN 2010

LIVING AS A CATHOLIC WITHIN A DIVERSE RELIGIOUS LANDSCAPE

Picture your closest friend. If you think about it, the close friendship that you share would not exist without each of you bringing your honest and true selves to the relationship. With such a close friend, you can be yourself. In fact, your friendship depends heavily on the honesty you both bring to your relationship with each other.

When the Catholic Church enters into conversation and partnership with other faith traditions, we must bring our true and honest selves into that dialogue. We express honestly and openly the beliefs and practices of our faith. We are true and faithful to who we are and to what we believe.

Good relationships with our fellow believers and non-believers emerge out of being able to share with one another authentically and honestly who we are. As in a solid friendship, honesty, truth, kindness and gentleness are the hallmarks of such sharing. As Catholics, we share the good news of our faith in Jesus Christ with people of all faith traditions.

Ecumenism is the name given to the efforts by Christians to restore unity among all Christians. 'Interreligious dialogue' is a term that refers to the Catholic Church's dialogue with non-Christian religions. (We will explore the Church's work of ecumenism and interreligious dialogue in greater depth in the next three sections of this chapter.)

OVER TO YOU

Imagine that your school appoints you as the Catholic representative to an interfaith student conference. At lunch, you find yourself in a conversation circle with students from Orthodox, Protestant, Jewish, Muslim, Hindu and Buddhist faith traditions. They ask you to share why you are a member of the Catholic Church.

- ⊙ What are the essential points about the beliefs and practices of the Catholic Church that you would be prepared to share?
- ⊙ What questions would you want to ask students of other faith traditions?
- ⊙ How would you explain your commitment to the Catholic Church?

One Body in Christ

In August 1993 Pope St. John Paul II traveled to Denver, Colorado for the eighth annual World Youth Day, to celebrate our faith in Christ with the thousands of young people, youth ministers and clergy gathered there. The theme song for World Youth Day Denver, 'We Are One Body', was composed by Dana Scallon. 'We Are One Body' has since become a widely popular song among Catholic youth, sounding out at retreats, youth groups, liturgies and at service and mission trips.

Scallon's song repeats this simple yet profound refrain about our identity as disciples of Jesus Christ: 'We are one Body, one Body in Christ, and we do not stand alone; we are one Body, one Body in Christ, and he came that we might have life.' Singing these words evokes such a deep connection between those singing that they are often moved to embrace and sway as one body to give expression to who they believe they are. 'We Are One Body' expresses in a powerful way our human desire for unity in God and the promise of Jesus Christ to fulfill this desire.

> **FROM THE WISDOM OF THE CHURCH**
> [T]he universal Church is seen to be 'a people brought into unity from the unity of the Father, the Son, and the Holy Spirit' [*Dogmatic Constitution on the Church*, no. 4, citing St. Cyprian].
>
> —CCC, no. 810

ECUMENISM: MOVEMENT TOWARD CHRISTIAN UNITY

On the night before he died, in his farewell reflections, Jesus prayed, 'that they may all be one. As you, Father, are in me and I am in you, may they also be in us, so that the world may believe that you have sent me' (John 17:21). The unity that Christ prayed for and desires for all his disciples 'subsists in the Catholic Church as something she can never lose, and we hope that it will continue to increase until the end of time' (Vatican II, *Decree on Ecumenism*, no. 4).

OPENING CONVERSATION

You are familiar with St. Paul's description of the Church as the **Body of Christ** in 1 Corinthians 12:1–31. This rich image carries many interconnected meanings.

- In what context do you most often hear the Church described as the Body of Christ?
- What are some things that come to mind when you think of the Church as the Body of Christ?
- How might you be able to connect these multiple meanings to one another?

To reunite all his children, scattered and led astray by sin, the Father willed to call the whole of humanity together into his Son's Church. The Church is the place where humanity must rediscover its unity and salvation.
—CCC, no. 845

Catholicism, Orthodoxy and Protestantism are all members within the one family of God, the one Body of Christ. In Baptism all Christians are siblings; they have put on Jesus Christ and are one in him. The Holy Spirit animates the whole family of the Body of Christ and is guiding it toward greater unity. St. Paul teaches:

[F]or in Christ Jesus you are all children of God through faith. As many of you as were baptized into Christ have clothed yourselves with Christ. There is no longer Jew or Greek, there is no longer slave or free, there is no longer male and female; for all of you are one in Christ Jesus.
—Galatians 3:26–28

All Christians must work for Christian unity with love for one another and faithfulness to Jesus. This work of all Christians is called ecumenism, or the Church's efforts to bring about unity and **communion** among Catholic, Orthodox and other members of the Body of Christ. One starting point for this work is recognizing and participating in actions and works that we share in common as disciples of Jesus. Among these works, '*conversion of heart*', '*prayer in common*', '*fraternal knowledge of each other*', '*dialogue among theologians and meetings among Christians*', '*ecumenical formation* of the faithful', and '*human service*' are especially important (see CCC, no. 821).

THINK, PAIR AND SHARE
- Work with a partner. List at least three actions that are characteristic of a person baptized in Christ.
- Share your list with the class.
- Work with the whole class and create one list.

The Catholic Church and the Orthodox Churches: The Great Schism of 1054 divided the Church into the East and the West. (See chapter 5 of this text.) In this **schism** the **Orthodox Churches** separated themselves from the authority of the Pope, the bishop of Rome, and the Catholic Church. Despite this division, a great unity in core beliefs, practices and other traditions remains between the Churches. Both Churches share a profound reverence for and a deep appreciation of worship and of the sacraments, and of the role of the Holy Spirit in the life of the universal Church and in the lives of the baptized. This is a reminder of the utter holiness of God, who is ever present in our lives.

OVER TO YOU

- ⊙ How aware are you of the presence and work of the Holy Spirit in your life?
- ⊙ How often do you pray to the Holy Spirit?

The Catholic Church and other Christian denominations, or ecclesial communities:
The Protestant Reformation gave birth to a diversity of many other Christian faith traditions, or ecclesial communities. (See chapter 5 of this text.) Since the Second Vatican Council (1962–65), Catholics and other Christians have been engaging in dialogue about such central teachings as the presence of Christ in the Eucharist, the role of faith and good works for salvation, and the nature and purpose of the Church. This dialogue with our other Christian brothers and sisters has also emphasized our common appreciation and understanding of the fundamental importance of reading and praying with the Bible and of the centrality of grace in our human efforts to live our faith in Christ.

WHAT ABOUT YOU PERSONALLY?

- ⊙ How regularly do you read the Bible?
- ⊙ When have you sensed the power of God's grace in your life? How did you respond to God's presence?

RECONCILIATION POSSIBILITIES FOR THE HUMAN FAMILY

'All women and men are called to belong to the new people of God' (Vatican II, *Dogmatic Constitution on the Church*, no. 13), so that, in Christ, 'men and women might form one family and one people of God' (Vatican II, *Decree on the Church's Missionary Activity*, no. 1). St. Paul the Apostle taught: '[I]f anyone is in Christ, there is a new creation. . . . All this is from God, who reconciled us to himself through Christ, and has given us the ministry of reconciliation' (2 Corinthians 5:17–18). All Christians share in this ministry of reconciliation, of healing the wounds dividing not only the Church but also the entire human family. For the 'Church is both the means and the goal of God's plan' (CCC, no. 778).

All the baptized are to be signs and instruments of this 'new creation' that God is bringing about in Christ through his Church and the reunion of all people into the one family of God. We are to work together to heal the divisions and discord that divide the Body of Christ and the entire human family.

OVER TO YOU

- ⊙ Think about your own family, school, circle of friends and local community, and whatever disharmony and discord exists within those groups. What are some possibilities to restore harmony? How can you be a reconciler among family or friends?
- ⊙ What efforts are you making to help bring about the reconciliation of people into the one family of God?

THE HOLY SPIRIT | NOTRE-DAME DE DEUIL-LA-BARRE, PARIS, FRANCE

Sharers in the covenant

At Mass in Eucharistic Prayer I the Catholic Church acknowledges Abraham to be 'our father in faith'. Catholics look to and reverence the Jewish people, the descendants of Abraham, as our ancestors in faith. Jesus, a Jew raised in the Jewish tradition, is the promised Messiah of all peoples. He is the new and everlasting covenant.

OPENING CONVERSATION

⊙ What is the relationship between Christians and Jewish people in your community?

⊙ Why is it important for Christians to remember that the roots of their faith are found in the faith and expectations of the Jewish people?

ABRAHAM, DAVID AND JOSEPH | ST. CLOTILDE, PARIS, FRANCE

> FROM THE WISDOM OF THE CHURCH
> When she delves into her own mystery, the Church, the People of God in the New Covenant, discovers her link with the Jewish People [Vatican II, *Declaration on the Relation of the Church to Non-Christian Religions*, no. 4].
> —CCC, no. 839

SHARERS IN GOD'S WORD AND THE COVENANT

Dialogue with our Jewish sisters and brothers is vital for our understanding of the Catholic faith. St. Paul, the zealous Jewish Pharisee and Christian Apostle to the Gentiles, taught us about the heart of the relationship that binds Jews and Christians. Read Romans 11:17–24.

In this passage St. Paul compared the relationship between the people of ancient Israel and the disciples of Jesus Christ to an olive tree. Israel is the root of the tree that keeps Christians, the new **People of God**, grounded and nourished in their fundamental covenantal relationship with God. The followers of Jesus Christ are like a wild olive shoot, grafted into the cultivated tree, where it continues to live and flourish. St. Paul admonished the early Church in Rome:

> [Do] not boast over the branches. If you do boast, remember that it is not you that support the root, but the root that supports you. . . . So do not become proud, but stand in awe.
> —Romans 11:18, 20

The Jewish people are our ancestors in faith. We inherit from them God's invitation to live in covenant with him, the Scriptures of the Old Testament, and a shared longing for the fulfillment of God's reign at the end of time. (See CCC, no. 840.)

Sacred Scripture: The Scriptures of ancient Israel are an indispensable part of **divine Revelation**. There is unity between the Old Testament and the New Testament that 'proceeds from the unity of God's plan and his Revelation' (CCC, no. 140). The Old Testament helps Christians understand more fully who Jesus Christ is and his mission in the world. 'All Scripture is but one book, and this one book is Christ, "because all divine Scripture speaks of Christ, and all divine Scripture is fulfilled in Christ" ' (Hugh of St. Victor, *Sermon on Noah's Ark*, 2, 8, quoted in CCC, no. 134).

The Covenant: The Scriptures of the Old Testament chronicle the establishment and the promise of the fulfillment of the **covenant**. The covenant is the solemn agreement God and his people entered. The Bible speaks of covenants that God made with Noah, with Abraham and with Moses and the Israelites. 'Israel is the priestly people of God, "called by the name of the Lord", and "the first to hear the word of God", the people of "elder brethren" in the faith of Abraham' (CCC, no. 63).

The prophets of ancient Israel constantly pointed to a messiah in whom God would enter a new covenant. This Messiah is Jesus Christ. 'Jesus did not abolish the Law of Sinai but rather fulfilled it [see Matthew 5:17–19] with such perfection [see John 8:46] that he revealed its ultimate meaning [see Matthew 5:33] and redeemed the transgressions against it [see Hebrews 9:15]' (CCC, no. 592). Jesus is the new and everlasting covenant.

Christians await the second and final coming of Christ, the risen and glorified Messiah, at the end of time. We join our **hope** for the completion of God's reign to the hope of the Jewish people, who still look for the coming of the Messiah. We remember that this world is temporary, and God's promise of justice, peace and the fullness of life for all creation still awaits complete fulfillment.

TALK IT OVER
- What does the covenant reveal about God's invitation to relationship with all people?

WHAT ABOUT YOU PERSONALLY?
- Where in your life do you have the greatest need for God's saving grace to help you overcome suffering?
- What is your greatest hope for God's liberating salvation?

THE SIN OF ANTI-JUDAISM
The current dialogue between Catholics and Jews includes overcoming and healing the effects of

JEWISH WORSHIPPER IN PRAYER AT THE WESTERN WALL, JERUSALEM

What Catholic spiritual practices do you know that are rooted in our Jewish ancestry?

a long history of bigotry and persecution of the Jewish people by Christians. This bigotry and persecution was based on the false judgment that all Jews of all time are responsible for the persecution and death of Jesus. The Catholic Church has acknowledged and apologized for this 'sin' against Jews; she condemns all forms of anti-Judaism (also called anti-Semitism) as a sin and contrary to the teaching of the Catholic Church and the love of God for all people. The Church clearly teaches:

[N]either all Jews indiscriminately at that time, nor Jews today, can be charged with the crimes committed during his passion. . . . [T]he Jews should not be spoken of as rejected or accursed as if this followed from holy Scripture.
—Vatican II, *Declaration on the Relation of the Church to Non-Christian Religions*, no. 4

Christians are to honor and respect the Jewish people as the people of the first covenant and as the root that gave life and nourishment to Christian faith. We are to have great esteem for and gratitude toward our Jewish brothers and sisters.

TALK IT OVER
- What Catholic spiritual practices do you know that are rooted in our Jewish ancestry?
- What acts of anti-Judaism are you aware of?
- How can you stand up against bigotry and prejudice toward Jews or people of other religions?

WHAT ABOUT YOU PERSONALLY?
- Have you ever experienced prejudice or bigotry because of your faith in Christ? How did you respond?
- What wisdom for your life did you learn from this experience?

God the Creator, the final destiny of all people of faith

Christian and Muslim youth in Birmingham, England participate in a celebration called 'the Feast'. The Feast brings Christian and Muslim teenagers together to join in service and fun; more importantly, it is an opportunity for them to grow in friendship and understanding. On one Christmas, the Feast hosted an event for the youth to meet up at a community Christmas party. Sharing in the festivities, the young people began to talk about the role of singing in their respective faith traditions; they shared ideas on how both Christmas carols and Muslim *nasheeds* express their respective faith and beliefs.

After the celebration the Christian and Muslim youth visited a home for the elderly to sing for the residents. Natasha, their youth minister, reflected, 'I was so touched to see how the youth responded to some of the elderly people there. They were really inspired by their visit and would like to go back again and do something more with and for the elderly. What I thought would be an exciting venture simply to see Christians and Muslims singing together turned into something much deeper than I could ever have hoped for!'

OPENING CONVERSATION
- What are your thoughts about the story of the 'Feast'?
- What made singing together—especially their singing for the elderly—so meaningful for both the Christian and Muslim young people?

OVER TO YOU
- When have you worked with youth from a diversity of faith traditions on a service project?

- How did your working together contribute to your understanding of and respect for one another?

CHRISTIANS AND MUSLIMS IN DIALOGUE
Music and song play a vital part in the life of the Catholic Church, as they do in all religious traditions. Song expresses the faith of a religion and can also deepen the unity among the members of a religion. For example, Maher Zain, a contemporary Lebanese-Swedish Muslim musician, and John Newton (1725–1807), an English Anglican clergyman, poet and hymn composer, have both expressed their faith in God in song. Though Zain's 'Thank You, Allah' and Newton's 'Amazing Grace' were written from different faith traditions and two hundred and thirty years apart, both songs express something profoundly similar about God. Both songs name God as their home and their refuge in facing the trials of life.

MAHER ZAIN IN CONCERT, 2011

Devout Muslims pause to pray five times a day

REFLECT AND SHARE

- Name your favorite hymns or other sacred songs. How do they help you express your faith in God?
- When have you been in a situation where you longed for God to bring you safely home?
- What is it like to be at home in God?

Abraham, one father in faith: In describing the relationship of the Church to non-Christians, the *Catechism* teaches: 'Many elements of sanctification and of truth are found outside [the Church's] visible confines' (CCC, no. 870). By their interreligious dialogue with Jews, Muslims and people of other non-Christian religions, Christians can help the members of the Church deepen their faith. For example, Christianity, Judaism and Islam stand together in their profession of faith in one God. Islam professes 'to hold the faith of Abraham, and . . . adore the one, merciful God, who will judge humanity on the last day' as Christianity does (Vatican II, *Dogmatic Constitution on the Church*, no. 16).

In the Qur'an, the holy writings of Islam, there are ninety-nine names and titles for God that express Islam's understanding of God. These include 'The Timeless One', 'The Unattainable One', 'The Everlasting One', 'The Manifest One', 'The Hidden One', 'The Friend', 'The Watchful One', 'The Source of Peace', 'The Compassionate One', 'The Bringer of Life' and 'The Bringer of Death'. While Islam does not accept Jesus to be the Incarnate Son of God, it holds Jesus in high respect as a great prophet of God, and honors Mary, his mother.

The spiritual practices of Islam are also central to a Muslim's profession of faith. Devout Muslims pause to pray five times a day. They embrace and seek to fulfill five great pillars of their faith throughout their life; these practices are: professing faith in Allah (the name Islam uses for God), daily prayers, fasting, almsgiving to the poor, and a holy pilgrimage to Mecca. Through the example of their faithful practice of these pillars of Islam, Muslims remind Christians of God's greatness and that submission to God's will is an essential part of the life of faith.

- How do Muslim images and titles for God mirror the images of God held by Christians?
- Which of these is most different from the Christian understanding of God?

OTHER NON-CHRISTIAN RELIGIONS

In addition to Christianity, Judaism and Islam, there are many other religions and faith traditions among the over six billion people of the world. At the time of the publication of this text, Christians, Muslims and Jews together make up the largest segment (55.7 percent) of that population.

While the fullness of the means of **salvation**—of sharing the saving events of Jesus' Death and Resurrection—are found in the Catholic Church, the Catholic Church acknowledges all that is good and true in the beliefs and practices of all religions. The goodness and truth of other religions are signs of God's presence among all peoples. When encountering non-Christian people of faith, these seeds of goodness and truth are starting points for dialogue and greater mutual respect and understanding. The truth and goodness of religious traditions help people make sense out of life and live God-centered lives. In their own way, the members of each religion with the grace of God seek to live in communion with him.

OVER TO YOU

Imagine that you are taking part in a conversation about faith with a Jewish, Muslim, Hindu or Buddhist friend. The conversation begins with a discussion on goodness and truth.
- What would you share about the beliefs and practices of the Catholic Church to begin the conversation?
- What would you like to learn from this person about his or her religious faith, about her or his beliefs and practices?
- Why might such a conversation foster respect among you and the other participants?

JUDGE AND ACT

REFLECT ON WHAT YOU HAVE LEARNED IN THIS CHAPTER

As you come toward the end of this chapter, pause and reflect on what you have come to understand to be the Catholic Church's relationship with the Orthodox Church, with Protestant ecclesial communities and with Judaism and other non-Christian faith traditions. Share your understanding of the teaching of the Catholic Church on these statements:

- ⊙ The Church founded by Jesus Christ is one and is both the means and the goal of God's plan for humanity.
- ⊙ The fullness of Christ's Church subsists in the Catholic Church.
- ⊙ All nations form but one community because God is the creator and the savior and the final destiny of all people.
- ⊙ All humanity is called to belong to the new People of God.
- ⊙ The Catholic Church recognizes all the goodness and truth found in other religions as preparation for the Gospel.
- ⊙ Christianity, Judaism and Islam are monotheistic religions.
- ⊙ Judaism holds a unique relationship to the Catholic Church.

OVER TO YOU

- ⊙ What is the best spiritual wisdom you have learned from this chapter?
- ⊙ What did you know already? What surprised you as a new insight or attitude?

LEARN BY EXAMPLE

The faith journey of Avery Cardinal Dulles, Jesuit priest and theologian

Avery Cardinal Dulles (1918–2008) was a Jesuit priest. Pope St. John Paul II named him a cardinal of the Church on February 21, 2001. Fr. Dulles was the first American theologian to receive this honor who was not a bishop.

Avery Dulles' journey to the Catholic Church involved a deep inner dialogue. While Avery was baptized a Presbyterian, his faith journey led him through a period during which he doubted the very existence of God. In 1936, while at Harvard University, he had a deeply moving experience that put those doubts to rest. Standing near the Charles River on a rainy day, the sight of a flowering tree opened his eyes to 'the existence of an all-good omnipotent God'. This moment marked the beginning of what Dulles called 'the long road to Rome'. He wrote, 'The more I examined, the more I was impressed with the consistency and sublimity of Catholic Doctrine'.

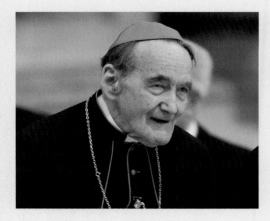

Cardinal Dulles has contributed to the ecumenical and interreligious dialogues of the Church. He published twenty-three books and wrote more than 750 articles on many theological subjects. Much of his writing efforts have focused on exploring the meaning and mission of the Church.

TALK IT OVER

- What is the role of doubt and the search for the truth in a person's faith journey?
- How did the faith journey of Cardinal Dulles reflect that search?
- How can doubt about the truths of the faith lead one to a deeper faith?

RESPOND WITH FAMILY AND FRIENDS

- Talk with family members and friends about some of the small ways in which religious intolerance and persecution begin
- Where might you encounter examples of religious intolerance in your school? In your community? Discuss what you could do, individually and together, to resist these.

WHAT WILL YOU DO NOW?

- What three simple things will you do to promote peace and harmony within your family?
- What three simple things will you do to promote peace and harmony among your friends?

- What three simple things will you do to promote peace and harmony within your school?
- What three simple things will you do to promote peace and harmony within your local community?

DECIDE FOR YOURSELF

- Imagine that your friend shares with you a joke that makes fun of another religious tradition. What might you do?
- What are the greatest obstacles in our world to unity and reconciliation among peoples of faith? How might you contribute to removing one of those obstacles?

LEARN BY HEART

[I]f anyone is in Christ, there is a new creation. . . .
All this is from God, who reconciled us to himself through Christ, and has given us the ministry of reconciliation.

2 CORINTHIANS 5:17–18

JESUS SPEAKS WITH THE SAMARITAN WOMAN | ENGRAVING AFTER ALEXANDRE BIDA

PRAYER REFLECTION

Pray the Sign of the Cross together.

Opening Prayer

LEADER
Loving God,
 you sent your Spirit of peace and unity among
  all people
 who abide in goodness and truth
 and who seek relationship with you
 and respond to you in faith.
Send us your Spirit of truth,
 to increase our faith and hope
 and make us signs of your loving presence
 for all peoples of faith.
We ask this in the name of Jesus Christ, your Son,
 the fullness of your presence and Revelation,
 and the source of our hope and joy,
 who lives and reigns with you and the Holy
 Spirit, one God, for ever and ever.

ALL
Amen.

The Word of God

READER
Proclaim Ephesians 4:1–6.
The word of the Lord.

ALL
Thanks be to God.

Intercessory Prayer

LEADER
Lord God, you are the one God of all.
With hope we call upon you.

All offer prayers for the unity of the Church and for the whole human family. After each petition, pray aloud, 'Spirit make us one'.

The Lord's Prayer

LEADER
Let us raise our voices in hope
and pray to God, the Father of all people,
for the coming of the Kingdom as Jesus taught
us.

All pray the Our Father *together and conclude with the doxology:*

For the kingdom, the power, and the glory are
yours, now and for ever. Amen.

All share a sign of peace.

Concluding Prayer

LEADER
Spirit of Unity,
gather in this humble prayer
 the prayers from all your people in the world,
that your peace, your justice and your mercy
  enfold us
 and enable us to live as one,
 the new humanity of peace.

ALL
Amen.

Pray the Sign of the Cross together.

CHAPTER 9

The Church in the World

THE CHURCH IS THE COMMUNITY OF THE DISCIPLES OF JESUS

THE CHURCH EXISTS TO EVANGELIZE

THE CHURCH BRINGS LIFE TO FAITH AND FAITH TO LIFE

LIGHTS IN THE WORLD

THE PEOPLE OF GOD ARE THE SACRAMENT OF GOD IN THE WORLD

WE ARE TO BRING THE LIGHT AND WISDOM OF JESUS TO THE WORLD

CHRIST FOUNDED THE CHURCH WITH A DIVINE purpose and mission. 'God created the world for the sake of communion with his divine life, a communion brought about by the "convocation" of men in Christ, and this "convocation" is the Church' (*Catechism of the Catholic Church*, no. 760). This chapter explores, in more detail, the work of the Church in and with the world. Each member of the Church has a part to play in continuing God's saving mission in Jesus in the world.

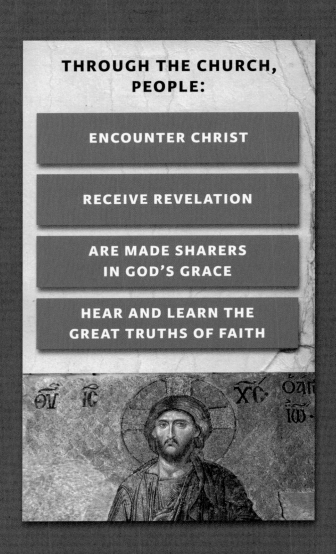

THROUGH THE CHURCH, PEOPLE:

ENCOUNTER CHRIST

RECEIVE REVELATION

ARE MADE SHARERS IN GOD'S GRACE

HEAR AND LEARN THE GREAT TRUTHS OF FAITH

Faith Focus: The teachings of the Catholic Church that are the primary focus of the doctrinal content presented in this chapter include:

- ⊙ Christ founded the Church with a divine purpose and mission.
- ⊙ The Church is the sign and sacrament of the communion of God with all people.
- ⊙ The Church is the visible sign and instrument of God's saving presence in the world.
- ⊙ Jesus—not the members—has endowed the Church with authority, power, and responsibility.
- ⊙ The Church continues Christ's salvation, preserves and hands on his teaching and has the mission and authority to bring the Gospel to the affairs of the world.
- ⊙ The Church scrutinizes 'signs of the times' and interprets them in light of the Gospel.

Discipleship Formation: As a result of studying this chapter and discovering the meaning of the faith of the Catholic Church for your life, you should be better able to:

- ⊙ commit yourself to follow Jesus Christ as the 'Light of the World';
- ⊙ welcome Jesus Christ into all aspects of your life;
- ⊙ be confident in asserting your religious beliefs in accordance with your basic human right to religious freedom;
- ⊙ respect the religious freedom of other people;
- ⊙ connect your faith with social and cultural issues;
- ⊙ identify your talents for and take part in the Church's mission of evangelization;
- ⊙ identify some unusual places where the Spirit of God may be calling you to evangelize.

Scripture References: These Scripture references are quoted or referred to in this chapter:
OLD TESTAMENT: **Psalms** 85:11–14
NEW TESTAMENT: **Matthew** 1:23, 5:14–16, 13:57, 24:14, 25:31–45, 28:1–10, 16–20; **Mark** 16:15; **Luke** 2:10–11, 9:1–6, 10:1–12 and 23; **John** 1:3–5, 8–12, 9:1–10; **Ephesians** 1:3–10, 3:1–12

Faith Glossary: Familiarize yourself with the meaning of these key terms. Definitions are found in the Glossary: **disciple, evangelization, missionary/missioner, *Urbi et Orbi*, Vatican**

Learn by Heart: Mark 16:15
Learn by Example: Pope St. John Paul II, evangelizer to youth

How should we witness to our faith?

One of the 'signs of the times' in the United States of America is the controversy and division arising from the diversity of religious beliefs and political philosophies. Many cable 'opinion shows' thrive financially on such controversy and foster that division. There is some wisdom in the First Amendment to the Constitution of the United States, which has established a clear separation between Church and State. This same Amendment also guarantees us the freedom to practice our religion and to share our religious faith and political views. The freedom to exercise fundamental human rights, while respecting the rights of others, is central and vital to the life of peoples of all nations. For people of faith, the separation of Church and State cannot mean a separation of faith from life.

OPENING CONVERSATION

⊙ When have you shared your faith with someone? How were your views received?

⊙ How do you try to witness to your own faith and convictions and, at the same time, respect others whose beliefs and convictions differ from yours?

Respecting Religious Freedom

Our country values religious and political freedom for good reason. Religious freedom is a basic human right and a foundational principle of the social doctrine of the Catholic Church because it belongs to the basic rights of each human being. (See *Catechism of the Catholic Church* [CCC], no. 1738.)

At the same time, this fundamental human right which is protected and assured by the Constitution might seem to put Catholics in the United States between a rock and a hard place. We might find it difficult to reconcile our belief that the Church is 'the instrument of the communion of God and men' (CCC, no. 780) with the religious freedom of people of other faith traditions and with people who do not believe in God. Exercising our right to religious freedom may seem impossible without violating the Constitution—without violating the rights of non-Catholics. We ask: how can we respect and honor the religious freedom of those around us and still obey Christ's mandate, 'Go therefore and make disciples of all nations' (Matthew 28:19)?

Even with the wise separation of Church and State in our country, we are called to live our faith publicly. We give witness

to our faith not only in our churches; we also live our faith in the marketplace. Our words and deeds invite but do not coerce a response. We recognize that faith in Christ and in his Church is a gift. It is both an invitation and a free response. We acknowledge that to force religious faith on anyone empties it of love, life and freedom. We see this clearly in the example of Jesus throughout his public life. While he constantly called people to discipleship, he left them entirely free to choose. He is the model of how we are to live our faith in the marketplace.

POPE FRANCIS DELIVERING *URBI ET ORBI* MESSAGE

THINK, PAIR AND SHARE

- Work with a partner. Select a current 'religious freedom' issue that we face in the United States. Imagine two scenarios: first, where one person shares his or her faith in an authentic, joyful and respectful way; and second, where a person shares his or her beliefs in an imposing way and without respecting the freedom of others.

- Act out the two scenarios, and then perform them for the class.

- Then, as a class, discuss what factors enable people to share their faith in a respectful, joyful and credible way.

URBI ET ORBI—'TO THE CITY AND TO THE WORLD'

Each year at Christmas and Easter the Pope delivers a message to all people of the world from the balcony of St. Peter's Basilica in Vatican City, Rome. His message begins with the words **Urbi et orbi**, which mean 'To the city and to the world'. The Pope, often speaking in many different languages, addresses some of the contemporary public issues that we face as a global family, and he interprets them in the light of the Gospel.

The Pope's recent *Urbi et Orbi* messages have addressed world hunger, nuclear disarmament, the plight of migrants and the human rights of all people. At times, when the world is facing wars or dealing with other catastrophes or great tragedies, the Pope will offer a message of hope, promoting peace and justice, and condemning violence and injustice. The Pope's messages reaffirm the Church's mission to protect the dignity and sacredness of all human life.

TALK IT OVER

⊙ Why is it important for the Pope to address global issues, such as injustice and war and genocide, in the light of Christ and the Gospel?

WHAT ABOUT YOU PERSONALLY?

⊙ Many Christians wear a cross on a chain around their neck. A non-Christian friend sees you wearing your cross and asks, 'Why do so many Christians wear crosses?'

⊙ How might you take that opportunity to share your faith in Christ and how living that faith makes a difference in your life and in the lives of others?

RESEARCH ACTIVITY

⊙ Research and discover the long list of issues that challenge the world which the Pope and the bishops of the Church in the United States have addressed.

⊙ Choose one issue and briefly summarize what the Pope or our bishops have taught on that issue.

⊙ Present your list of issues during the 'Judge and Act' section of this chapter.

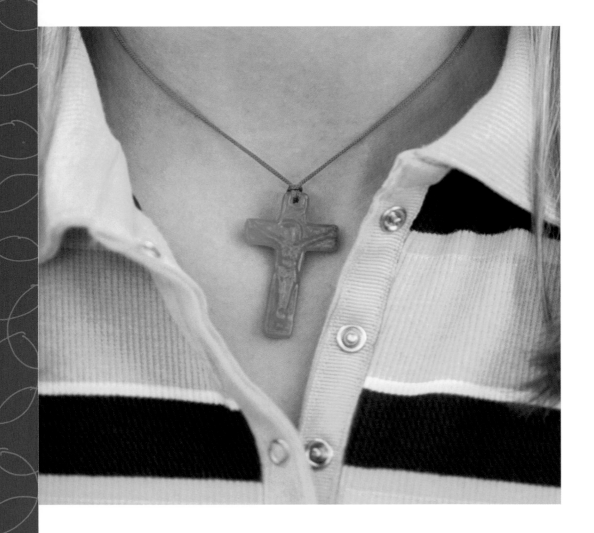

The Church in the ongoing story of humanity

The Pope is the Vicar of Christ and the Pastor of the universal Church on earth. He has the vocation, the mission and the authority to bring the Gospel to the affairs of the world and to invite the world into conversation with Christian faith. Through his *Urbi et Orbi* messages, his Apostolic Exhortations, his Encyclical Letters and all his teachings, the Pope proclaims the Church's faith to the world.

Pope Benedict XVI in his 2012 Christmas *Urbi et Orbi* message spoke about some of the places in the world where the good news of the Prince of Peace was needed:

In this *Year of Faith*, I express my Christmas greetings and good wishes in these words taken from one of the Psalms: 'Truth has sprung out of the earth'. Actually, in the text of the Psalm, these words are in the future: 'Kindness and truth shall meet; / justice and peace shall kiss. / Truth shall spring out of the earth, / and justice shall look down from heaven. / The Lord himself will give his benefits; / our land shall yield its increase. / Justice shall walk before him, / salvation, along the way of his steps' (Psalm 85:11–14).

Today these prophetic words have been fulfilled! In Jesus, born in Bethlehem of the Virgin Mary, kindness and truth do indeed meet; justice and peace have kissed; truth has sprung out of the earth and justice has looked down from heaven. . . . the Infinite has become a child, has entered the human family. . . .

Pope Benedict XVI continued:

Consequently there is hope in the world, a hope in which we can trust, even at the most difficult times and in the most difficult situations. Truth has sprung up, bringing kindness, justice and peace.

Pope Benedict XVI prayed that this truth made present in Christ would be a source of hope for the people of Syria, Israel and Palestine, Egypt, Nigeria, the Democratic Republic of Congo, Kenya and Mali, and for the People's Republic of China and Latin America.

More recently Pope Francis, in his Apostolic Exhortation *Evangelii Gaudium* (The Joy of the Gospel), called individuals, communities and nations to leave behind the ways of conflict and to recognize and avoid in themselves the tendencies that lead to war and division of all kinds:

How many wars take place within the people of God and in our different communities! In our neighbourhoods and in the workplace, how many wars are caused by envy and jealousy, even among Christians! Spiritual worldliness leads some Christians to war with other Christians who stand in the way of their quest for power, prestige, pleasure and economic security. (no. 98)

Our world is being torn apart by wars and violence, and wounded by a widespread individualism which divides human beings, setting them against one another as they pursue their own well-being. In various countries, conflicts and old divisions from the past are re-emerging. I especially ask Christians in communities throughout the world to offer a radiant and attractive witness of fraternal communion. Let everyone admire how you care for one another, and how you encourage and accompany one another: "By this everyone will know that you are my disciples, if you have love for one another" (John 13:35). This was Jesus' heartfelt prayer to the Father: "That they may all be one. . . in us. . . so that the world may believe" (John 17:21). Beware of the temptation of jealousy! We are all in the same boat and headed to the same port! Let us ask for the grace to rejoice in the gifts of each, which belong to all. (no. 99)

OPENING CONVERSATION

◉ What do these papal messages say to the world about the concern of the Church for all the people of the world?

WHAT ABOUT YOU PERSONALLY?

◉ Which sentiments from the words of Pope Benedict XVI or Pope Francis do you find to be the most challenging for you right now?
◉ What do they challenge you to do differently?

THE POPE: A WORLD LEADER

The Pope is a recognized head of state. The **Vatican** is among the smallest sovereign states in the world. The Pope regularly meets with presidents, prime ministers, other heads of state and diplomats. He offers opportunities to other world leaders to reflect on their decisions and policies in light of the wisdom of Christ.

In this work the Pope has the unique opportunity to challenge social policies that are making the world a dark and gloomy place in which to live. He lets the light of the Spirit of Christ shine in the world, leading humanity toward the fulfillment of their deepest hopes for justice and peace for the world. He provides a vision that will open the eyes of the world to see the truth and the path that will fulfill the prayer of all Christians, 'Thy will be done on earth as it is in heaven'.

The Pope is a recognized head of state. The Vatican is among the smallest sovereign states in the world

EXAMPLES OF COINAGE AND POSTAL STAMPS ISSUED BY THE VATICAN STATE

- What do you think the world can learn from the Church?
- What might the Church learn from the world?

LIGHTS SHINING IN DARKNESS

Recall these words from the Prologue of the Fourth Gospel describing Jesus, the Incarnate Word of God:

What has come into being in him was life, and the life was the light of all people. The light shines in the darkness, and the darkness did not overcome it.

—John 1:3–5

The Church is the community of the disciples of Jesus, the Light of the world. (Read John 8:12.) We have been given the responsibility and the grace to bring Christ the Light to the world.

The life of every Christian is to light up the way for people to work to bring about God's reign of peace and justice in the world. The Church is the visible manifestation of Christ in the world. She is the bearer of the 'light of all people' into the darkness of the world. Some might ignore the light; others might turn their eyes from its brightness; others might choose to follow the way of the light. A world without the Light of God is very blind; it sees no real hope, no afterlife, no eternity, no greater meaning to life. (Read John 9:1–10.)

The Church lives within the global human community, a world of believers and non-believers. Living as a disciple of Jesus, 'the light of all people' (John 1:4), in the global community or within a diverse society, such as the United States of America, can be challenging; but it is also an opportunity. It is an opportunity for living out our discipleship and for making visible the Spirit at work in the world. It enables the Church to show the way of turning darkness into light—bringing life to faith and faith to life. It is an opportunity to respond to the face of God in those around us, especially the poor, the suffering and the needy. (See Matthew 25:31–45.) When we live our faith in Christ, we become 'sacraments', visible signs and instruments of God for others.

REFLECT AND SHARE

- Work with a partner and list as many ways as you can think of that portray the world of a high school student as a world of darkness; for example, one of your friends has worked hard in school and applied to her dream university. As she is waiting for the reply, her anxiety takes over her life. She never stops doubting herself and she asks you over and over again, 'What if I get rejected? What will I do? What future will I have?'
- Choose several of the ways and share how faith in Christ can bring light to that darkness.

OVER TO YOU

- How is Jesus the light of *your* world?
- How can you share Jesus, the Light of your life, with others?

Living as a sacrament of God in the world

OPENING REFLECTION

Close your eyes and visualize your parish church or another 'sacred space'. Sacred spaces have a dimension that is beyond what the five senses can comprehend. They give us entry into a deeper dimension of reality, of 'what is'. Sacred spaces invite us into a moment where we can slow down and open our minds and hearts to the reality of the presence of God whose name is Emmanuel, 'God is with us' (Matthew 1:23).

- ◉ What makes a place sacred?
- ◉ How do you respond when you realize that you are in a 'sacred space'?
- ◉ Where do you find the sacred in your life?

The Church and the World: Sacred Spaces

For the Israelites the Temple in Jerusalem was both the center of the 'presence of God' in the world and a reminder that God was always present in their midst wherever they were. The holy of holies in the center of the Temple was the most sacred space of all. For Christians the church building is a particularly sacred space; and the tabernacle, which houses the Blessed Sacrament, is the most sacred of places. The sacred place of our parish church reminds us that the Church, the People of God who gather there, is the sacrament of God in the world.

LABYRINTH IN THE NORTHGATE COMMUNITY GARDEN, SEATTLE

The Church has a divine purpose and mission. She is the visible sign and instrument of God's saving presence in the world. The Church does not just tell the world about God; she invites and makes people sharers in God's effective, saving presence and love—in God's grace. Within and through the Church, people encounter Christ, receive Revelation through the Sacred Scripture and Sacred Tradition, are made sharers in God's grace through the sacraments, and hear and learn the great truths of faith as taught by the Church under the guidance of the Holy Spirit.

The Church is the instrument and goal of God's plan for all humanity. She is the sign and sacrament of the communion of God with all people, past, present and future. Listen to the words of Jesus, '[P]eople will come from east and west, from north and south, and will eat in the kingdom of God' (Luke 13:29). God has gathered the Church to be the visible sign of the invisible saving love of God, inviting all people—believers in Christ, other believers and non-believers, as well as agnostics and atheists—to the fullness of life in his family, in his kingdom.

ONE OF THE SEVEN WONDERS OF THE ANCIENT WORLD, THE TEMPLE OF ARTEMIS AT EPHESUS, WAS DESTROYED IN AD 401

Ephesus was a cosmopolitan city, much like New York City, Washington D.C. and Los Angeles

THINK, PAIR AND SHARE

- Think about these four ways the Church shares God's love with the world: teaching; community life; prayer and worship; works of justice and service.
- Share with a partner how you have experienced God's love through each of these four ways.
- Which of these do you participate in the most? Why?

FROM THE WISDOM OF THE CHURCH

Christians of the first centuries said, 'The world was created for the sake of the Church.' God created the world for the sake of communion with his divine life, a communion brought about by the 'convocation' of men in Christ, and this 'convocation' is the Church.

—CCC, no. 760

EYES OF FAITH

Jesus invited people to see with eyes of faith. For example, recall Jesus' words to his disciples, 'Blessed are the eyes that see what you see!' (Luke 10:23). The visible Church in the world issues the same invitation, as Pope Benedict XVI did in his Christmas 2012 *Urbi et Orbi* message. The life of the baptized should help people 'to see' God's presence and grace at work in daily life, 'to see' what can and should be done to advance the coming of God's reign of 'kindness and truth', 'justice and peace'. '[T]his good news of the kingdom [is to] be proclaimed throughout the world, as a testimony to all the nations' (Matthew 24:14). The early Church in Ephesus was such a living sign and instrument of God and his work in the world.

Ephesus, in modern Turkey, was a cosmopolitan city, much like New York City, Washington D.C. and Los Angeles. It had a magnificent library, a great theater and a temple dedicated to the goddess Artemis—so impressive was this structure that it is recognized to be one of the seven wonders of the ancient world! If you visit Turkey today, some of these buildings still stand. The early Church in Ephesus lived in and was part of this thriving city.

Christians lived in the midst of pagan visitors from all over the world who came to honor the goddess Artemis. How would they be a sign and instrument of God's love to those around them? How might they be an invitation to faith in Jesus Christ? St. Paul offered his advice:

Although I am the very least of all the saints, this grace was given to me to bring to the Gentiles the news of the boundless riches of Christ, and to make everyone see what is the plan of the mystery hidden for ages in God who created all things; so that through the church the wisdom of God in its rich variety might now be made known to the rulers and authorities in the heavenly places. This was in accordance with the eternal purpose that he has carried out in Christ Jesus our Lord, in whom we have access to God in boldness and confidence through faith in him.

—Ephesians 3:8–12

'Christ himself chose the apostles and gave them a share in his mission and authority' (CCC, no. 1575). The members of the hierarchy share in that authority through apostolic succession. Jesus—not the members—has endowed his Church with authority, power and responsibility to bring about that 'eternal purpose that he has carried out in Christ'. The Church is both the means and the goal of God's plan. The Church is to announce and make all people sharers in the hope, joy, fulfillment and new life offered to us through the life, Death and Resurrection of Jesus Christ. She is to make visible through her teaching, community life, prayer and worship, justice and service the reality that God is present in the work of bringing about his Kingdom and reign.

TALK IT OVER

⊙ Where do you see the Church making visible the invisible saving presence of God at work in the world?

WHAT ABOUT YOU PERSONALLY?

⊙ How are you taking part in that work of the Church?

CHRIST PANTOCRATER | HAGIA SOPHIA, ISTANBUL, TURKEY

Go everywhere! Tell the Good News to all people!

OPENING CONVERSATION

- When was the last time you had great news to share? What was the news?
- With whom did you share it? How did they respond?

GOSPEL = GOOD NEWS

Jesus Christ is God's Good News to the world. The four written accounts of the Gospel in the New Testament proclaim that 'Good News'. The Gospels are filled with 'good news' stories; for example, read Luke 2:10–11, Matthew 28:1–10 and Mark 16:15. Receiving the Good News of Christ transforms lives.

The Resurrection was the heart of the Good News that the **disciples** shared with both Jew and Gentile. Sharing their rock-solid faith that Jesus had risen became the foundation of the lives and identity of the disciples of Jesus. The same is true of Jesus' disciples today and will be true of disciples in the future. All the baptized receive a mandate to share the Gospel of Jesus with the world. They share that Good News not only through words but also by the way they live. God desires all people to know Christ and be saved; he loves every person unconditionally. For God chose us in Christ before the foundation of the world to be adopted through Jesus Christ and to restore all things in Christ through his blood according to the richness of his grace. (Reread Ephesians 1:3–10.)

REFLECT AND SHARE

- Where do you see Christians announcing the Gospel, the Good News of Jesus?
- How effective can social media be as a means for proclaiming the Gospel?

- Some young people include a Scripture verse under their signature on their emails. Might this be an effective way for you to share the Good News of Jesus with others?

JOURNAL EXERCISE

- Think about your faith in Christ.
- Describe why your faith in Christ, in his life, Death and Resurrection, is Good News for you.
- How do you bring that Good News into the lives of those around you?

MISSIONERS: MESSENGERS OF THE GOOD NEWS

In chapter 7 you learned about the Maryknoll Lay Missioners. The Church by her very nature is missionary; she is a community of **missioners**. One might think of Jesus himself as the exemplar missioner, the master missioner after whom his disciples fashion their lives.

JESUIT MISSIONARY FR. JACQUINOT SAVED COUNTLESS LIVES IN CHINA IN THE 1930S

faith in Christ and her missionary work, leaving the comforts of life in the United States to travel to Central America, and Dorothy Stang, a Sister of Notre Dame de Namur, who was murdered for her work for justice among the poor in the Amazon Basin in Brazil in 2005. All these and countless other missioner-evangelizers willingly sacrificed their lives to preach and live the Gospel of justice among the poor. The lives of these missioners are truly inspiring. But we do not need to travel to far-off places to serve the Gospel as missioners. We can do so wherever we live, just as St. Katharine Drexel and St. Elizabeth Ann Seton were missioner-evangelizers here in their native land.

Each summer many Catholic youth in the United States follow the example of these saints of the Church and become evangelizers. They leave their home parishes to live and worship with and to share faith stories and eat with other youth in Appalachia, in Native American tribal lands and in inner cities throughout the United States. Others travel to Mexico, Central America and Africa. These youth are missioners in the true sense of the word. They are taking part in the Church's primary work, **evangelization**, which you explored in chapter 7. Taking part in the work of evangelization is not just something the Church does; rather, it is something the Church is. The Church exists to evangelize. Sharing the Good News of Jesus Christ is central to our identity and mission as members of the Church, wherever we are. (Read Matthew 28:16–20, Luke 9:1-6, and Luke 10:1–12.)

When we hear the word 'missionary', or 'missioner', our minds often evoke images of St. Francis Xavier sailing off to the East in the first part of the sixteenth century, or of the eight North America Martyrs—Sts. Jean de Brébeuf, Noel Chabanel, Antoine Daniel, Charles Garnier, René Goupil, Isaac Jogues, Jean de Lalande, and Gabriel Lalemant—running the rivers and tracking the forests of the New World in the mid-seventeenth century. We think of St. Frances 'Mother' Cabrini, who died in 1947, leaving Italy to minister with the immigrant poor of the cities in the United States, or lay missioner Jean Donovan, who was raped and murdered in December 1980 for her

OVER TO YOU

⊙ Describe the opportunities your school or parish offers you to take part in the Church's work of evangelization, for example, in mission or service projects.

⊙ Have you ever participated in a mission trip or service project? If not, would you consider doing so?

JUDGE AND ACT

REFLECT ON WHAT YOU HAVE LEARNED IN THIS CHAPTER

As you come toward the end of this chapter, pause and reflect on what you have come to understand to be the primary mission of the Catholic Church. Share your understanding of the teaching of the Catholic Church on these statements:

- Religious freedom is a basic human right and a foundational principle of the social doctrine of the Catholic Church.
- God created the world for the sake of communion with his divine life, a communion brought about by the convocation of the human race in Christ, and this convocation is the Church.
- The Church is the community of the disciples of Jesus, the Light of the world.
- Jesus—not the members—has endowed the Church with authority, power and responsibility.
- The Church continues Christ's salvation, preserves and hands on his teaching, and has the mission and authority to bring the Gospel to the affairs of the world.
- The Church is missionary by nature; she is a community of missioners.

OVER TO YOU

- What is the best insight, truth or wisdom that you have learned from this chapter?
- What difference might it make to your own faith life?
- What one thing can you do right now to be a living sign of Jesus Christ to the people around you?

SPREADING THE GOOD NEWS BOLDLY

Karol Józef Wojtyła was born on May 18, 1920, in Wadowice, Poland. He lived under both Nazi and communist rule of Poland. People of faith living in communist countries often experienced persecution and oppression—sometimes even imprisonment, torture and death. When Cardinal Wojtyła was elected Pope on October 16, 1978, he took the name John Paul II. He did not forget about the suffering and persecution in his home country. He continued to read the signs of the times, interpreting the events in Poland and throughout the world in light of the Gospel.

Pope St. John Paul II's support of the people of his native land was instrumental in bringing down communism in Eastern Europe and Russia at the end of the 1980s. In his heroic work, John Paul II often faced resistance and threats, and he even experienced an attempted assassination on his life along the way. The Pope experienced first-hand the meaning of Jesus' words: 'Prophets are not without honor except in their own country and in their own house' (Matthew 13:57).

REFLECT AND SHARE

- What does the above passage from Matthew tell you about Pope St. John Paul II's commitment to be a missioner?
- What can you do or say so that those closest to you may be open to what you want to share with them?

STATUE OF POPE ST. JOHN PAUL II

The story of Pope St. John Paul II, evangelizer to youth

Pope St. John Paul II is a model for sharing the Gospel with the entire world. He often called Catholics to bring their faith into the world with joy and credible witness. Unlike many popes before him, he traveled the world. He visited 129 countries, including many places where no pope had officially gone before. He met with world leaders and leaders of other religions, some engaging with the Catholic Church for the first time. He spoke fourteen languages and was able to say brief greetings in many other languages in his regular *Urbi et Orbi* messages.

POPE ST. JOHN PAUL II IN DENVER, 1993

In 1984 Pope St. John Paul II established World Youth Day. Since then, International World Youth Day has been held every two or three years, has taken place in twelve different countries, and has drawn together more than sixteen million teens, young adults, priests and bishops to worship, celebrate and learn about the Catholic faith with the Pope and one another. From 1984 to 2002, the missioner Pope to the world's youth met with them in ten countries. Pope Francis canonized, or named, Pope John Paul II a saint on April 27, 2014.

PILGRIMS AT WORLD YOUTH DAY 2011 IN MADRID, SPAIN

International World Youth Days

1986: Italy (Rome)
1987: Argentina (Buenos Aires)
1989: Spain (Santiago de Compostella)
1991: Poland (Częstochowa)
1993: United States of America (Denver)
1995 Philippines (Manila)
1997: France (Paris)
2000: Italy (Rome)
2002: Canada (Toronto)
2005: Germany (Cologne)
2008: Australia (Sydney)
2011: Spain (Madrid)
2013: Brazil (Rio de Janeiro)

OVER TO YOU

Pope St. John Paul II was a new kind of person elected for a very old job. He knew what gifts God's Spirit had given him, and he was not afraid to use these to open up the Church to the world.

⊙ What gives you trust and courage to be able to share the Gospel with those around you?

⊙ Where are some unusual places the Spirit of God may be calling you to take the good news of God's love?

RESPOND WITH FAMILY AND FRIENDS

⊙ How can you be a light in the world and bring Christ, the Light of the World, into your home, into your school, among your friends?

WHAT WILL YOU DO NOW?

⊙ How will you announce the good news that Christ has brought into the world?

⊙ What will be your message?

LEARN BY HEART

'Go into all the world and proclaim the good news to the whole creation.'

MARK 16:15

PRAYER REFLECTION

Pray the Sign of the Cross together.

LEADER
God the Father, maker of all things,
    your Son Jesus Christ is the Light of the world.
Send us your Spirit,
    to help us become bright lights shining in the
    world. We ask this in Christ's name.

ALL
Amen.

READER
Proclaim Matthew 5:14–16.
The Gospel of the Lord.

ALL
Praise to you, Lord Jesus Christ.

LEADER
Each International World Youth Day has a special
theme and song to celebrate one aspect of the
Gospel, the Good News of Jesus Christ. For World
Youth Day Toronto 2002 Robert Lebel composed
the song 'Light of the World'.

ALL
Celui que de nos yeux nous avons vu,
Celui que de nos mains nous avons pu toucher,
Celui que nos oreilles ont entendu,
Celui que dans nos cœurs
nous avons rencontré. . . .
Voilà Celui que nous vous annonçons
Et qui a resplendi
Sur la terre ou nous vivons!

So many in our world drift into sleep,
while others only know a darkness without end.
Let brothers rise to call them from the deep!
Let sisters take their hands
to heal and be their friends.
Together, let us stand against the storm
and in the heart of night be the watchers of the
morn.

Refrain:
Lumière du Monde!

Sel de la Terre!
Soyons pour le Monde
Visage de l'Amour!
The light of the world,
Christ is our light.
We shine with his brightness,
The reflection of his light
From day to day!

Hay tantos que se pierden al buscar;
Sentido de vivir, razones para amar.
Si los pudiéramos acompañar,
Compartir su dolor, presentarles a Jesús,
Quizás ellos pudiesen comprender
Que es en el partir del pan
Que podemos renacer. *(Refrain)*

La gente dove andare più non sa,
In noi cercando va l'amore che non ha:
Il senso della vita troverà
Facendo insieme a noi la Comunità . . .,
Così potrà conoscere
Gesù Spezzando il pane che
Vita eterna donerà! *(Refrain)*

LEADER
Let us pray: *(Pause)*
Jesus, you are the Light of the world.
You call each of us by name
    to shine the light of your good news for those
        around us.
Send us your Spirit of truth and goodness,
    of courage and conviction
    and of kindness and compassion.
May our lights burn brightly
    that all may see the wonder and goodness of
        God, the God of all people.
Help us shine as a beacon for the world,
    for all who are lost, sad, suffering and needy
so that they clearly see that you are always
    present with them.

ALL
Amen.

Pray the Sign of the Cross together.

CHAPTER 10

Chosen and Called

GOD CALLS EACH ONE OF US

TO LIVE THE GOSPEL

TO LIVE IN COMMUNION WITH HIM

TO LIVE A LIFE OF FAITH IN CHRIST

TO BE HIS IMAGE IN THE WORLD

TO LIVE THE GREATEST COMMANDMENT

TO LIVE IN COMMUNITY

TO LIVE AS ONE PEOPLE OF GOD

THE HOLY SPIRIT GIVES ALL THE BAPTIZED CHARISMS, or specific graces, to participate in the life and mission of the Church. These charisms directly or indirectly benefit the Church and help the baptized to live out the Christian life and serve the common good in building up the Church. (See *Catechism of the Catholic Church*, nos. 799 and 951.) In this chapter we explore in more detail the visible structure of the Church. We study the vocation and responsibilities of all the baptized—the ordained, religious and laypeople.

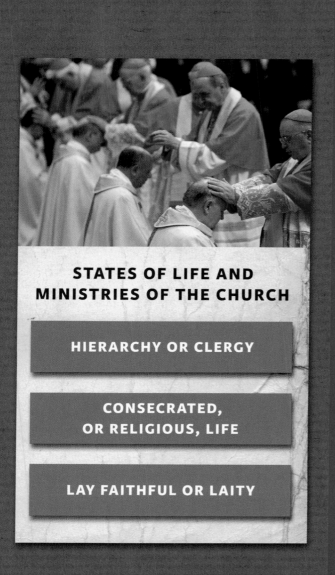

STATES OF LIFE AND MINISTRIES OF THE CHURCH

HIERARCHY OR CLERGY

CONSECRATED, OR RELIGIOUS, LIFE

LAY FAITHFUL OR LAITY

Faith Focus: The teachings of the Catholic Church that are the primary focus of the doctrinal content presented in this chapter include:

- ☉ The Church, the People of God, is both a visible and an invisible society.
- ☉ Christ himself is the source of ministry in the Church.
- ☉ All the baptized share in the threefold ministry of Christ according to their vocation of life in the Church, namely, hierarchy, laity or consecrated life.
- ☉ The various vocations within the Church serve both the mission and unity of the Church.
- ☉ The visible structure of the Church is a hierarchical communion.
- ☉ The Lord made St. Peter the visible foundation of his Church.
- ☉ The bishops in union with the Pope form the college of bishops, which is the expression of the diversity and universality and unity of the People of God.
- ☉ The Christian home is the domestic church.

Discipleship Formation: As a result of studying this chapter and discovering the meaning of the faith of the Catholic Church for your life, you should be better able to:

- ☉ develop discernment in identifying your vocation in life;
- ☉ grow in your appreciation of how belonging to the Catholic Church helps you live and nurture your faith;
- ☉ appreciate that each baptized person has a vital role to play in the life and mission of the Church;
- ☉ fulfill your own role as part of the ministry of the laity;
- ☉ assess how the faith life of your family has contributed to your growth as a member of the Church.

Scripture References: These Scripture references are quoted or referred to in this chapter:
OLD TESTAMENT: 1 Samuel 3:1–21, **Isaiah** 49:1–3, **Jeremiah** 1:4–10
NEW TESTAMENT: Matthew 5:13–16, 9:35–38, 13:31–32, 16:13–20; **John** 15:16; **Acts of the Apostles** 6:1–7; **1 Corinthians** 3:9, 11:25, 12:1–11; **Colossians** 1:15–18; **1 Timothy** 3:8–13; **1 Peter** 2:4–5, 9–10

Faith Glossary: Familiarize yourself with the meaning of these key terms. Definitions are found in the Glossary: **apostolate, bishop, celibacy, college of bishops, common priesthood of the faithful, consecrated life, deacon, domestic church, hierarchy, holiness, Holy Orders, laity, lay ecclesial ministers, Matrimony, ministerial priesthood, new evangelization, Ordinary, priest, Sacraments at the Service of Communion, vocation**

Faith Words: vocation; Holy Orders
Learn by Heart: John 15:16
Learn by Example: The Johnson family and Lay Mission-Helpers

How do we hear God's call?

OPENING REFLECTION

Have you ever heard someone say about another person, 'She is a born teacher' or 'He is a born dancer'? Have you ever heard anyone speak about having a 'vocation' or a 'calling' to do something? When a person finds their 'calling' in life, it can seem as if they are doing what they were born to do. It's as if a person is most fully alive when they follow where their heart, skills and talents lead.

⦿ Think about people you know who are really following their calling in life. Why does it seem that they were 'born' to do what they are doing?

⦿ What makes it clear to you that they have found and are following their calling?

LET'S PROBE DEEPER

While some people seem to know at an early age what they are being called to do, most people take longer to discover that calling. There are several really dramatic stories in the Old Testament of God calling people to take part in the work of God. The calling of the young teenager, Samuel, in 1 Samuel 3:1–21, is one of those stories. The calling of Jeremiah to be a prophet is another. Here is Jeremiah's account of his calling:

Now the word of the LORD came to me saying,
   'Before I formed you in the womb I knew you,
   and before you were born I consecrated you;
   I appointed you a prophet to the nations.'
Then I said, 'Ah, Lord GOD! Truly I do not
know how to speak, for I am only a boy.'
But the LORD said to me,
   'Do not say, "I am only a boy";
   for you shall go to all to whom I send you,
   and you shall speak whatever I command
       you.
   Do not be afraid of them,
   for I am with you to deliver you,
           says the LORD.'
Then the LORD put out his hand and touched
my mouth; and the LORD said to me,
   'Now I have put my words in your mouth.
   See, today I appoint you over nations and
      over kingdoms,
   to pluck up and to pull down,
   to destroy and to overthrow,
   to build and to plant.'
           —Jeremiah 1:4–10

THINK, PAIR AND SHARE

⦿ Read 1 Samuel 3:1–2. With a partner, compare and contrast the call of Samuel with the call of Jeremiah.

⦿ What are the similarities in each story? What are the differences?

⦿ What do each of the stories teach about God's call to people?

⊙ When have you experienced God reaching out to you and calling you to do something?

⊙ How did it happen?
⊙ How did you respond?

The Christian Vocation: Called to Live the Gospel

God creates everyone in his image and likeness. He calls every person to live in communion with him—to love and serve him—both in this world and in the life everlasting. The word 'vocation' comes from the Latin verb *vocare*, which means 'to call'. God gives everyone the fundamental **vocation** to be true to their identity and to live as an image of the God who created them. This fundamental human calling, or vocation, is the call to **holiness**. Christ calls the baptized to a life of holiness in the Church. 'It is in the Church, in communion with all the baptized, that the Christian fulfills his vocation' (*Catechism of the Catholic Church* [CCC], no. 2030). Our bishops of the Church in the United States reminded us of this truth in their document on **new evangelization**.

BAPTISMAL FONT, CLONFERT CATHEDRAL, IRELAND

One's vocation to holiness is strengthened through the gifts of the Church, namely, the grace of the sacraments, prayer, Scripture and the Church's teachings and traditions.
—*Disciples Called to Witness: The New Evangelization*, Part II

Christians fulfill the call to holiness by living and sharing the Gospel. When pondering the specific path God is calling you to follow to fulfill this fundamental vocation, know that it is a choice between many possible good paths. These may include a vocation to the priesthood, the laity or the consecrated life. Whatever God may be calling you to do in life, you can count on this: it is to live the Great Commandment in a particular way.

TALK IT OVER

⊙ Brainstorm the many ways you see people living the Gospel.
⊙ What vocations are they following?
⊙ Which of those vocations might appeal to you right now?

JOURNAL EXERCISE

⊙ Do you have a sense of what God might be calling you to do now? In the future?
⊙ To help you respond, ask yourself:
  – What am I really good at?

– What do I enjoy doing?
– Where is the greatest need for God's love around me?

⊙ Spend a few minutes reflecting on the above three questions; then make three columns, one for each question, and then write your reflections in your journal.
⊙ Take a look at what you have written. Ask yourself:
  – Do I see any connections between the responses in the three columns?
  – What might God be calling me to do?

Vocation

The term given to the call to each person from God; everyone has been called to holiness and eternal life, especially in Baptism. Each person can also be called more specifically to the priesthood or to religious life, to married life, and to single life, as well as to a particular profession or service.

—*United States Catholic Catechism for Adults* [USCCA], 531

CALLED TO LIVE IN COMMUNITY

God calls every baptized person to live out their vocation in and with the support of the Church, the People of God. It is in and through the Church that we receive the Word of God, the teachings of Christ and the graces of the sacraments, and learn the example of holiness from the saints and those who are faithfully living the Gospel. This is made clear at the beginning of the Rite of Baptism, when a family presents an infant or young child for Baptism.

Celebrant: What name have you given your child? *Parents say name aloud for the whole assembly to hear.*
Celebrant: What do you ask of God's Church for [Name]?

Parents: Baptism.
Celebrant: You have asked to have your child baptized. . . . Do you clearly understand what you are undertaking?
Parents: We do.
Celebrant (*addressing the godparents and assembly*)**:** Are you ready to help these parents of this child in their duty as a Christian mother and father?
Godparents and Assembly: We are.
Celebrant: (*addressing the infant/child to be baptized by name*): [Name], the Christian community welcomes you with great joy. In its name I claim you for Christ our Savior by the sign of his cross. I now trace the cross on your forehead, and invite your parents [and godparents] to do the same.

The gift and vocation to a life of holiness and faith in Christ is a gift that includes the call to life in community. God has 'willed to make women and men holy and to save them, not as individuals without any bond between them, but rather to make them into a people who might acknowledge him in truth and serve him in holiness' (Vatican II, *Dogmatic Constitution on the Church*, no. 9). This call first came to the Jewish people, with whom God first entered the covenant. All this was done in preparation for Jesus Christ, the new and everlasting covenant.

Christ instituted this new covenant, the new covenant in his blood (see 1 Corinthians 11:25); he called a people together made up of Jews and Gentiles which would be one, not according to the flesh, but in the Spirit, and it would be the new people of God.
—*Dogmatic Constitution on the Church*, no. 9

REFLECT AND SHARE

⊙ How does belonging to the Church, the community of the disciples of Jesus, assist one in growing and living as a person of faith? Living a holy life?

OVER TO YOU

⊙ What do you know about the day of your Baptism?
⊙ How would you describe the importance of your Baptism for your life?

- Might you think of celebrating your 'Baptism Day' each year as you celebrate your birthday?
- Whom would you invite? Why?

WE ARE GOD'S PEOPLE

When you hear the word 'church', many things can come to mind. For example, 'a great and ornate building with a cross and steeple on top', 'your local parish', 'the Vatican', 'the Pope, cardinals and bishops in Rome', 'youth groups', 'the people of a parish', and so on.

TALK IT OVER

- Brainstorm as many 'ideas' as you can to complete this statement: When I hear the word 'church', I think of. . . .
- What were the most common responses?

Vatican II's *Dogmatic Constitution on the Church*, whose Latin title is *Lumen Gentium*, which means 'The Light of Nations', teaches that the Church is first and foremost 'the People of God'. She is the community of all the people whom God has called and gathered in Christ, the Incarnate Son of God, who is 'the image of the invisible God, the firstborn of all creation; for him all things in heaven and on earth were created . . . all things have been created through him and for him. He himself is before all things, and in him all things hold together. He is the head of the body, the Church; . . .' (Colossians 1:15–18).

The First Letter of Peter describes God's will for the Church this way:

Come to [Christ], a living stone, though rejected by mortals yet chosen and precious in God's sight, and like living stones, let yourselves be built into a spiritual house, to be a holy priesthood, to offer spiritual sacrifices acceptable to God through Jesus Christ. . . . you are a chosen race, a royal priesthood, a holy nation, God's own people, in order that you may proclaim the mighty acts of him who called you out of darkness into his marvelous light.

Once you were not a people,
but now you are God's people. . . .
—1 Peter 2:4–5, 9–10

The Church is the new People of God. It is through our association with others who want to follow Christ in the Church that we can be whom God has chosen and called us to be. It is in the Church through a life of prayer, communion, charity, service and justice that we can be salt and light for the world. (See Matthew 5:13–16.)

WHAT ABOUT YOU PERSONALLY?

- Where do you see yourself among the 'living stones', among these 'people'? How are you using the talents and other blessings that God has given you to 'build up' the Church?
- What sacrifices are you making or willing to make to build up the People of God?

Come to [Christ], a living stone, though rejected by mortals yet chosen and precious in God's sight, and like living stones, let yourselves be built into a spiritual house

Called to be one people

OPENING CONVERSATION

- Think of a project that you have worked on with others, for example, publishing your school's yearbook or organizing a school service project.
- How did the diversity of people and of responsibilities contribute to the success of the project?

ONE PEOPLE OF GOD—A DIVERSITY OF VOCATIONS

The call to use our gifts and talents in service of the coming of God's reign in the world takes root in Baptism. We use our gifts and talents in one of the states of life and ministries of the Church, namely, as a member of the **hierarchy**, the **laity** or the **consecrated life**. Some of the faithful are teachers, speakers or interpreters of God's word. Others have creative or artistic talents to enrich worship. Some have a compassionate heart and minister with the ill and dying. Others have the courage and passion to speak out and act on behalf of the oppressed and marginalized. (Read 1 Corinthians 12:1–11.) No one vocation and no one member of the Church has everything that is needed to continue Jesus' mission. The whole Church, all the People of God, must work together. (Read 1 Corinthians 12:1–11.)

OVER TO YOU

- How can you, right now, bring your gifts to the life and mission of the Church?

CALLED TO SERVE THE WHOLE CHURCH

God calls some members of the Church to serve the whole Church. They receive the graces to

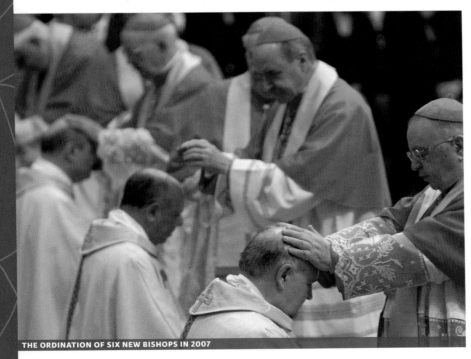

THE ORDINATION OF SIX NEW BISHOPS IN 2007

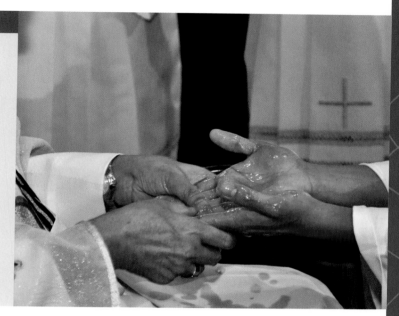

Holy Orders

The Sacrament in which a bishop ordains a man to be conformed to Jesus Christ by grace, to service and leadership in the Church. A man can be ordained a deacon, priest, or bishop. Through this Sacrament, the mission entrusted by Christ to his Apostles continues to be exercised in the Church. This Sacrament confers a permanent mark or character on the one who receives it.

—USCCA, 514–515

fulfill this vocation through the Sacrament of **Holy Orders** and the Sacrament of Marriage, or **Matrimony**. These two sacraments are called the **Sacraments at the Service of Communion**. 'The term *communion* refers to the Community of the Church. . . . This means [these two sacraments] are primarily directed toward the salvation of others. If they benefit the personal salvation of the ordained or married person, it is through service to others that this happens' (USCCA, 527).

In the Sacrament of Holy Orders a baptized man is ordained to serve the People of God as a **bishop, priest** or **deacon**. The ordained ministers of the Church exercise their service for the People of God by teaching, divine worship and pastoral governance. 'The ministries conferred by ordination are irreplaceable for the organic structure of the Church: without the bishop, presbyters, and deacons, one cannot speak of the Church' (CCC, no. 1593).

Through Holy Orders, priests and bishops share in a unique way in the one priesthood of Christ. This participation is called the **ministerial priesthood**, 'where the task is to serve in the name and in the person of Christ the Head in the midst of the community' (CCC, no. 1591). Through Baptism, all the faithful are also made sharers in the priesthood of Jesus Christ, but not in the same way as bishops and priests. The participation of all the baptized in the priesthood of Christ is called the '**common priesthood of the faithful**' (CCC, no. 1591).

Bishops: Bishops receive the fullness of the Sacrament of Holy Orders. Bishops, who are in union with the Pope, share in the authority and responsibilities that Christ gave to St. Peter and the other Apostles. The bishops are members of the **College of Bishops**, or the Episcopal College. 'All the bishops of the Church with the Pope at their head form a single "college", which succeeds in every generation the "college" of the Twelve Apostles, with Peter at their head, which Christ instituted as the foundation of the Church. This college of bishops together with, but never without, the Pope has supreme and full authority over the universal Church' (CCC, Glossary; see also CCC, nos. 861, 880 and 883).

The Pope, the bishop of Rome, is the Vicar of Christ and the visible head of the universal Church on earth. He has the ministry to care for the universal Church, for the People of God everywhere. Bishops are appointed by the Pope and oversee a 'particular Church entrusted to [them]' (CCC, no. 1594). They are the visible source and foundation of unity in their particular churches. Most often, this particular Church is called a **diocese**. Sometimes a diocese has

ST. PETER | SEVASTOPOL, UKRAINE

'And I tell you, you are Peter, and on this rock I will build my church.'

MATTHEW 16:18

TALK IT OVER
⊙ Read Matthew 16:13–20.
⊙ What do these verses tell you about the role of Peter among the Twelve?
⊙ What do they tell you about the role of the Pope among the other bishops in the Catholic Church today?

Priests: Through the Sacrament of Holy Orders, diocesan and religious priests are also made sharers in the ministerial priesthood. Bishops and priests are true co-workers. Together with their bishop(s), all priests serving the people of a diocese 'form . . . the presbyterium which bears responsibility with him for the particular Church' (CCC, no. 1595). The word 'presbyterium' comes from the Greek word *presbyteroi*, which means 'elders', a word used in the early Church to identify her ordained leaders.

Priests, as bishops do, act in the name and person of Christ. Priests serve the People of God by leading us in worship and administering the sacraments, teaching and preaching God's word, and by pastoral leadership, or governance. Only priests and bishops may administer the Sacraments of the Eucharist, Confirmation, Penance and Reconciliation, and Anointing of the Sick.

more than one bishop. The bishop who has been appointed to be the head of the diocese is called the local **Ordinary**. The bishops appointed to help the Ordinary are called auxiliary bishops.

Sometimes a bishop is honored with the title 'Cardinal'. Cardinals usually have the special task of helping and advising the Pope. When a Pope dies, cardinals, under the age of eighty, gather in a conclave to elect the new Pope. The word 'conclave' comes from the Latin prefix *cum* and the noun *clavis*, which literally means 'under key'. The Conclave of Cardinals received its name because the cardinals must remain 'under lock and key' until they elect the new Pope.

While a priest often shares in these responsibilities by serving the people of a parish to which the bishop has assigned him, a priest can serve the People of God in many other ways. Priests may serve the Church as teachers in schools and universities, as chaplains in hospitals and in the military, and as missioners at home and abroad. Both bishops and priests receive special graces and the guidance of the Holy Spirit to enable the whole community to live and work well together in 'holy order'.

OVER TO YOU
⊙ Ask your school chaplain or parish priest to describe the process he followed to become a priest.

Deacons: Deacons are not ordained to the ministerial priesthood. They are 'ministers ordained for tasks of service of the Church' (CCC, no. 1596). The word 'deacon' comes from the Greek word *diakonia*, which means 'to serve'. Deacons assist their bishop and priests in exercising and fulfilling their threefold office of teaching and pastoral leadership and worship. Deacons may administer the Sacrament of Baptism. At the Sacrament of Matrimony, deacons represent the Church and bless marriages. While deacons assist at the Eucharist and the other sacraments, they cannot administer, or are not the ordinary minister of, the Eucharist, Confirmation, Penance and Reconciliation, and Anointing of the Sick.

You are probably most familiar with the deacon or deacons who serve the people of your parish or in your school. These deacons, who may be married, are called 'permanent deacons'. There are other deacons who are 'transitional' deacons. Ordination to the diaconate is their final step on their way to priesthood.

LET'S PROBE DEEPER
⊙ Read Acts of the Apostles 6:1–7 and 1 Timothy 3:8–13.
⊙ What do these New Testament writings teach about the ministry of deacons?
⊙ How does the ministry of deacons give us insight into how the whole Church is to live the Great Commandment?

THINK, PAIR AND SHARE
⊙ Reflect on the ministry of bishops, priests and deacons.
⊙ What does the ministry of the ordained ministers of the Church say about the work of the whole Church?
⊙ What does it say about your work in the Church, right now?

OVER TO YOU
⊙ Think about the Pope, the bishop or bishops, and the priests and deacons who serve you. Take a moment and pray for them.
⊙ Research their social media sites; Tweet, post on Facebook or email them a word of thanks.

ORDINATION OF DEACONS, IOWA

At home in Christ

At the Norfolk State Prison in Massachusetts, a group of inmates are doing something truly extraordinary. Unable to leave the prison to go to church, the inmates have created church within the confines of the prison. They pray together every day and share their faith and understanding of the Gospel with one another. They pray the Liturgy of the Hours each morning and night, joining their prayers to the greater Church throughout the world. Following the Dominican tradition of spirituality, the inmates pray the Rosary each day and offer their prayers for the world and for those around them. Through their way of life, these inmates strive to live the Gospel of Jesus Christ in the prison.

With the help of their Catholic chaplain, Dominican Sr. Ruth, these extraordinary inmates have formed a Dominican Lay Chapter within the prison, with the official approval of the worldwide Dominican Order. Some seventeen inmates have made their final vows as Dominicans. These lay Dominicans make the Church present and visible where the Church's reach is otherwise limited. Sr. Ruth likes to say, 'The greatest sinners can become the greatest saints.'

OPENING CONVERSATION

⊙ How are these inmates living the vocation they received at Baptism?

⊙ What can you learn from this story for your own participation in the life of the Church?

> **FROM THE WISDOM OF THE CHURCH**
> In the Church, which is like the sacrament . . . of God's own life, the consecrated life is seen as a special sign of the mystery of redemption.
> —CCC, no. 932

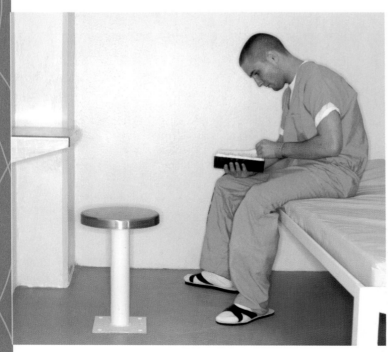

THE CONSECRATED, OR RELIGIOUS, LIFE

Sr. Ruth is a member of the Dominican Order. Religious orders (such as the Dominicans, Benedictines, Franciscans and Carmelites) and religious societies (such as the Jesuits, Vincentians, Missionaries of Charity, Maryknoll and Sisters of Mercy) respond to the vocation to live the Gospel in a variety of ways. 'Religious life in its various forms is called to signify the very charity of God in the language of our time' (CCC, no. 926).

Members of religious communities have the vocation to the consecrated life and may be ordained or members of the laity. They 'consecrate' their lives to serve God and the Church as members of a religious community approved by the Church. They give witness in a unique way to the holiness of life

to which Christ calls all the faithful. They vow or promise to live the **evangelical counsels**, or gospel counsels, of poverty, chastity and obedience. They serve in parishes, schools and universities and in hospitals and hospices. They serve runaways and the homeless; they serve as missioners at home and in countries other than their native lands.

By living the evangelical counsel of poverty, the faithful who have the vocation to the consecrated life witness that nothing created will distract them from keeping God at the center of their life. They live the counsel of chastity by a life of **celibacy** for the sake of the Kingdom of God. By living the counsel of obedience, they commit themselves always to seek to live by the will of God as it is made known through Scripture and the Church.

In addition, lay people who have the vocation to the consecrated life may choose not to live that vocation as members of a religious community. They may live their vocation in the world and give witness to the saving work of Jesus as members of secular institutes, of societies of apostolic life, of Third Orders or as consecrated virgins or widows. Others, without professing the three evangelical counsels, may live the vocation to the eremitic life, the life of a **hermit**. 'They manifest to everyone the interior aspect of the mystery of the Church, that is, personal intimacy with Christ' (CCC, no. 921) through 'a stricter separation from the world, the silence of solitude and assiduous prayer and penance' (*Code of Canon Law*, canon 603).

TALK IT OVER
⊙ What religious communities can you name?
⊙ If your school or parish was founded by a religious community, share what you know about the founder and the history of that community.
⊙ Where else in your community do you see members of the Church who have the vocation to the consecrated life giving witness to Christ and the Gospel? Describe the work they are doing to serve the people.

FROM THE WISDOM OF THE CHURCH
'The characteristic of the lay state being a life led in the midst of the world and of secular affairs, lay people are called by God to make of their **apostolate**, through the vigor of their Christian spirit, a leaven in the world' (Vatican II, *Decree on the Apostolate of the Laity*, no. 2).
—CCC, no. 940

LAYPEOPLE, OR THE LAITY

The inmates of Norfolk State Prison are laypeople, or members of the laity of the Church. Laypeople are the largest group among the People of God. Laypeople are the 'Church in the world'. Their anointing at Baptism with the consecrated oil of sacred chrism signifies that they have been made sharers in Christ the Prophet's ministry of teaching, Christ the Priest's ministry of sacrificial service and Christ the King's ministry of leadership.

The vocation to the married life or to the single life: God calls laypeople, both married and single, to participate in the Church's mission of evangelization and the sanctification of the world—in the marketplace of life. They are to witness to Christ 'in all circumstances and at the very heart of the community of mankind' and 'in all dimensions of their personal, family, social, and ecclesial lives, and so fulfill the call to holiness addressed to all the baptized' (CCC, nos. 942 and 941).

God calls married people and offers them the sacramental graces to be signs of Christ's love for the Church, the Bride of Christ, through the covenant relationship that unites them as husband and wife. Single laypeople give witness to Christ in the true and compassionate friendships they have. Because laypeople work and live in the world, they often have a chance to go and share the Good News in places that the Church would not reach otherwise.

Lay ecclesial ministers: Some laypeople have the vocation to serve the Church full time. In *Co-workers in the Vineyard of the Lord*, the Catholic bishops in the United States address this vital role of laypeople. *Co-Workers in the Vineyard of the Lord* uses the term 'lay ecclesial ministers' to describe those laypersons to whom the hierarchy 'entrust responsibilities for leadership in particular areas of ministry and thereby draw certain lay persons into a close mutual collaboration with the pastoral ministry of bishops, priests, and deacons. These men and women of every race and culture who serve in parishes, schools, diocesan agencies and Church institutions are identified by many different position titles' (*Co-Workers in the Vineyard of the Lord*, Introduction, page 7). The 'Introduction' concludes:

> *Co-Workers in the Vineyard of the Lord* expresses our strong desire for the fruitful collaboration of ordained and lay ministers who, in distinct but complementary ways, continue in the Church the saving mission of Christ for the world, his vineyard.

LET'S PROBE DEEPER

- Look up and read Matthew 9:35–38.
  - What does Jesus mean by 'the harvest is plentiful'?
  - What does Jesus mean by 'the laborers are few'?
  - Who is the 'Lord of the harvest'?
- How does *Co-workers in the Vineyard of the Lord* help you understand the role of laypeople in the Church? Might it open your eyes to ways of serving the Church?
- What wisdom do Jesus' words provide for all those members of the Church who are working together as the People of God?

WHAT ABOUT YOU PERSONALLY?

- Jesus told his disciples to 'ask the Lord of the harvest to send out laborers into his harvest'. How can you respond to this call?

The harvest is plentiful, but the laborers are few.
MATTHEW 9:37

Young people: chosen and called

OPENING REFLECTION

When asked about your 'vocation', you may have responded by naming a profession or career—nurse, teacher, graphic designer, accountant, coach, dancer. For most young people, the response will change many times, both before and during college, and sometimes well after college.

- ☉ By this time in your life, you certainly have been asked the question, 'What do you want to do with your life when you grow up?'
- ☉ Why do you think this is such an important question?

- ☉ What does this question presume?
- ☉ How do you usually respond—for now?

JOURNAL EXERCISE

- ☉ Reflect on these questions: Who are you now? What are some of the best things that make you who you are now as a child of God and a disciple of Jesus Christ?
- ☉ Now write about how you might use your gifts to give glory to God by serving the People of God over the next six months. Over the next ten years.

The Seed of Faith

Read the parable of the Mustard Seed in Matthew 13:31–32. The seed of faith has been planted in your whole being. You have been caring for and growing that seed in many ways. Youth, the young laity of the Church, are vital members of the People of God. The Church is not just a people of 'grown-ups'. The Popes since March 23, 1986 have gathered with Catholic youth from all corners of the Earth on International World Youth Day. The Popes' messages at these gatherings have both emphasized that point and encouraged and challenged youth to grow in their understanding of and living the gift of faith that God has planted within them. God calls them to go into the world and bear fruit.

As God called the teenage Samuel and the teenage Blessed Virgin Mary, he continues to call young people. As Jesus invited the teenage John, 'Come! Follow me', Jesus continues to invite young people today to be and live as his disciples. That includes you! You do not have to wait until you are out of college to be God's laborer in the world in which you live. God calls you to let your light shine now.

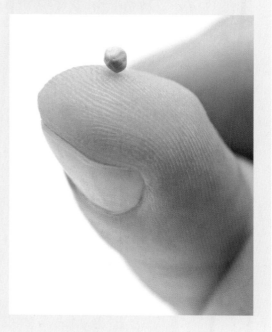

LET'S PROBE DEEPER

In John 15:16 Jesus reminds his disciples, 'You did not choose me but I chose you. And I appointed you to go and bear fruit, fruit that will last.' Your faith in Jesus is a gift. Your call to discipleship is a gift.

⊙ What is Jesus saying to you as you read his words?

⊙ How are you responding to Jesus? What are some of the ways you are accepting Jesus' 'appointment' to bear fruit?

FROM THE WISDOM OF THE CHURCH

[T]he home is the first school of Christian life and 'a school for human enrichment' [Vatican II, *Pastoral Constitution on the Church in the Modern World*, no. 52]. Here one learns endurance and the joy of work, fraternal love, generous—even repeated—forgiveness, and above all divine worship in prayer and the offering of one's life.

—CCC, no. 1657

THE DOMESTIC CHURCH—THE CHURCH OF THE HOME

The Christian home is the '**domestic church**', or 'church of the home'. Since the beginning of the Church, the Christian home has been the vital center of the Christian life. Your first vocation is to live as a disciple of Christ in your family, in both good times and bad times. The Acts of the Apostles and other New Testament letters report that the members of the early Church gathered in family homes. It was in these homes that the first Christians listened to the teachings of the Apostles, celebrated and shared in Eucharist, and shared their possessions to care for one another's needs. It was only as the Church grew in numbers and had the legal freedom to assemble that churches as we know them were built and became the gathering places of Christians. These home-churches were the origins of the parish churches in which we gather today.

It is in the Christian home that we first and most profoundly learn to live our vocation as disciples of Christ. All research about the lives of teenagers indicates that the home has the deepest and most lasting influence on their faith life. It is in the Christian family that we first learn about and experience faith. The Christian home has the vocation to be 'a community of grace and prayer, a school of human virtues and of Christian charity' (CCC, no. 1666). It is for this reason that the Catholic Church teaches that the Christian family is the 'domestic church', or the 'church of the home'.

OVER TO YOU

⊙ What has your family taught you about faith?

⊙ What are the ways and traditions by which your family honors God?

⊙ How do your family members share God's love with one another and with other people?

JUDGE AND ACT

REFLECT ON WHAT YOU HAVE LEARNED IN THIS CHAPTER

As you come toward the end of this chapter, pause and reflect on what you have come to understand about the variety of vocations, or states of life, within the Church. Share your understanding of the teaching of the Catholic Church on these statements:

- ⊙ The Church, the People of God, is both a visible and an invisible society.
- ⊙ Christ himself is the source of ministry in the Church.
- ⊙ Christ calls all the baptized to live the Gospel in and through the Church.
- ⊙ There are a variety of states of life within the Church.
- ⊙ Christ calls some members of the Church to serve the whole Church.
- ⊙ The visible structure of the Church is a hierarchical communion.
- ⊙ Bishops and priests share in the ministerial priesthood, which is essentially different from the common priesthood of the faithful.
- ⊙ The Lord made St. Peter the visible foundation of his Church; the bishops in union with the Pope form the college of bishops.
- ⊙ God calls some members of the Church, both clergy and laity, to the consecrated life.
- ⊙ Laypeople are the Church in the world.
- ⊙ The Christian home is the domestic church.

WHAT ABOUT YOU PERSONALLY?

- ⊙ Think about what you learned from studying this chapter.
- ⊙ What will help you build your relationship with the Church?
- ⊙ How does God's call to discipleship with Jesus give your life vision and purpose?

LEARN BY EXAMPLE

The story of the Johnson family and the Lay Mission-Helpers

Alicia and Chris Johnson heard God's call to serve the Church. They responded by volunteering to become Lay Mission-Helpers, members of an organization whose motto is 'We are God's helpers' (1 Corinthians 3:9). On their website, Lay Mission-Helpers describe themselves as 'Catholic lay people, single men and women, married couples, and families, called through our baptism to mission. We seek to walk with the poor of other countries sharing our gifts, living our faith, and learning from one another. Lay Mission-Helpers serve in a variety of different professions and strive to live a simple life close to the poor'.

The Johnson family served in the Diocese of Kumbo, Cameroon. During the first half of their assignment, Chris's job was to travel to the different diocesan health centers to assist the staff and to structure a set of protocol for the clinics. In the second half of his service, he worked at the new Cardiac Center of Shisong Hospital. Alicia taught English at

St. Augustine Secondary School. In addition to teaching, she helped form a student newspaper and ran a mobile library during the summer months. Their sons, Keaton and Quinn, attended the school as well. This is how Alicia Johnson describes her call.

From the time I was 18 years old, I kept feeling this nagging call that never went away and kept driving me toward the prospect of working in overseas missions. I felt excited when I would read about people doing mission work in Africa. Little did we know that my husband, Chris, would travel in a tiny jeep on some of the worst roads imaginable to reach village health centers and teach new nurses how to improve their skills. How fun to be a part of a community in a land with different customs, music and food. And for the time that our family served in Cameroon, it was incredibly fun and also incredibly difficult. The amazement of working 'in Africa' never wore off while we were there but also we experienced the daily struggles of limited electricity, scarce water, and the constant poverty in the community in which we lived. I was humbled; we were humbled. And at the same time, God used our very human weaknesses as a way to touch the lives of the people we were meant to serve. . . .

Reflecting back on our mission experience, Chris and I feel so blessed that we were able to do this work. The material sacrifices pale in comparison to the sense of peace of doing something that God wanted us to do.

TALK IT OVER
⊙ What other families or individuals do you know who are living out their baptismal call?
⊙ Name these people and describe how they are 'God's helpers' in the world.

RESPOND WITH FAMILY AND FRIENDS
⊙ Read and discuss the story of the Johnson family. Share responses to these questions:

– What might God be calling us to do together?
– How does this bring God's love into people's lives?

WHAT WILL YOU DO NOW?
⊙ How will you put into practice in your own life the wisdom you have learned from the Johnson family?

LEARN BY HEART

'You did not choose me but I chose you. And I appointed you to go and bear fruit, fruit that will last.'

JOHN 15:16

Invitation to Prayer

LEADER

God knows and calls each of us by name.
God gives each of us a vocation.
How can we come to know our vocation?
We come to know our vocation through the practice of discernment.
Discernment is a form of prayer. It is the placing of one's self in the presence of God,
asking God to make known his will for us,
listening to God in prayer,
and asking the Holy Spirit to guide us to respond to God's call.
Let us place our self in the presence of God.
(*Pause*)

Pray the Sign of the Cross together.

Opening Prayer

LEADER

God, you call each of us by name to follow your Son, Jesus Christ, in a life of discipleship.
Send us your Spirit now so that we can hear your call more clearly in our daily lives and follow your call.
We ask this in the name of Jesus Christ your Son.

ALL

Amen.

Proclamation of the Word of God

READER

Let us listen to God's word to Isaiah the prophet.
Proclaim Isaiah 49:1–3.

Discernment Reflection

All follow this process of discernment.

Step One

Become aware of God's goodness to you and reflect on these questions:
How have I experienced God's goodness and love today?
What gifts, great and small, have I already received this day?

Step Two

Become aware of your missed opportunities.
When did I recognize and respond to God's presence today?
When did I miss out?
What opportunities have I had to use my gifts and talents?
Was there a time today when I missed out on God's invitation to live as a disciple?

Step Three

Become more aware of your need to respond to the graces of the Holy Spirit.
What can I do to listen more attentively to God?
What can I do to respond to God?

Step Four

Pray to the Holy Spirit, your Advocate, Teacher and Guide.
Holy Spirit, give me the graces to hear God's call:
  – in what I am really good at;
  – in what I really enjoy doing;
  – among the people and places around me where there is need for God's love.

Concluding Prayer

LEADER
Let us now pray to Mary, the Mother of the Church.

ALL
Loving Mother, Our Lady of Guadalupe, you asked Juan Diego to help build a Church that would serve a new people in a new land.
You left your image upon his cloak as a visible sign of your love for us
so that we may come to believe in your Son, Jesus Christ.
Our Lady and St. Juan Diego, help us respond to God's call to build your Son's Church today.
Help us recognize our personal vocation to serve God as married or single persons or priests, brothers or sisters, as our way to extend the reign of God here on earth.
Help us pay attention to the promptings of the Holy Spirit.
May all of us have the courage to say 'Yes' to our personal call!
May we encourage one another to follow Jesus, no matter where the path takes us. Amen.

Pray the Sign of the Cross together.

SHRINE TO OUR LADY OF GUADALUPE, SANTA FE, NEW MEXICO

CHAPTER 11

Jesus, the Fullness of Grace and Truth

IN JESUS WE ENCOUNTER THE HUMAN FACE OF GOD, WHO IS TRUTH

JESUS CHRIST IS THE INCARNATE TRUTH

LIFE, LOVE AND TRUTH ARE INSEPARABLE IN THE LIFE OF A DISCIPLE OF JESUS

LIVING THE TRUTH SETS US FREE

THE CHURCH IS THE TEMPLE OF THE SPIRIT OF TRUTH

THE HOLY SPIRIT GUIDES THE MAGISTERIUM IN TEACHING FAITH AND MORALS

GOD IS TRUTH AND THE SOURCE OF ALL TRUTH

CHRISTIANS HAVE A SIMPLE YET COMPELLING answer to the question 'What is truth?' God is truth, and the fullness of the divine Revelation of truth has taken place in the Person of Jesus Christ, who declared 'I am the way, and the truth, and the life' (John 14:6). Christ has given his Church the responsibility and authority to pass on and teach authentically the truth of Revelation. This chapter explores the Church's transmission of divinely revealed truth.

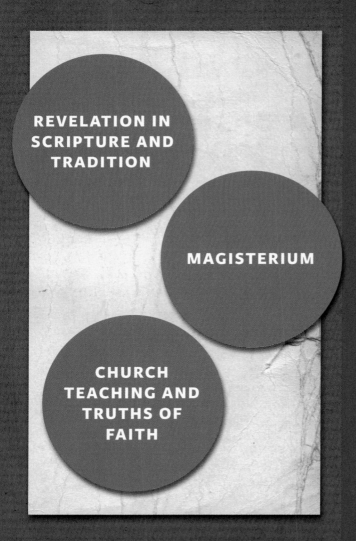

REVELATION IN SCRIPTURE AND TRADITION

MAGISTERIUM

CHURCH TEACHING AND TRUTHS OF FAITH

Faith Focus: The teachings of the Catholic Church that are the primary focus of the doctrinal content presented in this chapter include:
- ◉ God alone is truth.
- ◉ Jesus Christ is the incarnate truth, who is God.
- ◉ The Church is the temple of the Holy Spirit, the Spirit of Truth.
- ◉ Christ has entrusted to his Church, under the leadership of the Apostles and their successors, the mission of proclaiming and teaching the truth that he has revealed.
- ◉ There is a hierarchy among the truths revealed by God.
- ◉ The Magisterium is the authentic interpreter of Revelation, God's word in Scripture and Tradition.
- ◉ The Church scrutinizes the 'signs of the times' and interprets them in light of the Gospel.
- ◉ The Church will always teach the Gospel of Christ without error in spite of the defects of her members, both ordained and lay.
- ◉ The Holy Spirit blesses the Church with infallibility, or the unique gift to teach faith and morals without error and in fidelity to the Apostles.

Discipleship Formation: As a result of studying this chapter and discovering the meaning of the faith of the Catholic Church for your life, you should be better able to:
- ◉ follow the 'way' of Jesus Christ in discerning how to lead a life of truth;
- ◉ bear witness to the truth in the way you live and love;
- ◉ value and be guided by the Spirit of Truth within the community of the Church;
- ◉ trust in the presence of the Holy Spirit actively teaching through the Magisterium.

Scripture References: These Scripture references are quoted or referred to in this chapter:
OLD TESTAMENT: Psalm 119:160
NEW TESTAMENT: Matthew 5:3–10, 21:23–24, 28:20; **Mark** 1:22; **Luke** 4:36; **John** 1:14, 3:21, 8:31 and 38, 14:1, 6 and 15–17, 15:26, 16:13, 17:19, 18:37–38; **Acts of the Apostles** 24:16; **Romans** 2:8; **1 Corinthians** 13:6, 15:3–8 and 14; **1 Thessalonians** 2:13; **1 Timothy** 2:4; **2 Timothy** 1:8; **1 Peter** 1:22; **1 John** 2:20 and 27, 3:18–19; **Jude** 3

Faith Glossary: Familiarize yourself with the meaning of these key terms. Definitions are found in the Glossary: **apostolic constitution, charism, divine Revelation, Dogma, ecumenical council, indefectibility, infallibility, Magisterium, relativism,** *sensus fidelium,* **synod**

Faith Words: indefectibility; infallibility
Learn by Heart: John 14:16–17a
Learn by Example: The Samaritan woman

What is truth?

WHAT IS TRUTH? CHRIST AND PILATE | NIKOLAI GE

Diversity is a hallmark of the human family. Local customs and practices express truths common to all peoples. These truths are called universal truths. Universal truths are at the heart of the identity of all people. Universal truths are true always and everywhere. Truth transcends culture. Truth transcends a particular group of people living in a specific place at a given time. For example, 'telling the truth' has always been accepted universally as the right thing to do. Life within a society is built on truth.

OPENING REFLECTION

⊙ What universal truths do you know?
⊙ Why is both knowing and living by these truths vital to the human family?

'WHAT IS TRUTH?'

The search for what is true is universal; as with the search for happiness, we will only find truth in God, just as we can only find happiness in God. All 'truths' reflect and are rooted in God, who is truth and the source of all truth. The psalmist proclaims, 'The sum of your word is truth' (Psalm 119:160). In the Prologue of the Fourth Gospel, St. John describes Jesus as 'full of grace and truth' (John 1:14). At Jesus' trial, toward the end of that same account of the Gospel, Pontius Pilate, the fifth procurator of Judea (AD 26–36), asks Jesus to defend himself against the accusations that some of the Jewish leaders had made against him. The Evangelist writes:

Pilate asked him, 'So you are a king?' Jesus answered, 'You say that I am a king. For this I was born, and for this I came into the world, to testify to the truth. Everyone who belongs to the truth listens to my voice.' Pilate asked him, 'What is truth?'

—John 18:37–38

Jesus was silent. His entire life had already spoken 'with authority' (see Matthew 21:23–24, Mark 1:22, Luke 4:36).

THINK, PAIR AND SHARE

⊙ In what situations might Christians find themselves today that are similar to Jesus' encounter with Pilate?
⊙ When is silence more powerful than speaking? When might silence speak the truth clearly?

OVER TO YOU

⊙ Who and what helps you figure out the difference between truth and falsehood?
⊙ How does your faith in Jesus Christ guide you in making your decision about what is true and what is false? In your choices about what is good and what is evil?

PILATE'S ENCOUNTER WITH JESUS RETOLD

The interchange between Jesus and Pontius Pilate has been told and retold. The hit rock opera *Jesus Christ Superstar* reimagined the conversation. In the second act, the musical number 'Trial before Pilate' has the following imaginary exchange between Pilate and Jesus:

> **Pilate:** You're a king.
> **Jesus:** Yes you can see I am. / I look for truth / And find that I get damned.
> **Pilate:** What is truth? / Is truth unchanging law? / We both have truths. / Are mine the same as yours?

Jesus Christ Superstar tackles Pilate's question, 'What is truth?' in an interesting way. Pilate answers his own question. In his own response he points to the difference between the truth and the expression of truths that is relative to specific people and cultures. The Pilate of the musical implies that truth is relative, and that there are no universal truths, valid for all people, at all times and in all places. This view of truth is called **relativism**. Relativism is any 'doctrine which denies, universally or in regard to some restricted sphere of being, the existence of absolute values' (Online *Catholic Encyclopedia*)—all points of view and opinions are equal and relative to the individual.

The Church since her beginning has warned about the dangers of relativism. We can come to know truth with certainty. We can come to know truth through the use of our intellect and reasoning powers and, especially, through **divine Revelation**, through Sacred Scripture and Sacred Tradition. Pope Benedict XVI in his 2012 World Peace Day message described relativism as letting oneself be tossed and 'swept along by every wind of teaching' and he addressed the impact of relativism on people in our own time. He said:

> Today, a particularly insidious obstacle to the task of educating is the massive presence in our society and culture of that relativism which, recognizing nothing as definitive leaves as the ultimate criterion only the self with its desires. . . . And under the semblance of freedom it

CHRIST BEFORE PILATE | DUCCIO DI BUONINSEGNA

becomes a prison for each one, for it separates people from one another, locking each person into his or her own self.

TALK IT OVER

⊙ Where do you experience people today who say, as Pilate did in *Jesus Christ Superstar*, that there are no universal truths, or that all truth is relative?

⊙ What kind of society might we live in if there were no universal truths?

LET'S PROBE DEEPER

⊙ Encouraging his troubled disciples, Jesus invites them, 'Believe in God, believe also in me . . . I am the way, and the truth, and the life' (John 14:1 and 6). Look up and read John 3:21, 8:31, 15:26, 16:13 and 17:19.

⊙ What connection is Jesus making between truth and living one's life and himself?

WHO *IS* TRUTH?

St. John the Apostle and Evangelist teaches and passes on the faith of the early Church that truth is not a mere concept—not a set of beliefs and practices and moral principles— but a Person. John teaches that Jesus is 'full of grace and truth . . . From his fullness we have all received' (John 1:14, 16). Jesus is not a messenger bearing 'truths'. In Jesus we encounter the human face of God, who is truth. Jesus Christ is the incarnate truth, who is God. He is the fullness of the Revelation of God, who is truth. The Catholic Church summarizes this apostolic faith:

At the heart [of Christian faith] we find . . . a Person, the Person of Jesus of Nazareth, the only Son from the Father.
—*Catechism of the Catholic Church* (CCC), no. 426

TALK IT OVER

⊙ Where do you see the Church proclaiming and living the way of truth revealed in Jesus?

JOURNAL EXERCISE

⊙ Describe the truth about yourself that you have learned from your coming to know Jesus.

What kind of society might we live in if there were no universal truths?

How do we come to know the truth?

OPENING CONVERSATION
- What are some of your most deeply held truths?
- How have you come to believe and assent to these things being fundamentally true?
- Are these truths accepted by your friends? Explain.

OVER TO YOU
- When have you been challenged to defend these truths?
- How did you respond?

LIVING THE TRUTH THAT SETS YOU FREE

The Church, the Body of Christ, has the fullness of truth and the totality of the means of salvation. Scripture proclaims that life, love and truth are inseparable in the life of a disciple of Jesus. Love surrounds truth, and the truth of Jesus Christ is realized, ultimately, in living the Great Commandment of love of God, neighbor and oneself.

Jesus clearly connected 'truth' with living ('way' and 'life'). Speaking to his disciples, Jesus taught, 'If you continue in my word, you are truly my disciples; and you will know the truth, and the truth will make you free. . . . I declare what I have seen in the Father's presence; as for you, you should do what you have heard from the Father' (John 8:31, 38).

The Apostles took Jesus' words to heart. For example, St. Paul teaches: '[Love] does not rejoice in wrongdoing, but rejoices in the truth' (1 Corinthians 13:6). And in Romans 2:8 he writes about the consequences of not obeying the truth. The First Letter of Peter speaks of 'obedience to the truth' (1 Peter 1:22). The First Letter of John teaches, 'Little children, let us love, not in word or speech, but in truth and action. And by this we will know that we are from the truth . . .' (1 John 3:18–19).

TALK IT OVER
- What is the connection between truth and love?
- Where do you see that 'connection' being lived?
- What difference do you see people making when they live the truth–love connection?

GIVING WITNESS TO THE TRUTH

Reflecting on the encounter between the falsely charged Jesus and Pilate, the Church writes:

Before Pilate, Christ proclaims that he 'has come into the world, to bear witness to the truth'

THE SERMON ON THE MOUNT | ENGRAVING AFTER ALEXANDRE BIDA

[John 18:37]. The Christian is not to 'be ashamed then of testifying to our Lord' [2 Timothy 1:8]. In situations that require witness to the faith, the Christian must profess it without equivocation, after the example of St. Paul before his judges. We must keep 'a clear conscience toward God and toward men' [Acts of the Apostles 24:16].

—CCC, no. 2471

Jesus and the Father have sent the Holy Spirit, the Spirit of Truth, to be with the Church. The Church is the temple of the Spirit of Truth. The mission of the Church is to obey the mandate of evangelization and proclaim the truth revealed in Jesus Christ and to ensure the fidelity of the Church to the teachings of the Apostles. Vatican II taught:

The church is not motivated by earthly ambition but is interested in one thing only—to carry on the work of Christ under the guidance of the holy Spirit, who came into the world to bear witness to the truth, to save and not to judge, to serve and not to be served. . . . In every age, the church carries the responsibility of reading the signs of the times and of interpreting them in light of the Gospel, if it is to carry out its task. . . . We must be aware of and understand the aspirations, the yearnings, and the often dramatic features of the world in which we live.

—Vatican II, *Pastoral Constitution on the Church in the Modern World*, nos. 3 and 4

The Catholic Church speaks to these issues 'in light of the Gospel'. She gives witness to the truth that Christ 'came into the world to bear witness'. By proclaiming in both word and deed the truth revealed in Jesus, we take part in the one goal of the Church, namely, 'to carry on the work of Christ under the guidance of the holy Spirit'.

WHAT ABOUT YOU PERSONALLY?
- Where in your life do you hear God speak most clearly to you?
- How do you respond?

SCRUTINIZING THE SIGNS OF THE TIMES
The Pope, the bishop of Rome, and bishops around the world who are in union with the Pope are the authentic interpreters of God's word in Sacred Scripture and Tradition. They have the authority and responsibility to proclaim and teach authentically the truth revealed in Jesus Christ. They fulfill this ministry by preaching the truths of faith and the moral life to both the people entrusted to their pastoral care and leadership and to the world. The bishop, or local Ordinary, of a diocese teaches the people of his diocese in the name of Jesus Christ. The bishops of the Church in the United States support one another in fulfilling this ministry. They work together in the United States Conference of Catholic Bishops (USCCB). The mission of the Conference is carried out by a staff of more than 300 laypeople, priests, deacons and religious who work with and support the bishops. The USCCB scrutinizes the 'signs of the

times', that is, the circumstances of the Church in the United States. Our bishops carefully study issues in light of the Gospel and look at the impact of those issues on the lives of people. They publish the results of their discussions in print and online. Among the issues, or signs, that have been addressed by the USCCB are marriage and the family, human life and dignity, religious liberty, violence in the home and in society, economic justice, cultural diversity, war, environmental justice, agriculture and the responsibilities of faithful citizenship.

THINK, PAIR AND SHARE

⊙ Brainstorm with a partner a list of issues that impact the life of people, Catholic and non-Catholic, in the United States of America.

⊙ Name one issue in your community or country.

⊙ What can you do to address that issue? Who will you ask to work with you?

OVER TO YOU

⊙ Check out the USCCB website and research the bishops' work of reading the 'signs of the times' and addressing the issues on your list.

Finding truth as community

THE LAST SUPPER | DOMENICO GHIRLANDAIO

OPENING CONVERSATION

- ◉ When seeking to know and live the truth, why might it be that 'two heads are better than one'?
- ◉ What have you learned or understood recently with the help of others?

FROM THE WISDOM OF THE CHURCH

God 'desires all men to be saved and to come to the knowledge of the truth' [1 Timothy 2:4]; that is, God wills the salvation of everyone through the knowledge of *the truth*. Salvation is found in the truth.

—CCC, no. 851

THE SPIRIT OF TRUTH

At the Last Supper Jesus promised, 'I will ask the Father, and he will give you another Advocate, to be with you for ever. This is the Spirit of truth, whom the world cannot receive, because it neither sees him nor knows him. You know him, because he abides with you, and he will be in you' (John 14:15–17). The Holy Spirit is the Spirit of Truth, who abides in the whole Church and in all the faithful. He is 'the principal agent of the whole of the Church's mission' (Pope St. John Paul II, *The Mission of the Redeemer*, no. 21).

The Catholic Church responds to and interprets Revelation with the guidance of the Spirit of Truth. This does not mean that 'individual' interpretation of the Word of God by the faithful is 'on target', or authentic, and faithful to the teachings of the Apostles on matters of faith and morals. The authentic interpretation of the true meaning of Revelation has been given to the **Magisterium**. The Magisterium has been given the **charism** to discern the faith of the Church and 'ensure fidelity to the teachings of the Apostles on faith and morals'. The Magisterium does not exercise its responsibility and teaching office in a vacuum. It listens and discerns the 'sense of the faithful' (*sensus fidelium*). On this point the Church teaches:

> The whole body of the faithful who have received an anointing which comes from the holy one (see 1 John 2:20 and 27) cannot be mistaken in belief. It shows this characteristic through the entire people's supernatural sense of the faith, when 'from the bishops to the last of the faithful,' it manifests a universal consensus in matters of faith and morals. By this sense of the faith, aroused and sustained by the Spirit of truth, the people of God, guided by the sacred magisterium which it faithfully obeys, receives not the word of human beings, but truly the word of God (see 1 Thessalonians 2:13), 'the faith once for all delivered to the saints' (Jude 3). The people unfailingly adheres to this faith, penetrates it more deeply through right judgment, and applies it more fully in daily life.
> —Vatican II, *Dogmatic Constitution on the Church*, no. 12

The Spirit of Truth is always present with and in the Church so that she will always teach the Gospel of Christ authentically and without error. The Spirit guides the Church in this work, even in spite of the defects of her members, both ordained and non-ordained. In other words, the defects of the members of the Church will not prevent or deter the Church from fulfilling the teaching mission the risen Christ gave her. This gift of the Spirit, called **indefectibility**, assures that the Church under the guidance of her Magisterium will faithfully and authentically fulfill her mission until the reign of God comes about, when Christ comes again in glory at the

FAITH WORD

Indefectibility

Indefectibility means that the Church does not and cannot depart from proclaiming the authentic Gospel without error in spite of the defects of her members. The Lord Jesus ensures that his Church will remain until the Kingdom is fully achieved.

—*United States Catholic Catechism for Adults* (USCCA), 515

end of time. (*We will explore the Magisterium of the Church in more detail in the next section of this chapter.*)

OVER TO YOU

⊙ What would you do to stand up for the truth revealed by Jesus Christ and passed on through the Church?

Sharing in the truth as Church

Have you ever been to a concert or a symphony performance? If you arrived a little early, you may have noticed and heard the musicians tuning their instruments, creating a cacophony of sounds, entirely in discord with one another. While the tuning is taking place, all of the instruments have their say, but all they make is noise. When the performance begins, it is a whole different experience. Each musician, following the guidance of the conductor, interprets the score for his or her instrument. Working together in harmony, all the individual sounds of each of the instruments blend to produce 'music' and not simply 'the noise' of notes.

OPENING CONVERSATION
⊙ What do you think makes a leader great?
⊙ What does a great leader add to a group?

THE MAGISTERIUM: THE TEACHING OFFICE OF THE CHURCH
God gives the members of the Church different instruments—different charisms—to take part in the life and mission of the Church. The Spirit of Truth guides all the faithful to use (to play) those instruments according to their role in the Church for the good of the Church and all humanity.

We can use the image of an orchestra to help us understand the Church's mission to teach all peoples to obey everything that Jesus commanded. (See Matthew 28:20.) The teaching office, or Magisterium, of the Church has the primary responsibility to teach; all other members of the Church are to teach in harmony with the Magisterium. The word 'magisterium' comes from the Latin word *magister*, which means 'teacher'. The Magisterium is the 'living teaching office of the Church, whose task it is to give authentic interpretation of the word of God, whether in its written form (Sacred Scripture), or in the form of Tradition' (CCC, Glossary).

> [S]acred tradition, sacred scripture, and the magisterium of the church are so connected and associated that one of them cannot stand without the others. Working together, each in its own way under the action of the one holy Spirit, they all contribute effectively to the salvation of souls.
> —Vatican II, *Dogmatic Constitution on Divine Revelation*, no. 10

The Pope and other bishops of the Church form the Magisterium. They are 'the authoritative teachers in the Church' (USCCA, 519). The Holy Spirit guides the Magisterium in fulfilling its responsibilities. Trusting in the presence of the Holy Spirit in the Church, we accept the teachings of the Magisterium even when they are not pronounced in a definitive, or infallible, manner.

ST. PETER'S SQUARE, VATICAN CITY

TALK IT OVER

⊙ How does the image 'Orchestra of Christ' help us understand the Church?

The Pope and bishops work together in many ways to fulfill their teaching office; for example, by gathering in an **Ecumenical Council** or in **synod**. A synod is a meeting of some bishops, called together by the Pope to discuss an important faith question or moral issue facing the Church and humanity. In a synod the Pope and bishops scrutinize the 'signs of the times' and the Church's efforts to address those 'signs'. For example, the Pope and bishops meeting in synod have carefully looked at the Church in various parts of the world: America in 1997, Europe in 1991 and 1999, Africa in 1994 and 2009, and the Middle East in 2010. Synods have also addressed such specific issues as 'Justice in the World' (1971), 'The Christian Family' (1980), 'The Lay Faithful' (1987), and the New Evangelization (2012). After each synod the Pope issues a document summarizing the teachings of the synod. These documents can be found on the Vatican website.

LET'S PROBE DEEPER

⊙ Work with a partner and research the various synods of the Church on the Vatican website.

⊙ Choose one of the synods and write a summary of its teaching.
⊙ Present your research to the whole class.

HIERARCHY OF THE TRUTHS OF FAITH

There is a hierarchy of truths revealed by God and taught by the Church. While some truths are more foundational to the faith of the Church than others, all the truths of faith are connected. 'The mutual connections between dogmas, and their coherence, can be found in the whole of the Revelation of the mystery of Christ' (CCC, no. 90). From the time of the Apostles, the mystery of the Holy Trinity 'is the most fundamental and essential teaching in the "hierarchy of the truths of faith" [*General Catechetical Directory*, no. 43]' (CCC, no. 234).

The Resurrection of Jesus Christ is also central to the faith of the Church. St. Paul gave testimony to the place of the Resurrection in the hierarchy of truths as believed and professed by the apostolic Church. St. Paul wrote:

I handed on to you as of first importance what I in turn had received: that Christ died for our sins in accordance with the scriptures, and that he was buried, and that he was raised on the third day in accordance with the scriptures, and that he appeared to Cephas, then to the twelve. Then he appeared to more than five hundred brothers and sisters at one time, most of whom are still alive, though some have died. Then he appeared to James, then to all the apostles. Last of all, as to someone untimely born, he appeared also to me. . . . [I]f Christ has not been raised, then our proclamation has been in vain and your faith has been in vain.

—1 Corinthians 15:3–8, 14

THINK, PAIR AND SHARE
⊙ Look over the Apostles' Creed.
⊙ What does the Apostles' Creed teach about God the Father? God the Son? God the Holy Spirit?

INFALLIBILITY OF THE CHURCH
Finding true answers to the greatest questions of our faith is an amazingly daunting task. The Holy Spirit always guides the Church and gives her the ability to teach faith and morals without error. This charism, or grace of the Holy Spirit, is called **infallibility**.

The gift of infallibility is at work in the Church in two ways. First, the Pope can teach infallibly (a) when he teaches alone on faith and morals, and (b) when the teaching is held in common by the bishops of the world, and (c) when the Pope declares that he is teaching *ex cathedra*. The term *ex cathedra* means 'from the chair'. The bishop's chair in his cathedral is the symbol of his pastoral authority. The Pope teaches infallibly (*ex cathedra*) when he explicitly intends to teach authoritatively as the successor of St. Peter and the supreme Pastor of the universal Church and the Vicar of Christ. For example, on November 1, 1950 Pope Pius XII infallibly defined and taught the **Dogma** of the Assumption in his **apostolic constitution** *Munificentissimus Deus*.

Second, the Pope and bishops can teach infallibly (a) when they teach together in regular teaching throughout the world, or (b) when gathered in an Ecumenical Council. For example, Pope Pius IX proclaimed and Vatican Council I approved the Dogma of infallibility to be divinely revealed.

When we place our trust in the Magisterium and assent to its teaching, we are trusting in the Spirit of Truth who is guiding the Church. Even when we do not fully understand a Dogma or other teaching of the Church, we assent to the teaching, even when it is not pronounced in a definitive manner.

REFLECT AND SHARE
⊙ Why is it important to know and believe that the Holy Spirit guides the Church to a true and authentic understanding of the truths of faith?

WHAT ABOUT YOU PERSONALLY?
⊙ How does your faith in the Holy Spirit help you believe the teachings of the Church that you do not fully understand?

FAITH WORD

Infallibility
This is the gift of the Holy Spirit to the Church whereby the pastors of the Church—the pope, and bishops in communion with him—can definitively proclaim a doctrine of faith and morals, which is divinely revealed for the belief of the faithful. This gift flows from the grace of the whole body of the faithful not to err in matters of faith and morals. The pope teaches infallibly when he declares that his teaching is *ex cathedra* (literally, 'from the throne'); that is, he teaches as supreme pastor of the Church.

—USCCA, 516

JUDGE AND ACT

REFLECT ON WHAT YOU HAVE LEARNED IN THIS CHAPTER

As you come toward the end of this chapter, pause and reflect on what you have come to understand about the Church's commission and responsibility to teach all nations to obey all that Jesus taught. Share your understanding of the teaching of the Catholic Church on these statements:

- ◉ Salvation is found in truth.
- ◉ Truth is not simply a concept; it is more than a set of beliefs, practices and moral principles.
- ◉ The Church is the temple of the Holy Spirit, the Spirit of Truth.

- ◉ The Pope and the bishops in union with him are the authoritative teachers in the Church.
- ◉ There is a hierarchy among the truths revealed by God.
- ◉ The Holy Spirit assures us that the Church will always teach faith and morals without error and in fidelity to the Apostles.

WHAT ABOUT YOU PERSONALLY?

- ◉ What have you learned this week that you want to bring with you throughout life?
- ◉ What does Jesus Christ, who is the truth of God, mean for all people, believers and non-believers?

LEARN BY EXAMPLE

The Samaritan woman, the story of a woman searching for and finding the truth

You can read the Gospel account of the Samaritan woman at the well in John 4:1–42. Here is a brief reflection on her coming to know Jesus, who is the truth.

Jesus, tired out by his travels with his disciples, was sitting by a well. It was noon and he was alone as he waited for his disciples who had gone into the city to buy food. Noticing a woman approaching the well, Jesus asked her, 'Give me a drink.' The woman, startled by Jesus' request, asked, 'How is it that you, a Jew, ask a drink of me, a woman of Samaria?' (John 4:9). Remember that Jews considered Samaritans to be heretics who had separated themselves from Judaism, and that it was not customary for men and women to interact like this in public.

Jesus, overriding the Samaritan woman's objection, astounded her even more, saying, 'If you knew the gift of God, and who it is that is saying to you, "Give me a drink," you would have asked him, and he would have given you living water' (John 4:10).

Seeing that Jesus had no bucket, the woman said, 'Sir, you have no bucket, and the well is deep. Where do you get that living water? Are you greater than our ancestor Jacob, who gave us the well, and with his sons and his flocks drank from it?' (John 4:11–12).

Jesus said to her, 'Everyone who drinks of this water will be thirsty again, but those who drink of the water that I will give them will never be thirsty. The water that I will give will become in them a spring of water gushing up to eternal life' (John 4:13–14).

The woman said to him, 'Sir, give me this water, so that I may never be thirsty or have to keep coming here to draw water' (John 4:15).

The Gospel account of the Samaritan woman's encounter with Jesus implies that the woman was, at least, curious when this Jewish man struck up a conversation. Jesus' questions and responses—simple, yet direct—obviously moved her to want to learn more from him and about him.

Now take the time to read the remainder of the story in John 4:16–42.

TALK IT OVER
- ⊙ What do you make of the Samaritan woman leaving her water jar and going back into the city to tell people about her experience?
- ⊙ Where did the Samaritan woman's encounter with Jesus lead her?

OVER TO YOU
- ⊙ Where do you long for truth the most in your life?
- ⊙ How does your faith in Jesus speak to that longing?
- ⊙ What burdens do you long to lay down, wishing for his truth to set you free?

REFLECT AND DISCERN
- ⊙ Each day in our society we encounter many issues and questions. Working with a partner or a small group, list some of these questions and issues.
  - – Identify society's responses to those issues, reflected in the laws and public policies of our country, of the state and place where you live.
  - – What is the Church's teaching about those issues?
- ⊙ Compare and contrast society's responses with the teaching of the Church.
- ⊙ Which responses truly set people free?

RESPOND WITH FAMILY AND FRIENDS
- ⊙ Talk to your family and/or your friends about some of the issues you studied in class. Discuss and share responses to these questions with them:
  - – How can we put into practice the teachings of the Church?
  - – How can our living that truth set us and others 'free'?

WHAT WILL YOU DO NOW?
- ⊙ How is the truth of Jesus Christ good news for you and for other young people today?
- ⊙ Where do you most need the guidance of the Spirit of Truth in your life? Will you ask for it?

LEARN BY HEART

'I will ask the Father, and he will give you another Advocate, to be with you forever. This is the Spirit of truth.'

JOHN 14:16–17A

GOD THE FATHER | FIDELIS SCHABET

PRAYER REFLECTION

LEADER

In the Sermon on the Mount we find many of Jesus' teachings about the 'truth' of being his disciples. Among these teachings, the Beatitudes are central to the life and identity of a disciple of Jesus.

Let us reflect on the truths revealed in the Beatitudes and make living those truths part of our daily life. (*Pause*)

THE SERMON ON THE MOUNT | KÁROLY FERENCZY

God of goodness and love, you alone are truth and the source of all truth.
You sent your Son, Jesus Christ, 'full of grace and truth', to live among us so that we may come to know the fullness of the truth you wished to reveal.
Send the Holy Spirit, the Spirit of Truth, to lead us to you so that we may grow in truth and wisdom.
We make our prayer in the name of your only Son, Jesus, who is the fullness of your Revelation of the truth.

ALL

Amen.

READER

Lord Jesus, you said,

'Blessed are the poor in spirit, for theirs is the kingdom of heaven.'

—Matthew 5:3

Keep us from being preoccupied with falsehoods of excessive shopping, money and worldly goods, which hinder us from living the truths of justice.

All pause and reflect, and then respond aloud together:
Lord God, send us your Spirit of Truth!

READER

Lord Jesus, you said,

'Blessed are those who mourn, for they will be comforted.'

—Matthew 5:4

Grant us patience as we carry our burdens and guide us to share your compassion so as to help those around us carry theirs.

All pause and reflect, and then respond aloud together:
Lord God, send us your Spirit of Truth!

READER

Lord Jesus, you said,

'Blessed are the meek, for they will inherit the earth.'

—Matthew 5:5

Guide and strengthen us to work toward eliminating the discord and violence that exists in the world around us.

All pause and reflect, and then respond aloud together:
Lord God, send us your Spirit of Truth!

READER
Lord Jesus, you said,

'Blessed are those who hunger and thirst for righteousness, for they will be filled.'
—Matthew 5:6

Make us thirst for you, the fountain of all truth and holiness, and actively share your good news of justice with those around us.

All pause and reflect, and then respond aloud together:
Lord God, send us your Spirit of Truth!

READER
Lord Jesus, you said,

'Blessed are the merciful, for they will receive mercy.'
—Matthew 5:7

Grant that we may be quick to share the power of the truth of love by forgiving others.

All pause and reflect, and then respond aloud together:
Lord God, send us your Spirit of Truth!

READER
Lord Jesus, you said,

'Blessed are the pure in heart, for they will see God.'
—Matthew 5:8

Free us from all the deceit and lies that hurt or damage the beauty and dignity of ourselves or of your creation.

All pause and reflect, and then respond aloud together:
Lord God, send us your Spirit of Truth!

READER
Lord Jesus, you said,

'Blessed are the peacemakers, for they will be called children of God.'
—Matthew 5:9

Help us live your life-giving way of truth and make peace in our families, in our school, in our Church and in the world around us.

All pause and reflect, and then respond aloud together:
Lord God, send us your Spirit of Truth!

READER
Lord Jesus, you said,

'Blessed are those who are persecuted for righteousness' sake, for theirs is the kingdom of heaven.'
—Matthew 5:10

Give us the courage to speak the truth on behalf of those who are powerless,
and do not let us discriminate against our neighbors or oppress and persecute them.

All pause and reflect, and then respond aloud together:
Lord God, send us your Spirit of Truth!

LEADER
Let us pray. (*Pause*)
Come, Holy Spirit,
and set our hearts on fire for Jesus Christ,
who is truth-made-flesh and lived among us.
Help us come to know and always to rejoice in the truth.
We ask this in the name of Jesus Christ, our Lord.
ALL
Amen.

Conclude by praying the Sign of the Cross together.

CHAPTER 12

The Church: A Wisdom Community

WISDOM IS ONE OF THE SEVEN GIFTS OF THE HOLY SPIRIT

THE SCRIPTURES AND THE TEACHINGS OF THE CHURCH ARE SOURCES OF DIVINE WISDOM

GOD, WHO IS WISDOM, COMES LOOKING FOR US

ALL TRUE HUMAN WISDOM COMES FROM GOD JESUS IS THE WISDOM AND KNOWLEDGE OF GOD MADE FLESH

JESUS IS THE WAY OF WISDOM AND KNOWLEDGE OF GOD

THE CHURCH HELPS US GROW IN WISDOM AND HOLINESS OF LIFE

PRAYER IS VITAL TO GROWING IN WISDOM

GOD IS WISDOM AND ALL TRUE HUMAN WISDOM comes from God. The Catholic Church passes on this life-giving wisdom revealed in Sacred Scripture and Sacred Tradition. In this chapter we explore the governing and sanctifying offices of the Catholic Church, which help us celebrate and live the way of Jesus, who is the 'wisdom and knowledge of God' (Romans 11:33).

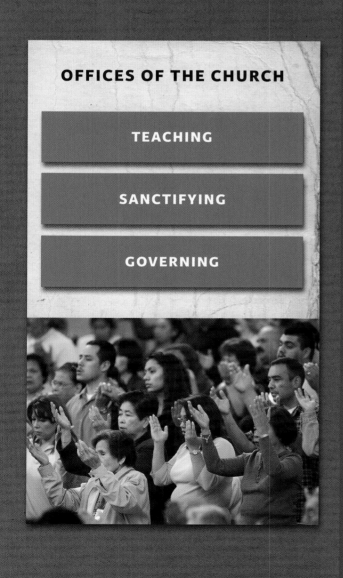

OFFICES OF THE CHURCH

TEACHING

SANCTIFYING

GOVERNING

Faith Focus: The teachings of the Catholic Church that are the primary focus of the doctrinal content presented in this chapter include:

- ⊙ Christ established his Church to continue his presence and work in the world.
- ⊙ Bishops and priests sanctify the Church by prayer, work and the ministry of the Word and the sacraments.
- ⊙ The Eucharist is the center of life in the Church.
- ⊙ The Catholic Church worships throughout the whole year; this year of grace and celebration is called the liturgical year.
- ⊙ Bishops and priests have the responsibility to govern the Church and to exercise their authority and sacred power with the Good Shepherd as their model.
- ⊙ The Pope, the bishop of Rome, exercises supreme, ordinary and immediate jurisdiction over the universal Church.
- ⊙ Bishops have the responsibility to govern the particular Church to which the Pope has appointed them.

Discipleship Formation: As a result of studying this chapter and discovering the meaning of the faith of the Catholic Church for your life, you should be better able to:

- ⊙ recognize God, who is wisdom, at work in the world;
- ⊙ value Jesus as the embodiment of wisdom;
- ⊙ understand wisdom to be an integral part of Christianity;
- ⊙ identify that true human laws, of both the Church and society, are rooted in the wisdom of God;
- ⊙ value living by the wisdom offered to you by the teachings of the Catholic Church;
- ⊙ value the wisdom of participating in the Eucharist and of praying regularly;
- ⊙ commit yourself to standing up for God's truth and wisdom by striving for justice.

Scripture References: These Scripture references are quoted or referred to in this chapter:
OLD TESTAMENT: Exodus 20:8–10, 25:10–22, 37:1–9; **Leviticus** 17:1—26:46, 19:17–18; **Deuteronomy** 6:4–5 and 12–13, 30:11–14; **2 Samuel** 6:1–23; **1 Kings** 3:7–12; **Psalms** 119:105; **Wisdom** 6:12–20, 7:22–26
NEW TESTAMENT: Matthew 5:17–22, 27–28, 31–34, 38–39 and 43–44, 12:1–21, 42, 22:34–40; **John** 1:9, 8:12, 13:35, 21:16; **Romans** 11:33; **1 Corinthians** 1:20–31, 4:10; **Galatians** 4:19, 6:2; **Colossians** 1:9–10; **1 John** 4:7–12

Faith Glossary: Familiarize yourself with the meaning of these key terms. Definitions are found in the Glossary: **gifts of the Holy Spirit, liturgical year, Liturgy, Lord's Day, prayer, precepts of the Church, religion, Sabbath, wisdom**

Faith Word: Precepts of the Church
Learn by Heart: Wisdom 6:20
Learn by Example: St. Teresa Benedicta of the Cross

Where do we find true wisdom?

You have more than likely read and analyzed 'The Road Not Taken', which was written by Robert Frost in 1920.

The Road Not Taken

Two roads diverged in a yellow wood,
And sorry I could not travel both
And be one traveler, long I stood
And looked down one as far as I could
To where it bent in the undergrowth;

Then took the other, as just as fair,
And having perhaps the better claim,
Because it was grassy and wanted wear;
Though as for that the passing there
Had worn them really about the same.

OPENING REFLECTION

- Recall a time when you found yourself at a 'fork in the road' of life.
- What were your options?
- How did you decide which road to take?
- What part did your faith in Christ play in your decision?

FROM THE WISDOM OF THE CHURCH

The Church is the Temple of the Holy Spirit. The Spirit is the soul, as it were, of the Mystical Body, the source of its life, of its unity in diversity, and of the riches of its gifts and charisms.

—*Catechism of the Catholic Church* (CCC), no. 809

CHOOSING WISELY

We need guidance to make wise decisions.

Deciding on the wise path can be confusing and, at times, a daunting challenge. Often we have an idea of where we want to go, but we are not so sure how to get there. Thankfully, the People of God, the Church, past and present, is our greatest and most reliable source of spiritual wisdom for our life journey.

The People of God have always been searching for wisdom to make wise choices to live their covenant with God. That search is guided by the Holy Spirit, whom the Father and the Son have sent to be our teacher and guide. At Baptism we are made sharers in the wisdom of God. We receive the seven **gifts of the Holy Spirit**. **Wisdom** is one of those gifts. It is the gift that gives us the grace to see ourselves and the world and everything in it as God sees them. The Scriptures and teachings of the Church pass on to us and teach and guide us in using that great gift.

The inspired sacred author of the Book of Wisdom compares wisdom to a graceful, feminine figure

When you respond to and cooperate with the Spirit of Wisdom, you can also be a source of wisdom for other people.

THINK, PAIR AND SHARE

- Talk to a partner about some of the people of wisdom in your life. Why do you identify them as 'wise'?
- Discuss how one might become wise and learn to choose wisely.
- Share your best insights with the class.

OVER TO YOU

- What is the best wisdom someone has shared with you?
- How did and does that wisdom guide you in making decisions?

THE WISDOM WRITINGS IN THE OLD TESTAMENT

Sacred Scripture is the Revelation of the wisdom of God. Jesus Christ, the Incarnate Word of God, is the fullness of that Revelation. He is the 'wisdom and knowledge of God' (Romans 11:33). There is a basic unity between the Old Testament and the New Testament. Jesus Christ is the source of that unity. The wisdom revealed in the Old Testament prepares the way for him.

The Wisdom writings in the Old Testament include the Books of Job, Psalms, Proverbs, Ecclesiastes, Song of Songs (Song of Solomon), Wisdom (Wisdom of Solomon), and Sirach (Ecclesiasticus). The Book of Wisdom describes wisdom:

Wisdom is radiant and unfading,
and she is easily discerned by those who love
    her,
and is found by those who seek her.
She hastens to make herself known to those
    who desire her.
One who rises early to seek her will have no
    difficulty,
for she will be found sitting at the gate.
To fix one's thought on her is perfect
    understanding,
and one who is vigilant on her account will soon
    be free from care,
because she goes about seeking those worthy of
    her,
and she graciously appears to them in their
    paths,
and meets them in every thought.
                                    —Wisdom 6:12–16

In this passage, the inspired sacred author compares wisdom to a graceful, feminine figure.

Solomon is acknowledged to be one of the greatest wisdom figures in the Old Testament

SOLOMON | SAINT-EUSTACHE CHURCH, PARIS, FRANCE

She is a personification of God, appearing readily to those who look for her. She is God's goodness and truth, and the way to live life to the fullest. Lady Wisdom 'hastens to make herself known' and 'goes about seeking those worthy of her'.

TALK IT OVER
- ⊙ What might the image of Holy Wisdom in the Book of Wisdom reveal about God?
- ⊙ What does this passage reveal to those who desire to be wise?

WHAT ABOUT YOU PERSONALLY?
- ⊙ What wisdom are you seeking? Where are you seeking it?
- ⊙ How does the wisdom you seek compare to the description of wisdom in the Bible?

THE WISDOM OF SOLOMON

While we seek 'wisdom' in and for our lives, the truth is that wisdom is God, who seeks us. God takes the initiative and comes looking for us, 'meeting us in every thought'. The Old Testament story of King Solomon reveals this truth about God.

Solomon succeeded his father, King David, as king of the Israelites. Solomon, who was king of the Israelites from 961 to 922 BC, is acknowledged to be one of the greatest wisdom figures in the Old Testament. Early on as king, Solomon traveled to Gibeon, where the Ark of the Covenant resided before it was moved to the Temple in Jerusalem (see 2 Samuel 6:1–23), to worship God. The Ark of the Covenant was the elaborately decorated container (see Exodus 25:10–22 and 37:1–9) in which the Israelites kept the tablets of the Ten Commandments. The Israelites reverenced the Ark as the sign of God's presence with his people.

The night after worshiping God in Gibeon, Solomon had a vivid dream. In the dream, God told Solomon that he was eminently pleased with him, and said, 'Ask what I should give you.' Solomon replied:

'And now, O LORD my God, you have made your servant king in place of my father David, although I am only a little child; I do not know how to go out or come in. And your servant is in the midst of the people whom you have chosen, a great people, so numerous they cannot be numbered or counted. Give your servant therefore an understanding mind to govern your people, able to discern between good and evil; for who can govern this your great people?'

—1 Kings 3:7–9

Solomon could have asked God for the power to conquer and rule over other kingdoms, or for boundless wealth, or for a long life with good health. Solomon did not go there. Instead, he asked for 'an understanding mind', or *lev shemea* in Hebrew, which literally means a 'listening heart'. Solomon asked for the ability to know and understand the will of God and 'to discern between good and evil' so he could govern God's people. Solomon's request 'pleased the Lord', and God said to him:

'Because you have asked this, and have not asked for yourself long life or riches, or for the life of your enemies, but have asked for yourself understanding to discern what is right, I now do according to your word. Indeed I give you a wise and discerning mind.'

—1 Kings 3:10–12

Solomon is revered for his wisdom. Three of the writings in the Hebrew Scriptures, namely, Ecclesiastes, Song of Songs and the Book of Wisdom, pass on this 'wisdom'.

KING DAVID WITH THE ARK OF THE COVENANT | 19TH-CENTURY CHROMOLITHOGRAPH

REFLECT AND DISCUSS

- What did Solomon's request reveal about him?
- How does 'an understanding mind and listening heart' fit with your understanding of wisdom?
- How would a leader with 'an understanding mind and listening heart' govern his or her people?

OVER TO YOU

- Name the qualities of a wise person whom you know.
- When has this person helped you make a wise decision?

JESUS: 'THE WISDOM OF GOD' MADE FLESH

Jesus Christ, the Incarnate Word of God, is the fullness of Revelation. He is the Revelation of the 'wisdom and knowledge of God'. In speaking to the scribes and Pharisees, Jesus proclaimed:

'The Queen of the South will rise up at the judgment with this generation and condemn it, because she came from the ends of the earth to listen to the wisdom of Solomon, and see, something greater than Solomon is here!'

—Matthew 12:42

Jesus revealed himself to be greater than Solomon. Jesus is the fulfillment of the wisdom of ancient Israel. All the wisdom of the Old Testament and the wisest of the wise of ancient Israel prefigure him. St. Paul summarizes this belief of the apostolic Church when he teaches that Jesus is 'the wisdom and knowledge of God' (Romans 11:33). Later, to the Church in Corinth, Paul taught that Jesus is 'the power of God and the wisdom of God' . . . who 'became for us wisdom from God' in order to bring about our salvation. (Read 1 Corinthians 1:20–31.)

JOURNAL EXERCISE

- Give examples of people who put the wisdom of Jesus into practice.
- Write about how the wisdom of Jesus guides you to make 'wise' decisions about your life.

Name the qualities of a wise person whom you know

The greatest of gifts

Christian art has contributed to our understanding of the wisdom of God. Among the most famous examples are the Eastern Orthodox icons of Holy Wisdom. A favorite icon depicts an angelic or feminine figure wearing a crown and dressed in royal robes, seated on a throne. Sometimes angels and saints surround her; sometimes the image of Christ is above or near her; sometimes the icon artist includes a representation of the Holy Spirit and Jesus Christ side by side.

OPENING CONVERSATION

⊙ Examine and reflect on the image of the icon of Holy Wisdom. Pay close attention to the details.

⊙ How does the icon expand or open up your understanding of wisdom?

WHAT ABOUT YOU PERSONALLY?

⊙ What religious art gives you insight into the mystery of God?

⊙ What religious art inspires you to seek to live your faith in Christ?

⊙ Recall and visualize those images. Ask the Holy Spirit to deepen your gift of wisdom.

THE TORAH AND WISDOM

In addition to the Wisdom writings, the Torah is a primary source of wisdom for all God's people. The divinely inspired written Torah, or Pentateuch, includes the first five books of the Old Testament in the Bible. In Sacred Scripture, people of wisdom are identified as those who obey the Law and the Commandments of the covenant in all aspects of their day-to-day life. Scripture identifies those who do not live by the wisdom of God as 'fools'. For example, the Book of Deuteronomy, the fifth book of the Pentateuch, speaks of the Commandments and their wisdom for life. The Hebrew name for this book of the

RUSSIAN ICON OF SOPHIA, THE HOLY WISDOM, 17TH CENTURY

Scriptures is *debarim*, meaning 'words'. This name points to the fact that Deuteronomy contains the main discourses (words) of Moses' teaching on what the Israelites were to obey.

The word *deuteronomy* means 'second law'. The Book of Deuteronomy was written as an interpretation and adaptation of the law of the covenant. It applied the Law revealed to Moses and the Israelites to new situations in order to guide God's people in living the covenant. Here is how Deuteronomy describes the relationship between obeying the Commandments and wisdom:

Surely, this commandment that I am commanding you today is not too hard for you, nor is it too far away. It is not in heaven, that you should say, 'Who will go up to heaven for us, and get it for us so that we may hear it and

THE SCROLLS OF THE TORAH

developed around it) is to foster the full commitment of individuals and of the whole community to live the covenant—to live in intimacy and communion with the Lord God and with one another.

> Hear, O Israel: The LORD is our God; the LORD alone. You shall love the LORD your God with all you heart, and with all your soul, and with all your might.
>
> —Deuteronomy 6:4–5

> You shall not hate in your heart anyone of your kin; . . . You shall not take vengeance or bear a grudge against any of your people, but you shall love your neighbor as yourself: I am the LORD.
>
> —Leviticus 19:17–18

Living the Law of Love was true to the **religion** of both the ancient Israelites and the Jews of Jesus' day; it is the commandment Jesus gave to his Church, which has been the foundational law for the Church since her beginning. (Read Matthew 22:34–40, John 13:35 and 1 John 4:7–12.)

The Israelites developed and wrote codes, such as the holiness code, to provide a practical interpretation of the Law that would guide God's people in living the covenant. In fact, some laws of the Church today, such as the obligation on Catholics to worship God and keep Sunday as the **Lord's Day**, are the Church's expression of the laws of the covenant.

> observe it?' Neither is it beyond the sea, that you should say, 'Who will cross to the other side of the sea for us, and get it for us so that we may hear it and observe it?' No, the word is very near to you; it is in your mouth and in your heart for you to observe.
>
> —Deuteronomy 30:11–14

TALK IT OVER
⊙ Where have you seen God's wisdom at work in people? In events in the world?
⊙ How did that wisdom make a difference?

WHAT ABOUT YOU PERSONALLY?
⊙ When have you recently experienced God's wisdom as being 'very near to you'?

CODES OF ANCIENT ISRAEL: GUIDES TO LIVING THE WISDOM OF GOD
The heart and purpose of the Law God revealed to his people (and of the human laws that

TALK IT OVER
⊙ Name a human law or several human laws that help you live the Law of Love.

The Holiness Code: The Holiness Code in Leviticus 17:1—26:46 is one of the central codes, or systems of laws, in the Torah. This code prescribes laws that govern worship, justice, charity and chastity as well as the penalties for breaking those laws. In the Holiness Code the laws of worship include precise prescriptions for celebrating Passover and the Feast of the Unleavened Bread; Pentecost, or the Feast of

Weeks; New Year's Day, or Rosh Hashanah; the Day of Atonement; the Feast of Booths, or Tabernacles; as well as the Jubilee Year. Additional prescriptions were later added to adapt the Holiness Code to the life of the Jewish people in later generations.

THINK, PAIR AND SHARE

⊙ Talk with a partner about the laws of the Catholic Church that guide you in worshiping God, celebrating the sacraments and living a just, chaste and loving life. How do these laws guide you in living any of the Ten Commandments?

The Law of the Sabbath: Jews today, as Jews in Jesus' day, celebrate the **Sabbath** from sundown on Friday night to sundown on Saturday evening. Over time, the Jewish authorities developed man-made prescriptions that required Jews to adhere faithfully to the Law of the Sabbath. For example, 'Remember the sabbath day, and keep it holy. Six days you shall labor and do all your work. But the seventh day is a sabbath to the LORD your God; you shall not do any work' (Exodus 20:8–10; see also Deuteronomy 6:12–13). Jesus fulfilled and revealed the true meaning of these laws. It was Jesus' not following these man-made Sabbath prescriptions to the 'letter of the law' that was at the root of his well-known confrontation with the Pharisees in Matthew 12:1–8. (Take a moment to read the passage.)

In this episode, Jesus' actions were not a denial of the purpose and wisdom of the Sabbath Law. Rather, he was inviting the Pharisees to re-evaluate whether the many burdensome, man-made prescriptions that were attached to the Sabbath Law were negating the very purpose of the Sabbath Law. Admonishing the Pharisees, Jesus revealed his authority, concluding, 'For the Son of Man is lord of the sabbath' (Matthew 12:8).

Jesus then moved on and entered the synagogue, where some Pharisees confronted him again, trying to get the evidence to accuse him of breaking the Law. They asked, 'Is it lawful to cure on the sabbath?' Jesus responded by healing a man with a 'withered hand'. The Pharisees, in turn, 'went out and conspired against him, how to destroy him' (from Matthew 12:9–14). The leaders of the Pharisees, scribes and priests of the Temple rejected the authority of Jesus and were blind to the wisdom of his teaching. The Pharisees and scribes, who regarded themselves as experts in interpreting the Law, were not always 'wise' teachers.

THINK, PAIR AND SHARE

⊙ Read and reflect on Matthew 5:17–20.
⊙ Discuss how the passage from chapter 5 of Matthew's Gospel opens up the meaning of Matthew 12:1–14.
⊙ Check your response against Matthew 12:15–21.

OVER TO YOU

⊙ How does coming to know Jesus and his teachings guide you in understanding and living the Sabbath Law, which for Christians is 'Keep the Lord's Day holy'?

THE DISCIPLES PICK CORN ON THE SABBATH | GUSTAVE DORÉ

accomplished. Therefore, whoever breaks one of the least of these commandments, and teaches others to do the same, will be called least in the kingdom of heaven; but whoever does them and teaches them will be called great in the kingdom of heaven. For I tell you, unless your righteousness exceeds that of the scribes and Pharisees, you will never enter the kingdom of heaven.

—Matthew 5:17–20

In the remaining sections of the Sermon on the Mount Jesus reveals his authority as the giver of the new law. He declares many times, 'You have heard that it was said . . . But I say to you. . .' (See Matthew 5:21–22, 27–28, 31–32, 33–34, 38–39, 43–44.) For Jesus' disciples and many others who witnessed him teaching, Jesus taught and spoke with authority, the authority of God. They came to him not simply to hear and discuss his ideas, but to find hope and a new direction for their lives. They came to hear the wisdom and knowledge of God, which he himself was living.

The Church has received the Law as part of divine Revelation, revealed in Sacred Scripture and Sacred Tradition. She addresses modern issues in light of faith, according to the faith she has received. With the guidance of the Holy Spirit the Church applies the demands of the Law to the concrete circumstances of daily life.

REFLECT AND DISCERN

- What contemporary issues are you aware that the Church is addressing?
- With what authority does the Church address those issues?
- From what you have been learning, what is the source of that authority?

WHAT ABOUT YOU PERSONALLY?

- Name someone in authority whom you respect.
- Why do you respect that person?

JESUS, THE NEW MOSES AND GIVER OF THE NEW LAW

Jesus Christ is the fulfillment of the Law. He is the Revelation of the spirit of the Law, of the deepest and authentic meaning of the Law. He 'fulfilled it with such perfection that he revealed its ultimate meaning and redeemed the transgressions against it' (CCC, no. 592). Jesus is the new and everlasting covenant. He is the way of wisdom and knowledge of God.

Matthew wrote his account of the Gospel primarily for Jews who had become believers in Jesus. In his Gospel Matthew invites his readers to see that Moses prefigured Jesus. He leads them to see Jesus as the 'new Moses', the giver of the new law. As Moses received the Ten Commandments on a mountain, Matthew portrays Jesus teaching the demands of the new law, the Law of the Gospel, on a mountainside. In the Sermon on the Mount, Jesus declares:

Do not think that I have come to abolish the law or the prophets; I have come not to abolish but to fulfill. For truly I tell you, until heaven and earth pass away, not one letter, not one stroke of a letter, will pass from the law until all is

The Church, Mother and teacher

OPENING REFLECTION

- Think about your teachers who have encouraged you to integrate what you learn in the classroom into your daily life.
- What difference have they made to your living your 'life–faith–life' journey?
- In what ways is the Church your 'teacher'?

FROM THE WISDOM OF THE CHURCH

The way of Christ 'leads to life'; a contrary way 'leads to destruction' [Matthew 7:13; see Deuteronomy 30:15–20]. The Gospel parable of the *two ways* . . . shows the importance of moral decisions for our salvation: 'There are two ways: the one of life, the other of death; but between the two, there is a great difference' [*Didache*, 1,1].
—CCC, no. 1696

THE CHURCH: OUR MOTHER AND TEACHER

The Church is our Mother and teacher of the faith. She guides us in integrating into our daily lives the wisdom that God has revealed most fully in the Incarnate Word of God, Jesus Christ. Jesus' whole life is a 'continual teaching'. All the events of his life 'are the actualization of his word and the fulfillment of Revelation' (Pope St. John Paul II, *On Catechesis in Our Time*, no. 9, quoted in CCC, no. 561). It is in and through the Church that we encounter Jesus and conform ourselves to him.

It is in the Church, in communion with all the baptized, that the Christian fulfills his vocation. From the Church he receives the Word of God containing the teachings of 'the law of Christ' [Galatians 6:2]. From the Church he receives the grace of the sacraments that sustains him on the 'way'.

From the Church he learns the *example of holiness* and recognizes its model and source in the all-holy Virgin Mary; he discerns it in the authentic witnesses of those who live it; he discovers it in the spiritual tradition and long history of the saints who have gone before him and whom the liturgy celebrates in the rhythms of the sanctoral cycle.
—CCC, no. 2030

In chapter 10 we explored the different callings (vocations) and gifts (charisms) the spirit gives to the baptized. In chapter 11 we learned about the Magisterium, the teaching office of the Church. We now explore in more detail the 'sanctifying office' and the 'governing office' of the Church. All three offices of the Church—teaching, sanctifying and governing—serve the communion of the whole Church. All three offices guide the Church in her efforts to discern authentically the spiritual wisdom of our faith and the ways to integrate that faith into our daily lives.

STATUE OF THE VIRGIN MARY, ST. EUFEMIA, ROVINJ, CROATIA

Through the exercise of these offices the Pope and the other bishops in communion with him provide pastoral norms for living the faith and the moral life. Among these norms are the **precepts of the Church**.

The precepts of the Church are positive laws. The wisdom at the heart of the precepts is to guide the faithful in living the indispensable 'minimum in the spirit of prayer and moral effort, in the growth in love of God and neighbor' (CCC, no. 2041). The precepts name these serious responsibilities of the faithful.

⊙ The first precept is: 'You shall attend Mass on Sundays and on holy days of obligation and rest from servile labor.' Sunday is the Lord's Day, the day on which the Church commemorates the Resurrection; holy days of obligation celebrate the principal mysteries of the life of Christ, and of the Virgin Mary and the saints. In the United States of America there are six holy days of obligation, namely, the Solemnity of Mary, the Mother of God (January 1); Ascension of the Lord (the Thursday forty days after Easter; may be celebrated on the Sunday after that Thursday); Solemnity of the Assumption of Mary (August 15); All Saints' Day (November 1); Solemnity of the Immaculate Conception (December 8); and Christmas (December 25).

⊙ The second precept is: 'You shall confess your sins at least once a year.' This precept ensures that we prepare ourselves for the reception of the Eucharist and we continue our lifelong conversion to Christ that began at Baptism.

⊙ The third precept is: 'You shall receive the sacrament of the Eucharist at least during the Easter season.' The Eucharist is the center of the Christian life. This precept requires that, at the minimum, we receive the Eucharist during the Easter season, which is at the center of the Church's celebration of the saving mystery of Christ's Death and Resurrection.

⊙ The fourth precept is: 'You shall observe the days of fasting and abstinence established by the Church.' The disciplines of fasting and abstinence help us repent and live the Gospel more fully in the freedom of the children of God.

⊙ The fifth precept is: 'You shall help to provide for the needs of the Church.' From the Church's beginning, members of the Church have cared for the needs of the Church according to one's ability.

—Based on CCC, nos. 2042–2043

Many of the responsibilities of these laws and other disciplines of the Church have been adjusted by the hierarchy to meet the changing circumstances of the life of the Church.

The second precept is: 'You shall confess your sins at least once a year.'

Precepts of the Church

Laws made by the Church that indicate basic requirements for her members.
—*United States Catholic Catechism for Adults (USCCA)*, 524

JOURNAL EXERCISE

⦿ Read and reflect on the Precepts of the Church. What wisdom and guidance do the Precepts of the Church provide for living your life in Christ?

⦿ Write your reflections in your journal. Return to this exercise often.

FROM THE WISDOM OF THE CHURCH

The Church is holy: the Most Holy God is her author; Christ, her bridegroom, gave himself up to make her holy; the Spirit of holiness gives her life.
—CCC, no. 867

THE SANCTIFYING OFFICE OF THE CHURCH: BECOMING A HOLY PEOPLE

Christ entrusted the Word and the sacraments to the Church for our salvation. We receive Christ's redemption as members of his Body, the Church. You will recall that the Church is a communion of saints, of holy things, 'above all the Eucharist', by which the faithful form one body in Christ, the Holy One of God. The Bible often represents becoming wise and becoming holy as two sides of the same coin. The Church helps us grow in wisdom and holiness of life. Bishops and priests sanctify the Church by administering the sacraments, by proclaiming and preaching the Word of God, and by prayer and work. The participation of the faithful in the sacramental life of the Church, above all in the Eucharist, is a vital source of grace—of encountering and responding to God the Holy Trinity.

The Sacrament of the Eucharist is the center of the life of the Church. The Church recommends that 'the faithful receive Holy Communion when they participate in the celebration of the Eucharist; [and] she obliges them to do so at least once a year' (CCC, no. 1417). Encountering Christ really, truly and sacramentally present in the Eucharist and receiving the Body and the Blood of Christ in Holy Communion strengthens the communicant's union with the Lord and with the Church.

Christ gives us in the Eucharist the pledge of glory with him. Participation in the Holy Sacrifice [of the Mass] identifies us with his Heart, sustains our strength along the pilgrimage of this life, makes us long for eternal life, and unites us even now to the Church in heaven, the Blessed Virgin Mary, and all the saints.
—CCC, no. 1419

The Eucharist properly received has the power to transform us from the inside out—to conform us to Christ until he is formed in us (see Galatians 4:19). Receiving Christ in Holy Communion gives us the graces to live as faithful disciples of the Incarnate Son of God, as children of God the Father and as temples of God the Holy Spirit. Regular participation in Mass is essential for learning, for transformation, for growing in wisdom in living the way of Christ. It is essential for growing closer to God and for making better sense of our lives through loving God and neighbor as ourselves.

Participating in the celebration of Mass is like entering the biblical gate, where Wisdom sits waiting for us. We encounter Christ, the risen and glorified incarnate wisdom of God, in many ways. The readings, the prayers, the homily, the songs can all help us grow in wisdom and be more

CHINESE WORSHIPERS RECEIVE THE EUCHARIST IN BEIJING

perfectly conformed to him who is the wisdom of God. To help the faithful participate in Mass more fruitfully, the prayers in the *Roman Missal* have been revised so as to more closely reflect the original Latin. The Church in the United States began using the revised *Roman Missal* on the First Sunday of Advent 2011.

WHAT ABOUT YOU PERSONALLY?

⊙ Think of the last time you participated in the celebration of Mass. What did you learn through the readings, prayers, sermon, songs, rituals and gestures?

⊙ How did this help you live in a more loving way toward God and neighbor?

A PEOPLE OF PRAYER

The Church is a people of prayer, and the Christian life is a life of prayer. Our Lord forms, teaches, guides, consoles and blesses us through prayer. Christian prayer is 'the living relationship of the children of God with their Father who is good beyond measure, with his Son Jesus Christ and with the Holy Spirit' (CCC, no. 2565). It is an expression of our living in communion and intimacy with God. The sanctifying office of the Church supports and guides us in living as people of prayer.

The Church celebrates the Christian mysteries throughout her liturgical year. The liturgical year established by the Church gives a rhythm of prayer to the year and to each day of the year. Each week of the year is centered in Sunday, the Lord's Day, the day of the Resurrection. Sunday is 'the pre-eminent day of the liturgical assembly, the day of the Christian family, and the day of joy and rest from work' (CCC, no. 1193) and the day to celebrate a life centered in God. Worship of God has both a personal and a communal dimension: personal, private worship is encouraged to complement communal worship.

The seasons of Advent and Christmas, Lent and Easter remember and celebrate the 'whole mystery of Christ from his Incarnation and Nativity through his Ascension, to Pentecost and the expectation of the blessed hope of the coming of the Lord' (CCC, no. 1194). During Ordinary Time we remember and take part in the events of the Lord's public life and ministry; we travel the roads of Palestine with him. We listen and watch as our Lord and master teaches us to live the 'way' he lived. The Church also gives us the opportunity throughout the year to remember and celebrate the lives of Mary, the Mother of God, and the Apostles, martyrs, holy virgins, confessors and other saints. We learn from them, seek their intercession, and join with them in giving glory to God in 'the liturgy of heaven' (CCC, no. 1195). We call the yearly celebration of these feasts the sanctoral cycle, or 'cycle of the saints', of the liturgical year.

TALK IT OVER

- In what ways do your parish and your home celebrate the seasons and feasts of the Church? Share specific ways in which these celebrations reflect the cultural heritage of the people of your parish or of your family.

THE PASTORAL OFFICE OF GOVERNING THE CHURCH: SHARING IN THE WORK OF THE GOOD SHEPHERD

'The law of God entrusted to the Church is taught to the faithful as the way of life and truth' (CCC, no. 2037). Christ the Good Shepherd is the model for the pastors of the Church in the exercise of their governing, or pastoral, office.

The Pope is the Pastor of the universal Church on earth. The word 'pastor' comes from a Latin word meaning 'shepherd'. The Pope is the vicar of the Good Shepherd and the successor of St. Peter, whom Christ commissioned, 'Tend my sheep' (John 21:16). The Holy See, also known as the Vatican, is the 'seat', or place of governance, of the whole Church. Members of the Curia, or administrative offices of the Vatican, assist the Pope. Pope Benedict XVI was the Prefect, or head, of the Congregation for the Doctrine of the Faith, one of the Curia's offices, from 1981 until 2005, when he was elected the 265th Pope on April 19, 2005.

Bishops carry a crosier, a shepherd's staff, as they enter and leave the liturgical assembly for the celebration of the Liturgy. This practice reminds bishops that they are to exercise their authority and sacred power with the Good Shepherd as their model. In their exercise of their pastoral office, bishops interpret and apply the law

of God to changing circumstances of the Church. They fulfill their pastoral office so that 'together with the flock entrusted to them, they may attain eternal life' (Vatican II, *Dogmatic Constitution on the Church*, no. 26).

OVER TO YOU

- Check out the website of your diocese. If you do not know the name of the bishop of your diocese, find it out.
- Then check out your bishop's coat of arms. The symbols and the motto your bishop has chosen will tell you what his vision is for his pastoral leadership.
- Always remember to pray for your bishop.

JOURNAL EXERCISE

- Create your own leadership coat of arms, using symbols and a motto.
- Post your coat of arms near your bed or in your Bible. Refer to it often and live by it.

THE GOOD SHEPHERD | ABBEY SAINT-ETIENNE, ALSACE, FRANCE

Our search for wisdom

light, which enlightens everyone (see John 1:9). Jesus himself revealed the same truth when he declared, 'I am the light of the world' (John 8:12).

Jesus commanded his disciples to be lights in the world. (Read Matthew 5:14–16.) The light for the path of life, the wisdom revealed in Jesus Christ, continues to be made present in the Church. Through the teaching, sanctifying and governing offices of the Church we receive insight and guidance for following Jesus. We receive the wisdom and grace 'to walk always as children of the light . . . [and] keep the flame of faith alive in [our] hearts' (from *Rite of Baptism for Several Children*, no. 64).

As Solomon asked for understanding and a listening heart, to be enlightened by the wisdom of God, so must we. In the Book of Wisdom we read:

The beginning of wisdom is the most sincere
    desire for instruction,
and concern for instruction is love of her,
and love of her is the keeping of her laws,
and giving heed to her laws is assurance of
    immortality,
and immortality brings one near to God;
so the desire for wisdom leads to a kingdom.
                                —Wisdom 6:17–20

Finding wisdom is an encounter between our desire for God and God's desire that we lead good and holy lives. We express our desire for wisdom through the lengths we go to seek wisdom: learning and listening, seeking and questioning, praying and practicing. Learning, like you are doing now, is part of a bigger picture of one's response to God, who is wisdom.

OPENING CONVERSATION

- When have you seen a drawing of a 'light bulb' over the head of a person? Was it in a cartoon? In a TV commercial?
- What does the 'light bulb' symbolize?
- When was your last 'light bulb' moment? Share your thoughts with a partner.
- Now think of an image that points to a 'wisdom moment'. Draw it and share it with a partner.

WISDOM: GOD'S GIFT AND OUR RESPONSE

In Sacred Scripture light is used as a symbol of God and the wisdom of God. Psalm 119 is a prayer of praise in which the psalmist acknowledges obeying the Law. In verse 105 the psalmist declares, 'Your word is a lamp to my feet / and a light to my path'. The Fourth Gospel declares that Jesus, the Incarnate Word of God, is the true

THINK, PAIR AND SHARE

- How is the Church a source of wisdom?
- Share your response with a partner.

> **Prayer is the living relationship of the children of God with their Father who is good beyond measure, with his Son Jesus Christ and with the Holy Spirit**

WISDOM LITTLE BY LITTLE

The Church is our Mother and teacher of faith who guides and nourishes us in living as Christ, the wisdom of God. Growing in wisdom is a lifelong journey. None of us becomes 'wise' overnight. We grow into wisdom little by little. For example, infants become toddlers step by step. They observe and imitate. They take more tentative steps, struggle to find their balance, and sometimes fall down. As toddlers grow into children, they learn safety rules about walking, such as, 'Don't run out in the street', 'Look both ways before crossing', 'Cross at the green light and not in between'. When learning to make our way in the world, learning our first steps and respecting rules help us to get to where we want to go—safely and surely.

Disciples of Jesus must also commit themselves to learning, step by step, the way to living a life of wisdom. Praying regularly is vital to growing in wisdom. 'Prayer and *Christian life* are *inseparable*' (CCC, no. 2745). Prayer helps us to understand the teachings of Jesus Christ and his Church in a deeper way and to live them more fully.

The Christian family, the church of the home, is the first place for learning and developing the habit of prayer. Prayer is being with God and speaking 'heart to heart' with God. You will recall that prayer is 'the living relationship of the children of God with their Father who is good beyond measure, with his Son Jesus Christ and with the Holy Spirit' (CCC, no. 2565). God is always with us; we can pray anywhere and at any time. We live in the presence of God. Praying regularly deepens our relationship with God and gives us insight into the ways of God, into the wisdom of God.

Little by little, we learn to walk the way of Jesus, the incarnate wisdom of God. This task and responsibility often includes choosing the 'road not taken' by many. God gives us gifts and graces to make that choice wisely. Among those gifts is the gift of the Church, our Mother and teacher. Through the Church we receive the truth and grace of God to live a life of wisdom. We receive the 'knowledge and wisdom' to keep God at the center of our life, to see ourselves as God sees us, and to see the world as God sees it. Joined to Christ, we 'are wise in Christ' (1 Corinthians 4:10). Filled 'with the knowledge of God's will in all spiritual wisdom and understanding', we strive to live in a manner 'worthy of the Lord, fully pleasing to him', as we 'bear fruit in every good work and as [we] grow in the knowledge of God' (Colossians 1:9–10).

OVER TO YOU

⊙ What are the wisest lessons you have learned from the faith of the Church?

⊙ How have these lessons helped you make your life–faith–life journey?

JUDGE AND ACT

REFLECT ON WHAT YOU HAVE LEARNED IN THIS CHAPTER

As you come toward the end of this chapter, pause and reflect on what you have come to understand about the Church's work of sanctifying and governing the faithful. Share your understanding of the teaching of the Catholic Church on these statements:

◉ Christ established his Church to continue his presence and work in the world.

◉ Bishops and priests sanctify the Church by prayer, work and the ministry of the Word and the sacraments.

◉ The Eucharistic is the center of life in the Church.

◉ The Catholic Church worships throughout the whole year; this year of grace and celebration is called the liturgical year.

◉ The Church is a people of prayer.

◉ Bishops and priests have the responsibility to govern the Church and to exercise their authority and sacred power with the Good Shepherd as their model.

◉ Growing in wisdom is a lifelong journey of following the 'way' of Jesus, the incarnate wisdom of God.

◉ The Christian family is the first place for learning and growing in faith.

OVER TO YOU

◉ What have been some of the best lessons you have learned for living the 'way' of Jesus from studying this chapter?

LEARN BY EXAMPLE

St. Teresa Benedicta of the Cross (Edith Stein)

In her search for wisdom, Edith Stein was really passionate about understanding our world and its great mysteries.

Edith Stein was born into an observant Jewish family in Breslau in the German Empire in October 1891. She always loved learning about the world around her. She was gifted and smart, and excelled in school. Learning was not just a task for her, she genuinely felt a sense of wonder and awe about all of God's creation. She worked diligently to discover the greater cause of things and the connections between them. At the age of twenty-five, Edith was awarded a doctorate in philosophy, a subject that literally means 'the love of wisdom'. The more she journeyed in search of wisdom, the greater her sense that there might be more to understanding our world than what we can learn in school or from ordinary experience. She had a deep

feeling that 'there is more to life than meets the eye'.

One day in 1921, while on holiday, Edith came across *The Interior Castle*, St. Teresa of

Ávila's autobiography. While reading it, Edith had a 'light bulb' moment. She sensed that the saint's perspective was pointing her to answers about our world that she had been seeking for a long time. Edith became a Catholic within a year and left her university to forge a new path. Still pursuing wisdom, Edith explored the wisdom of the Catholic faith more deeply. She also found courage to bring her new-found faith not only to comment on the evil of the Nazi regime but to resign from teaching.

Edith discerned God's call for her to enter religious life. She joined the Carmelite order in 1933, took on the name of Teresa Benedicta of the Cross, which signified her decision to live a new way of life, and vowed to live the Gospel according to the way of the Carmelites. As a Carmelite, Teresa Benedicta continued to think and write about the world, bringing the wisdom of Christian faith to illumine how best to live one's life. On July 26, 1942, she was arrested by the Nazis and taken to Auschwitz because of her Jewish heritage. She died there in the gas chamber on August 9, 1942, at the age of 50. Pope St. John Paul II canonized her in 1998.

St. Teresa Benedicta of the Cross is a model in faith. She courageously pursued wisdom until she found her answers to the great questions in life, discerning with wisdom what would allow her to live life to the fullest. She moved beyond philosophy to follow the 'way' of Jesus Christ.

TALK IT OVER
- How can St. Teresa's example give you courage to stand up for God's truth and wisdom?

RESPOND WITH FAMILY AND FRIENDS
- What injustices in the world do you think the Church should address most urgently?
- Where do you need to speak up for justice in your life? How will you do it?

WHAT WILL YOU DO NOW?
- How will you live the way of wisdom and show compassion to those around you?

LEARN BY HEART

[T]he desire for wisdom leads to a kingdom.

WISDOM 6:20

ENVIRONMENTAL PROTEST IN HALIFAX, CANADA

Pray the Sign of the Cross together.

LEADER

Let us place ourselves in the presence of Jesus, the wisdom and knowledge of God. (*Pause*)

Loving God, you alone are true wisdom, you have sent your Word of Wisdom, your Son, Jesus Christ, to us.
We desire your wisdom to show us the way to live in and respond to your love.
Send us your Spirit of Wisdom now, as these holy icons remind us of your presence.

ALL

Amen.

READER

Read aloud Wisdom 7:22–26. (Pause)
The word of the Lord.

ALL

Thanks be to God.

LEADER

Spend a few minutes prayerfully reflecting on the icons. As you reflect, be aware of the presence of God. (*Pause*)
Think about your needs and hopes. Bring them into the presence of God as you continue to pray and to reflect on the icons. (*Pause*)
Think about how the icons help you become more aware of God's wisdom to you. (*Pause*)
Seeking you, God of Wisdom, we ask, 'Show us the Way of Wisdom'.

READER

We pray for the Pope, bishops, priests, deacons and ecclesial ministers of our Church, that the Holy Spirit of Wisdom will continue to guide them in serving our communities, so that we may all grow in wisdom and holiness. (*Pause*)
God of Wisdom, hear our prayer.

ALL

Show us the Way of Wisdom.

ICONOSTASIS AND ALTAR IN KIEV, UKRAINE

VIRGIN OF THE HOLY MONASTERY OF KYKKOS

READER

We pray that we may also become living icons, revealing God's wisdom and truth to those around us. (*Pause*)
God of Wisdom, hear our prayer.

ALL

Show us the Way of Wisdom.

READER

We pray that we may find Wisdom and that she may grant us courage to stand up for God's justice and truth. (*Pause*)
God of Wisdom, hear our prayer.

ALL

Show us the Way of Wisdom.

READER

We pray that our learning of the faith of our Church may lead us to true wisdom, to live our lives to the fullest in sharing God's love with those around us. (*Pause*)
God of Wisdom, hear our prayer.

ALL

Show us the Way of Wisdom.

LEADER

Let us now offer our prayers silently in our hearts for our own needs and hopes.
God of Wisdom, hear our prayer. (*Pause*)

ALL

Show us the Way of Wisdom.

LEADER

Let us now pray together.

ALL

Great is the Wisdom of the Lord!
God Almighty, your Wisdom includes
an understanding of what is fair,
what is logical, what is true,
what is right and what is lasting.
It mirrors your pure intellect!
I entreat you to grant me such Wisdom,
that my labors may reflect your insight.
Your Wisdom expands in your creations,
displaying complexity and multiplicity.
Your Wisdom is an eternity ahead of man.
May your Wisdom flourish forever.
Amen.

—Blessed John Henry Newman

Conclude by praying the Sign of the Cross together.

ICON OF CHRIST PANTOCRATOR

THE TRANSFIGURATION | THEOPHANES THE GREEK

CHAPTER 13

The Call to Discipleship

—Transforming the World in Christ

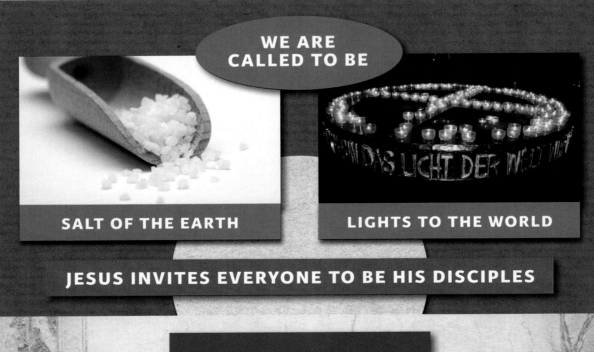

WE ARE CALLED TO BE

SALT OF THE EARTH

LIGHTS TO THE WORLD

JESUS INVITES EVERYONE TO BE HIS DISCIPLES

THE CHURCH INVITES ALL PEOPLE TO SALVATION

JESUS IS GOD'S 'GOOD WORD' OF SALVATION TO THE WORLD

THE CHURCH PROCLAIMS THE GOOD WORD OF SALVATION AND REDEMPTION

SACRED SCRIPTURE AND TRADITION PASS ON THE GOOD NEWS OF SALVATION

THE HOLY SPIRIT GUIDES US TO PROCLAIM THE LIGHT OF THE GOSPEL

AT THE BEGINNING OF HIS PUBLIC MINISTRY, Jesus said to Peter and his brother Andrew, 'Follow me, and I will make you fish for people' (Matthew 4:19). Among the risen Lord's last words to the Apostles was the command to 'make disciples of all nations' (Matthew 28:19). In this final chapter we explore our response to Jesus' invitation to discipleship. The Church is the community of Jesus' disciples who cooperate with the Spirit of Christ to transform their own lives and the lives of others in Christ.

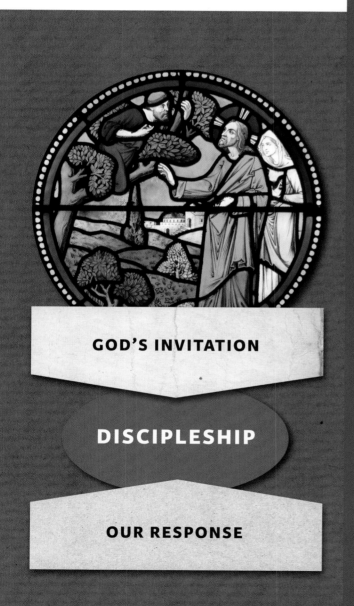

GOD'S INVITATION

DISCIPLESHIP

OUR RESPONSE

Faith Focus: The teachings of the Catholic Church that are the primary focus of the doctrinal content presented in this chapter include:

- ◉ God wills the Church to be the ordinary means of salvation and redemption.
- ◉ Christ entrusted the Word and the sacraments to the Church for our salvation.
- ◉ The Church has the fullness of truth and the totality of the means of salvation.
- ◉ Jesus Christ enriches us through the Church.
- ◉ Living as members of the Church, the Body of Christ, means we live as disciples, proclaiming the Lord Jesus and his teachings to others.
- ◉ As the disciples of Christ, we are salt and light wherever we are.

Discipleship Formation: As a result of studying this chapter and discovering the meaning of the faith of the Catholic Church for your life, you should be better able to:

- ◉ develop positive attitudes that reflect the common dignity of every human being;
- ◉ witness to your faith in Jesus, the Savior and Redeemer of all people;
- ◉ appreciate that the Gospel is for everyone;
- ◉ identify and commit to ways of living as 'salt of the earth' and a 'light for Christ' in the world;
- ◉ value the sacraments as encounters with Christ;
- ◉ seek to live as a person through whom others encounter Christ;
- ◉ bring the 'salt' and 'light' of justice and compassion to the world in which you live.

Scripture References: These Scripture references are quoted or referred to in this chapter:
NEW TESTAMENT: Matthew 4:18–19, 5:13–16, 9:26, 14:13–21, 15:32–39, 18:20, 19:26, 26:26, 28:19–20; **Mark** 6:30–44, 8:1–10 and 19, 16:15; **Luke** 19:1–17, 24:13–35; **John** 1:9, 6:5–59, 8:12; **1 Corinthians** 10:16–17, 11:23–24; **1 Timothy** 2:4

Faith Glossary: Familiarize yourself with the meaning of these key terms. Definitions are found in the Glossary: **breaking of bread, racism, sacrament, sin, social sin**

Faith Word: breaking of bread
Learn by Heart: Matthew 18:20
Learn by Example: Venerable Mother Henriette Delille

Who is invited to salvation?

ROSA PARKS AFTER HER ARREST IN 1955

Rosa Parks courageously challenged the 'Whites Only' segregation policies in Alabama. On December 1, 1955, after working all day in downtown Montgomery, Rosa boarded the same bus that she regularly traveled home in for more than twelve years. She took a seat in the first row in the 'colored' section, just behind the seats reserved for white passengers. When a white passenger boarded the bus and there were no more seats in the section reserved for white passengers, the driver, James F. Blake, told Rosa to give up her seat. (Blake was the same driver who in 1943 had made Rosa get off the bus, follow the law and re-enter the bus through the back door. After she exited, Blake drove off, leaving her in the rain.) Rosa refused to give up her seat and was arrested. The incident led to Rosa being fired from her job. You know the rest of Rosa's story well.

As historians have come to know the story of Rosa's life, they have come to see that Rosa Parks was far more than a civil rights activist; she was a woman of deep faith. She once said, 'In Church I learned that people should stand up for their rights just as the children of Israel stood up to Pharaoh.' For Rosa, faith without works is dead.

OPENING CONVERSATION

◉ Name a time or times when you were excluded from a group for doing the right thing. Can you remember and describe your feelings?

◉ Have you excluded someone from being part of 'your group'? How did the person react?

FROM THE WISDOM OF THE CHURCH

'Since something of the glory of God shines on the face of every person, the dignity of every person before God is the basis of the dignity of man before other men' [Vatican II, *Pastoral Constitution on the Church in the Modern World*, no. 84]. Moreover this is the ultimate foundation of the radical equality and brotherhood among all people, regardless of their race, nation, sex, origin, culture, or class.

—*Compendium of the Social Doctrine of the Church*, no. 144

JESUS INVITES EVERYONE TO BE HIS DISCIPLES

The story of the treatment of Rosa Parks by Blake and the Montgomery police is a story of the evil of bigotry, prejudice and **racism**. Racism is the **sin** of judging and treating people as innately less in value than members of one's own race. Bigotry, prejudice and racism attack the God-given dignity of every person; these personal sins and **social sins** deny both the fundamental God-given dignity of people as children of God and the fundamental rights that flow from that dignity.

Jesus reached out to and valued everyone, especially those who were scorned and marginalized by society. The Gospel account of Jesus and Zacchaeus in Luke 19:1–10 exemplifies this truth in a dramatic way. Zacchaeus was the chief tax-collector in Jericho. Tax-collectors in Palestine in Jesus' day worked for the Romans. They not only had the authority to collect the taxes that were legally owed; they also took advantage of Roman law and added a surcharge to the tax as part of their salary. As a consequence, Jews regarded tax-collectors as oppressors of their own people.

One day there was a buzz in the streets of Jericho. News had reached the town that Jesus, the Teacher and wonder-healer from Nazareth (he had just healed a blind beggar as he approached Jericho), was coming their way! The residents of Jericho, including Zacchaeus, were intrigued and anxious to see Jesus and were jockeying for positions to get close to him. Ever wonder how Zacchaeus was treated as he made his way toward the sycamore tree?

LET'S PROBE DEEPER

- Work in groups of three. Read Luke 19:1–10, Jesus' encounter with Zacchaeus. One group member retells the story from the perspective of Jesus, one from the perspective of Zacchaeus, and the third from the perspective of the crowd.
- Discuss any new insights the members of the group got from hearing the story from the three different perspectives.

THE CHURCH INVITES ALL PEOPLE TO SALVATION

The Gospel account of Jesus and Zacchaeus is but one story that reveals that Jesus' mission was to all people. Surely, if salvation could come to the home of a tax-collector, God was inviting all people to share in his saving love— God excludes no one. The risen Savior commissioned the Apostles and his Church to do the same; we are to invite all people to become his disciples. Christ willed the Church to

be the ordinary way and means of salvation. In a way known to God alone, all people are offered the possibility of salvation through the Church.

The four accounts of the Gospel and other New Testament writings clearly attest that the members of the early Church grew in their understanding of the universal dimension of Christ's mission—that 'all women and men are called to belong to the new people of God' (Vatican II, *Dogmatic Constitution on the Church*, no. 13), so that, in Christ, 'men and women might form one family and one people of God' (Vatican II, *Decree on the Church's Missionary Activity*, no. 1).

Jesus revealed that he is the Savior and Redeemer of all people. God offers his saving

God invites all people to salvation

love to all people, to Jews and Gentiles. This revealed truth was not always accepted by some Christians. For example, in the fourth century St. Augustine, Bishop of Hippo and Doctor of the Church, defended this teaching of the Church against Donatism. Donatism taught that only 'saints' could belong to the Church and that there was no room for sinners. You will recall from chapter 5, in our discussion of heresy and schism, that a religious teaching, such as Donatism, that denies or contradicts truths revealed by God, is a heresy. When Christians are adamant in their convictions that are contrary to the Church's teachings and separate themselves from the Pope and his authority, a schism results.

God offers his saving love in Christ to all people, to saints and sinners. Some people may reject God's offer of salvation in Christ; other people, through no fault of their own, may not come to know of God's gift of salvation in Christ. In ways known to God alone, they may be saved.

The Church exists for all people and is the means of salvation for all people. 'The Church prays that no one should be lost: . . . If it is true that no one can save himself, it is also true that God wills "all men to be saved" [1 Timothy 2:4], and that for him "all things are possible" [Matthew 19:26]' (*Catechism of the Catholic Church* [CCC], no. 1058).

TALK IT OVER
- ⊙ When have you heard people excluding others from God's saving love?
- ⊙ What were they saying? How did you respond?

OVER TO YOU
- ⊙ Take a look around. Who are the people neglected or even cast aside by others? Why does this happen?
- ⊙ What can you do to reach out to these people? What can you do to let them know that God loves them?

SCULPTURE OF ST. AUGUSTINE

The Church: salt of the earth and Good News for all people

'I'm Gonna Sit Right Down and Write Myself a Letter' is one of the most popular songs of all time in the *Great American Songbook*. Here are its opening lyrics:

> I'm gonna sit right down and write myself a letter
> And make believe it came from you.

OPENING CONVERSATION

⊙ What 'good words' have you shared with others today?

⊙ What difference did your 'good words' make to them?

PROCLAIMING THE WORD OF GOD

Words are part of our life. We speak them, write them, text them, read them and live them. True and honest words are the building blocks of our life-giving relationships. Exchanging 'mean and false words' usually weakens but can even destroy relationships. We need to share and hear good words—words of love and support, words of truth and honesty, words of compassion and justice.

Jesus gave the Church the work of preaching and teaching the truth with love. He gives the baptized a share in his own mission, each according to their role in the Church. The primary mission of the Church, which the risen Christ first gave to the Apostles, is to proclaim the 'Good Word' of salvation and redemption in Christ by her words and works. Jesus said, 'Blessed rather are those who hear the word of God and obey it' (Luke 11:28). Through the Church the Spirit of God invites all people to obey everything Christ taught, to become his disciples and to enter into life in the Church.

Christ sends the Church to all people to proclaim the fullness of faith, truth and love and she 'administers the totality of the means of salvation' (CCC, no. 868) and plants the seeds of the reign of God. She undertakes this mission so that the Good News will be heard and responded to by all people and all generations until the end of time. Her words and actions of truth and love work to bring about in Christ the healing (the root meaning of the verb 'to save') of the communion with God and unity among all peoples.

OVER TO YOU

⊙ When was the last time someone shared the Good News of the Gospel with you? What was that news?

⊙ When was the last time you shared the Good News of the Gospel with someone? How was that Good News received?

Jesus, the Incarnate Word of God: Jesus Christ is the Word of God made flesh, who 'came down from heaven, / and by the Holy Spirit was incarnate of the Virgin Mary, and became man' (Nicene Creed). Jesus, the Son of God, is the Son of Mary, is true God and true man. He is the Revelation of God, who is truth and love. No word or words from God could be better or more complete than God's Word revealed and made present in Jesus. The divine Word-made-flesh lived among us. Jesus is God's 'Good Word' of salvation to the world. He is, as Pope Benedict XVI described him in his February 3, 2013 Vatican Radio address, the prophet of truth and love. By his teaching and preaching, his healing and serving people, his dying and rising from the dead, Jesus made present and revealed God's saving love; he invited, as the Holy Spirit continues to invite, people to belief in him to be the Savior and Redeemer of the world.

Sacred Scripture and Sacred Tradition: Sacred Scripture and Sacred Tradition pass on this Good News of salvation in Christ. Christ entrusted to the Apostles and their successors the responsibility and authority of authentically interpreting and passing on his Good Word. The Church fulfills this mission 'in its doctrine, life, and worship' (Vatican II, *Dogmatic Constitution on Divine Revelation*, no. 8). She proclaims Scripture during the celebration of every **sacrament**. Through participation in the sacraments, the faithful are made sharers in the saving work of Jesus. In Scripture 'the pilgrim Church contemplates God, the source of all her riches' (CCC, no. 97).

THINK, PAIR AND SHARE
- Share your favorite Gospel story with a partner.
- Identify the words in the passage that strike you the most.
- What do those words say to you?

RESEARCH AND DISCERN
- Look up the Gospel reading that was proclaimed at Mass last Sunday or the Gospel reading that will be proclaimed this coming Sunday. Hint: You can find them on the website of the United States Conference of Catholic Bishops.
- Read and reflect on the Gospel proclamation you selected.
- What is God's Word saying to you?

OVER TO YOU
- Recall the last words you spoke to a member of your family or school community, or to a friend.
- Were your words 'good words', life-giving words? Explain.

BEING THE SALT OF THE EARTH
Jesus used the image of 'salt' to help his disciples understand the mission he was giving them. In the Sermon on the Mount Jesus challenged his disciples to be the 'salt of the earth'. Immediately after his teaching on the Beatitudes, Jesus used

16TH-CENTURY WOODCUT SHOWING THE MANUFACTURE OF SALT

The disciples would be 'salt of the earth' by proclaiming the Gospel of Christ

the image of salt to describe the work of his disciples:

You are the salt of the earth; but if salt has lost its taste, how can its saltiness be restored? It is no longer good for anything, but is thrown out and trampled under foot.

—Matthew 5:13

In order to understand the power of this image, we need to remember that, in Jesus' time, salt was a very valuable substance. There was plenty of salt in the province of Judea, where it was harvested from the Dead Sea. As it is today, salt was important for cooking and flavoring foods, but salt had other uses as well. The people of the ancient Mediterranean used salt as a preservative in the absence of refrigeration. For health and wellness, salt was a useful disinfectant for cleaning out wounds. For trading and commerce, salt was a commodity of value, used as a standard unit for exchanging or measuring against other goods, similar to gold today.

The disciples would be 'salt of the earth' by proclaiming the Gospel of Christ, by both their words *and* their deeds. In so doing they would bring 'the Good News of Jesus Christ' into the lives of people. They would be inviting people to discover the need for the 'salt' of the Gospel for their lives.

How can we keep our 'saltiness'? Living as Christ the Light of the world calls and teaches is known in and through the Church. We are to pay careful attention to the words we speak and hear as Church; we are to speak truthfully and lovingly. We are to study and learn from the teachings of the Church. We are to explore the meaning of the documents of the Pope and the documents of our bishops in the United States. (You are doing just that in your discussions in theology class.) We are to listen to the teaching of the bishop of our diocese and seek the advice of our parish priest and others in our parish and school who have the ministry to guide us in growing in our faith. Above all, we are to share our faith with our family and in our home. When we make these things part of our life, we are also learning to share God's Good Word with others.

TALK IT OVER

- Think of a time when you tasted really bland food. What might the addition of salt have done to improve the taste?
- What does it mean for a disciple of Christ to be 'salt of the earth'?
- What people would you describe as 'salt of the earth', and why?

THE CHURCH'S INVITATION TO YOUTH

Pope St. John Paul II, in his address to youth at Toronto World Youth Day 2002, described the youth of the Church as 'salt of the earth, light of the world':

As the salt of the earth, you are called to preserve the faith which you have received and to pass it on intact to others. Your generation is being challenged in a special way to keep safe the deposit of faith. . . . Discover your Christian roots, learn about the Church's history, deepen your knowledge of the spiritual heritage which has been passed on to you, follow in the footsteps of the witnesses and teachers who have gone before you! Only by staying faithful to God's commandments, to the Covenant which Christ sealed with his blood poured out on the Cross, will you be the apostles and witnesses of the new millennium.

Pope St. John Paul II (as the Popes that succeeded him) challenged youth not only to be 'salt of the earth' but also to hold on to their saltiness. John Paul II pleaded with the youth not to lose their identity as 'salt'; he encouraged them to keep growing in faith and in the love of God, and to learn from the wisdom and Tradition of the Church about the full meaning of the Good News of Jesus Christ. The Pope was inviting youth, as the Church invites you today, to live faithfully as disciples and bring out the 'flavor of life' in the lives of others by encouraging others in faith and friendship.

Catholic youth around the world continue to respond to this invitation. They take part in such parish and diocesan service projects as tutoring, feeding elderly and families who struggle to find the money to buy healthy foods, and joining with organizations to build homes. They quietly and generously help care for family members who are sick or weakened by old age. Each summer Catholic youth in high schools and parishes travel on mission trips both within and outside the country. In these and numerous other ways Catholic youth are living as Christ calls at home, at school, in the parish and in their community.

THINK, PAIR AND SHARE

- Think of a person whom you would describe as 'salt of the earth'. Talk with a partner about why you have chosen that person.

JOURNAL EXERCISE

- What are you doing that shows you are accepting Jesus' invitation to be 'salt of the earth'? What can you do more faithfully?
- Describe some practical things you can do to grow in your identity as 'salt of the earth'.

WORLD YOUTH DAY CELEBRATIONS IN MANILA, PHILIPPINES

The Church: light in the world

In many Hispanic cultures, teenage girls celebrate *La Quinceañera*, or *Fiesta de Quince*. The word 'quince' means 'fifteenth'. Family and friends come together to celebrate their daughter's or granddaughter's, sister's or niece's, or friend's fifteenth birthday—a birthday that marks a turning point on the journey from being a teenager to becoming a woman.

OPENING REFLECTION

- Reflect on a memorable celebration of a 'turning point' in your life.
- What did you celebrate? What did the celebration say about who you are?
- Whom did you invite to share in the celebration? Why?

DISCIPLESHIP: A LIFELONG CELEBRATION OF OUR LIFE IN CHRIST

Discipleship is a lifelong celebration of who we are and of who we are called to be. We began that celebration in Baptism. After we were baptized in water, anointed with sacred chrism and clothed in a white garment, we were given a candle lighted from the Easter candle. If you were baptized as an infant, the celebrant gave someone from your family the lighted candle, saying:

Parents and godparent (or godparents), this light is entrusted to you to be kept burning brightly. This child of yours has been enlightened by Christ. He (she) is to walk always as a child of the light. May he (she) keep the flame of faith alive in his (her) heart. When the Lord comes, may he (she) go out to meet him with all the saints in the heavenly kingdom.
> —*Rite of Baptism for One Child*, no. 100

Throughout his ministry on earth Jesus revealed the 'who', 'what', 'when', 'where', 'why' and 'how' of responding to his invitation, 'Follow me'. In addition to describing the vocation of disciples to be 'salt of the earth', Jesus used the image 'light' to describe the identity and mission of a disciple. He said:

'You are the light of the world. A city built on a hill cannot be hidden. No one after lighting a lamp puts it under a bushel basket, but on a lampstand, and it gives light to all in the house. In the same way, let your light shine before others, so that they may see your good works and give glory to your Father in heaven.'
> —Matthew 5:14–16

'I AM THE LIGHT OF THE WORLD' | CANDLES IN BREMEN CATHEDRAL, GERMANY

'I am the light of the world. Whoever follows me will never walk in darkness but will have the light of life.'

JOHN 8:12

We see the significance of this teaching in Matthew when we connect it to Jesus' description of himself in the Fourth Gospel. Admonishing the scribes and Pharisees, Jesus said:

'I am the light of the world. Whoever follows me will never walk in darkness but will have the light of life.'

—John 8:12

Jesus' whole life speaks to us of the commitment to be light in and for the world. Jesus, the Incarnate Son of God, embodied that commitment; he put flesh and blood on how we are to live out that commitment. In Jesus we see how we, his disciples, are to join with Christ and the Holy Spirit and preach the Gospel and work toward gathering all people into one family and one People of God.

TALK IT OVER

- ⊙ Talk about how God's invitation to live in loving relationship with him, and the human response to that invitation, are revealed in Jesus.

WHAT ABOUT YOU PERSONALLY?

- ⊙ When in your life did you experience God inviting you to be 'light' among your friends?
- ⊙ How did your response make a difference?

THE CHURCH: THE LIGHT OF NATIONS

Throughout *Credo* we have often referenced the *Dogmatic Constitution on the Church*, one of the major documents of Vatican II, which begins:

Christ is the light of the nations and consequently this holy synod, gathered together in the holy Spirit, ardently desires to bring to all humanity that light of Christ which is resplendent on the face of the church, by proclaiming his Gospel to every creature [see Mark 16:15].

—*Dogmatic Constitution on the Church*, no. 1

Jesus Christ, Incarnate Son of God, is 'the light of nations', who lived and walked among us two thousand years ago in the land of Palestine, an insignificant outpost of the Roman Empire. There, Jesus invited his first disciples, as he continues to invite his Church throughout the ages, to keep him, 'the true light' (John 1:9), 'the light of the world' and 'the light of life' (John 8:12), burning brightly in the world until he comes again in glory at the end of time.

The Holy Spirit, who is depicted in Sacred Scripture as 'fire', now fills and enlivens the People of God, whom he has gathered in the name of Christ, the Church. The fire of the Holy Spirit guides us and enflames us with zeal to proclaim the light of the Gospel. We let the light of our just and merciful and compassionate deeds shine before others, so that they may experience the love of God and give him glory.

THINK, PAIR AND SHARE

⊙ Talk with a partner about where you see members of your school community bringing the light of Christ to one another and to people outside of your school community.

⊙ How might your school let the light of its faith shine more brightly? Share your ideas.

JOURNAL EXERCISE

⊙ Write about how you can take part in the life of your parish and let the flame of your faith in Christ, the light of the world, shine more brightly.

Encountering the Light of Christ

CHRIST OF THE BREADLINES | FRITZ EICHENBERG

OPENING CONVERSATION

⊙ What first comes to mind when you hear the word 'bread'?

⊙ What other meanings might the word 'bread' have?

JESUS, THE BREAD OF LIFE

Jesus used the image 'bread' to identify himself. The Jews of Jesus' time would have understood the deeper meaning of this image. Jesus feeding the multitude with bread is so central to the Gospel that all four Gospel accounts describe this 'miracle' (see Matthew 14:13–21, 15:32–39; Mark 6:30–44, 8:1–10; Luke 9:10–17; John 6:5–59). In John's account, Jesus says to the crowd:

'Very truly, I tell you, you are looking for me, not because you saw signs, but because you ate your fill of the loaves. Do not work for the food that perishes, but for the food that endures for eternal life, which the Son of Man will give you. . . . I am the bread of life. Whoever comes to me will never be hungry, and whoever believes in me will never be thirsty.'

—John 6:26–27, 35

The phrase 'to break bread' means 'to share a meal'. Welcoming a friend or stranger into one's home was a sign of hospitality and inclusion in Jesus' time and culture, as it is in our time and culture. Jesus often broke and shared bread at a meal with his disciples and with the Pharisees, with Jews and Gentiles, and with 'saints and sinners'. At the Last Supper Jesus went beyond sharing simple bread. Jesus, the bread of life, took 'a loaf of bread, and when he had given thanks, he broke it and said, "This is my body that is for you. Do this in remembrance of me" ' (1 Corinthians 11:23–24).

- What does Jesus mean when he says, 'I am the bread of life'?
- Where do you see the Church being 'bread' for people'?
- How can you join with the Church—your family, your school, your parish—and be 'bread of life' for others?

BREAKING BREAD

Very early in the life of the apostolic Church the term **breaking of bread** pointed to the Last Supper and became synonymous with the Eucharist. We see this in Luke's account of the encounter of the two disciples with Jesus on the road to Emmaus.

Luke tells us that after the Crucifixion, burial and Resurrection of Jesus, two unnamed and dejected disciples from Emmaus were returning home. The risen Christ, whom they did not recognize, joined up with them, and the disciples expressed their disappointment over Jesus' death. In response, this 'stranger' helped them understand the teachings of Scripture about the Messiah. It was only when they came to Emmaus, and the risen Christ 'was at table with them, [and] he took bread, blessed and broke it, and gave it to them [were] their eyes . . . opened and they recognized him' (Luke 24:30–31). By accepting the invitation to 'break bread' with his disciples after the Resurrection, Jesus made it possible for them to recognize that he had risen, and so he transformed their lives.

Our risen Lord walks through life with us, too. True to his promise, 'I am with you always, to the end of the age' (Matthew 28:20), he is always with us on the road of our life. Christ is present with us 'in his word, in his Church's prayer . . . in the poor, the sick, and the imprisoned, in the sacraments of which he is the author . . .' (CCC, no. 1373). Wherever we encounter the Lord, the Bread of Life, he invites us, 'Follow me.' We follow Jesus when we faithfully strive to be bread to others. We follow Jesus when we show every person—family and friend, neighbor and stranger, and even our 'enemies'—to the table of our life and welcome them into the one family of God.

FAITH WORD

Breaking of Bread

Jesus used this rite, part of a Jewish meal, when as master of the table he blessed and distributed the bread, above all at the Last Supper. It is by this action that his disciples will recognize him after his Resurrection, and it is this expression that the first Christians will use to designate their Eucharistic assemblies; by doing so they signified that all who eat the one broken bread, Christ, enter into communion with him and form but one body in him. (CCC, no. 1329)

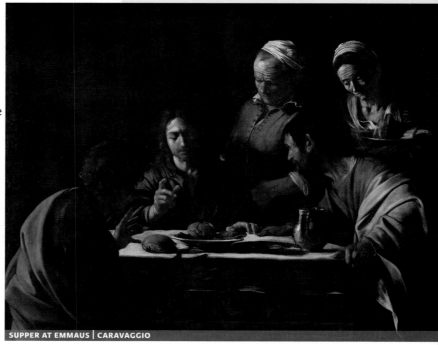

SUPPER AT EMMAUS | CARAVAGGIO

⊙ Imagine recognizing the face of Christ wherever you go today: what an extraordinarily joyful way to live life! What difference would this make in your day-to-day life?

FROM THE WISDOM OF THE CHURCH

The seven sacraments touch all the stages and all the important moments of Christian life [see St. Thomas Aquinas, *Summa Theologiae*, III, 65, I]: they give birth and increase, healing and mission to the Christian's life of faith.

—CCC, no. 1210

SACRAMENTS—ENCOUNTERS WITH CHRIST

The Emmaus story gives us insight into the presence of Christ with his Church when she gathers to listen to the Scripture and celebrate the sacraments. Jesus taught, '[W]here two or three are gathered in my name, I am there among them' (Matthew 18:20)—some translations have 'until the end of time'. For celebrating the sacraments is the work of the Body of Christ, the Church, of whom Christ is the head. Encountering Jesus Christ in and through the Church, in his presence in the Word and in the regular reception of the sacraments, is essential for members of the Church. When the faithful participate in the celebration of the Seven Sacraments, they are joined closer to Christ and his Church. They receive the graces of the sacraments to proclaim Christ, the Light of Nations and the Bread of Life, by the witness of their lives.

TALK IT OVER

⊙ Work with a partner and briefly review the Seven Sacraments.
⊙ Which of the Seven Sacraments have you received?
⊙ How do those sacraments help you live as a disciple of Jesus?

THE EUCHARIST: SACRAMENT OF SACRAMENTS

The Eucharist is the 'Sacrament' of sacraments to which all the other sacraments 'are ordered' (Pope Paul VI). The Eucharist 'is the sum and summary of our faith: "Our way of thinking is attuned to the Eucharist, and the Eucharist in turn confirms our way of thinking" ' (St. Irenaeus, quoted in CCC, no. 1327). The Eucharist is the 'heart and the summit of the Church's life' (CCC, no. 1407).

The Church offers us authentic worship in spirit and in truth when we unite ourselves with Christ's self-offering in the Mass. At every celebration of the Eucharist, Christ is present in the assembly, in the proclamation of the Word and in the person of the priest, who acts in Christ's name and person. But 'he is present . . . most *especially in the Eucharistic species* [Vatican II, *Constitution on the Sacred Liturgy*, no. 7]' (CCC, no. 1373), in his Body and Blood.

The great St. Augustine (354–430) taught: 'Go and live as what you have received, the body of Christ.' Receiving Holy Communion regularly deepens our friendship and union with Christ and his Church. The Eucharist strengthens us with the wisdom and compassion to see Christ in the poor and to reach out to them as he did. It offers us the grace to overcome temptations to sin; and we receive forgiveness for venial sins and the strength to avoid mortal sin. At the end of Mass, the priest or deacon sends us forth with these or similar words, 'Go in peace, glorifying the Lord by your life.' When we receive the Bread of Life, we receive the grace to live in the world as faithful disciples of him who is the 'bread of life' (John 6:48), 'the living bread that came down from heaven . . . [who gave his flesh] for the life of the world' (John 6:51).

THINK, PAIR AND SHARE

- ⊙ Talk with a partner about situations or people in whom you have encountered Christ.
- ⊙ Share how any of those experiences strengthened you to bring the Gospel to others by being 'bread' for them.

JOURNAL EXERCISE

- ⊙ Reflect on your life this past week. When might people have encountered Christ in you?
- ⊙ What can you do to let Christ, the 'light of the world' and the 'bread of life', shine on and nourish the lives of your family and friends?
- ⊙ Write your reflections in your journal. You might also make your reflections part of your daily examen, or examination of conscience.

JUDGE AND ACT

REFLECT ON WHAT YOU HAVE LEARNED IN THIS CHAPTER

As you come toward the end of this chapter, pause and reflect on what you have come to understand about your vocation as a disciple of Jesus Christ to be 'salt', 'light' and 'bread' for all people. Share your understanding of the teaching of the Catholic Church on these statements:

- ⊙ The Church in Christ is like a sacrament—a sign and instrument of communion with God and of unity among all peoples.
- ⊙ Jesus gave the Church the work of preaching and teaching the truth with love.
- ⊙ The Church has the mission to shine 'the light of Christ' in the world.

- ⊙ The Church exists for all people and is the means of salvation for all people.
- ⊙ Christ is present with us in the Church in his Word, in the sacraments and prayer, in the poor, the sick and the imprisoned.
- ⊙ The call to discipleship in Christ includes the vocation to cooperate with the Holy Spirit to transform the world in Christ.

OVER TO YOU

- ⊙ How has studying this chapter strengthened you to fulfil Jesus' command to his disciples to be 'salt of the earth' and 'light to the world'?
- ⊙ What wisdom did you receive for being 'bread' for others that nourished their faith in God?

LEARN BY EXAMPLE

Venerable Mother Henriette Delille, exemplar of love and service to neighbor

Henriette Delille is the first United States-born African American whose cause for canonization has been officially opened by the Catholic Church.

The Sisters of the Holy Family were 'dancing for joy' on March 29, 2010. They had just received 'the great and joyous news' that Pope Benedict XVI had approved the continuation of the canonization process of their African-American founder Mother Henriette Delille (1812–62). Sr. Evan Regina Martin, the congregational leader of the Sisters of the Holy Family, summed up the legacy of Mother Henriette: 'If you work with God's grace, this can come about. All of us are called to be saints through the practice of love and service to neighbor.' Sr. Evan's words echoed the Pope's description of Mother Henriette as a person of 'heroic virtue', which is another way of saying that she was indeed 'salt of the earth', 'light to the world'.

Henriette was a 'woman of color' who lived during the time of slavery and the Civil War. She was a light in the world during a time of darkness in the history of the United States of America. The designation 'woman of color' was used for a person of African-American descent who was not a slave and whose parents were of mixed races. This often resulted in 'women of color' being marginalized from the life of society and sometimes from full life in the Church. Henriette experienced this firsthand: first, by her mother, and then when the religious communities she sought to enter rejected her application.

Henriette's experience of the death of her second child was a 'light bulb moment' and, in the words of Charles Nolan, the archivist of the Archdiocese of New Orleans, 'she took a whole different course in life' and decided 'to live and die for God'. At first she worked alone, living the Gospel among the elderly, the sick and the poor. Soon Juliette Gaudin and Josephine Charles, two other 'women of color', joined with her. And in 1842, with Henriette, they founded the Congregation of the Sisters of the Holy Family. Together, they 'heroically' continued to educate slaves and free Blacks in New Orleans, even though, according to the Louisiana law of the time, they faced the possibility of life imprisonment or death for doing so.

Today, the Sisters of the Holy Family are an African-American Congregation who continue the ministries begun in the 1840s in New Orleans. The Sisters 'bring healing comfort to children, the elderly, the poor, and the powerless, especially those of African descent . . . confront racism, all forms of injustice, discrimination and economic oppression through evangelization and education . . . who are empowered by the Spirit of God and sustained by the Eucharist and the Word of God' (from Mission Statement and Spirituality Statement of the Sisters of the Holy Family). The Sisters are 'salt of the earth' and 'light to the world' in Louisiana, Texas, California and Washington D.C. in the United States, and in Belize, Central America and Nigeria in West Africa.

TALK IT OVER
- Name and describe the ways that God may be calling you personally and as a member of your school community to serve and stand up for justice.

RESPOND WITH FAMILY AND FRIENDS
- How are we working together to bring healing comfort to children, to the elderly, to the poor and to the powerless?
- How are we confronting racism, all forms of injustice, discrimination and economic oppression through evangelization and education?
- What might we do better to be 'salt', 'light' and 'bread' for others?

OVER TO YOU
- Think about your relationship with your local Church community. How does that relationship support you in using your gifts to the fullest to live as a disciple of Jesus Christ?
- How can you contribute to supporting your school and parish communities in fulfilling their calling to be 'salt of the earth' and 'light to the world'?

- How can your regular participation in the Eucharist help you to do that work?

WHAT WILL YOU DO NOW?
- What will you do now to bring the 'salt' and 'light' of justice and compassion to the world in which you are living?

LEARN BY HEART

'Where two or three are gathered in my name, I am there among them.'

MATTHEW 18:20

PRAYER REFLECTION

Pray the Sign of the Cross together.

LEADER
Lights and holds up high a candle, if fire laws and school policy permit; if not, holds up an unlighted candle and proclaims:

Christ, be our light. (*Pause*)

Places candle in a bowl of sand which has been put in a central place among the students and says,

Reflect on the presence of Jesus Christ in your life, especially as you have encountered him through the Church. Ask yourself: How is Christ speaking to me now? (*Pause*)

READER
The Holy Spirit inspires us and gives us the grace to fulfill our commitment to live as faithful disciples of Christ, the Light of Nations. After each petition, respond, 'Lord, hear our prayer'. We pray:
Come, Spirit of Christ, guide, teach and strengthen us to be lights in the world by living the Spiritual Works of Mercy. (*Pause*)
Christ, you are the Light of Nations, hear our prayer.
ALL
Lord, hear our prayer.

READER:
Give us the wisdom and courage to:
help those who sin to see the need for changing their ways; (*Pause*)
teach those who are seeking the truth; (*Pause*)
advise those who have doubts about your love; (*Pause*)
comfort those who are suffering; (*Pause*)
be patient with all people; (*Pause*)
forgive those who trespass against us; (*Pause*)
pray for the living and the dead. (*Pause*)
Christ, you are the Light of Nations, hear our prayer.

All pray the response and reflect on the ways the Spirit is calling us to live the Spiritual Works of Mercy.

READER
Come, Spirit of God, guide, teach and strengthen us to be lights in the world by living the Corporal Works of Mercy. (*Pause*)
Christ, you are the Light of Nations.
Give us the wisdom and courage to:
feed the hungry; (*Pause*)
give drink to the thirsty; (*Pause*)
shelter the homeless; (*Pause*)
clothe the naked; (*Pause*)
visit the sick and those in prison; (*Pause*)
bury the dead; (*Pause*)
give alms to the poor. (*Pause*)

All pray the response and reflect on the ways the Spirit is calling us to live the Corporal Works of Mercy.

LEADER
Let us pray. (*Pause*)

ALL
Lord God,
who sent your Son into the world as the true Light.
Pour out the Spirit he promised
to sow seeds of truth constantly in people's hearts,
to awaken in them obedience to the faith,
so that, being born to new life in Baptism,
all may become part of your one People.
We ask this in the name of our Lord Jesus Christ, your Son, who lives and reigns with you in the unity of the Holy Spirit, one God for ever and ever. Amen.

Pray the Sign of the Cross together.

CATHOLIC PRAYERS, DEVOTIONS AND PRACTICES

SIGN OF THE CROSS

In the name of the Father,
and of the Son,
and of the Holy Spirit. Amen.

OUR FATHER (LORD'S PRAYER)

Our Father who art in heaven,
hallowed be thy name;
thy kingdom come,
thy will be done
on earth as it is in heaven.
Give us this day our daily bread,
and forgive us our trespasses,
as we forgive those who trespass against us;
and lead us not into temptation,
but deliver us from evil. Amen.

GLORY PRAYER (DOXOLOGY)

Glory be to the Father,
and to the Son,
and to the Holy Spirit;
as it was in the beginning
is now, and ever shall be,
world without end. Amen.

PRAYER TO THE HOLY SPIRIT

Come, Holy Spirit, fill the hearts of your faithful.
Enkindle in them the fire of your love.
Send forth your Spirit and they shall be created.
And you shall renew the face of the earth.

O God, by the light of the Holy Spirit you have
    taught the hearts of your faithful.
In the same Spirit, help us to know what is truly
    right and always to rejoice in your consolation.
We ask this through Christ, our Lord. Amen.

HAIL MARY

Hail Mary, full of grace,
the Lord is with thee.
Blessed art thou among women
and blessed is the fruit of thy womb, Jesus.
Holy Mary, Mother of God,

pray for us sinners,
now and at the hour of our death. Amen.

APOSTLES' CREED

I believe in God,
the Father almighty,
Creator of heaven and earth,
and in Jesus Christ, his only Son, our Lord,
who was conceived by the Holy Spirit,
born of the Virgin Mary,
suffered under Pontius Pilate,
was crucified, died, and was buried;
he descended into hell;
on the third day he rose again from the dead;
he ascended into heaven,
and is seated at the right hand of God the Father
    almighty,
from there he will come to judge the living and
    the dead.

I believe in the Holy Spirit,
the holy catholic Church,
the communion of saints,
the forgiveness of sins,
the resurrection of the body,
and life everlasting. Amen.

NICENE CREED

I believe in one God,
the Father almighty,
maker of heaven and earth,
of all things visible and invisible.

I believe in one Lord Jesus Christ,
the Only Begotten Son of God,
born of the Father before all ages.
God from God, Light from Light,
true God from true God,
begotten, not made, consubstantial with the
    Father;
through him all things were made.
For us men and for our salvation
he came down from heaven,

and by the Holy Spirit was incarnate of the Virgin
    Mary,
and became man.

For our sake he was crucified under Pontius Pilate,
he suffered death and was buried,
and rose again on the third day
in accordance with the Scriptures.
He ascended into heaven
and is seated at the right hand of the Father.
He will come again in glory
to judge the living and the dead,
and his kingdom will have no end.

I believe in the Holy Spirit, the Lord, the giver of life,
who proceeds from the Father and the Son,
who with the Father and the Son is adored and
    glorified,
who has spoken through the prophets.

I believe in one, holy, catholic and apostolic
    Church.
I confess one Baptism for the forgiveness of sins
and I look forward to the resurrection of the dead
and the life of the world to come. Amen.

JESUS PRAYER
Lord Jesus Christ, Son of God, have mercy on me,
    a sinner. Amen.

ACT OF FAITH
O my God, I firmly believe that you are one God
in three divine Persons, Father, Son, and Holy
Spirit. I believe that your divine Son became man
and died for our sins and that he will come to
judge the living and the dead. I believe these and
all the truths which the Holy Catholic Church
teaches because you have revealed them, who
are eternal truth and wisdom, who can neither
deceive nor be deceived. In this faith I intend to
live and die. Amen.

ACT OF HOPE
O Lord God, I hope by your grace for the pardon
of all my sins and after life here to gain eternal
happiness because you have promised it, who are
infinitely powerful, faithful, kind, and merciful. In
this hope I intend to live and die. Amen.

ACT OF LOVE
O Lord God, I love you above all things and I love
my neighbor for your sake because you are the
highest, infinite and perfect good, worthy of all
my love. In this love I intend to live and die. Amen.

PRAYER FOR VOCATIONS
Loving Mother, Our Lady of Guadalupe,
you asked Juan Diego to help build a Church that
    would serve a new people in a new land.
You left your image upon his cloak as a visible
    sign of your love for us,
so that we may come to believe in your Son, Jesus
    the Christ.
Our Lady of Guadalupe and St. Juan Diego,
help us respond to God's call to build your Son's
    Church today.
Help us recognize our personal vocation to serve
    God as married or single persons or priests,
    brothers or sisters as our way to help extend
    the Reign of God here on earth.
Help us pay attention to the promptings of the
    Holy Spirit.
May all of us have the courage of Juan Diego to
    say 'Yes' to our personal call!
May we encourage one another to follow Jesus,
    no matter where that path takes us. Amen.

Daily Prayers

Morning Prayer
CANTICLE OF ZECHARIAH (THE BENEDICTUS)
(based on Luke 1:67–79)
Blessed be the Lord, the God of Israel;
for he has come to his people and set them free.
He has raised up for us a mighty Savior,
born of the House of his servant David.
Through his prophets he promised of old
    that he would save us from our enemies,
    from the hands of all who hate us.
He promised to show mercy to our fathers
and to remember his holy covenant.
This was the oath he swore to our father Abraham:
to set us free from the hand of our enemies,
free to worship him without fear,
holy and righteous in his sight
    all the days of our life.

You, my child, shall be called the prophet of the
Most High,
for you will go before the Lord to prepare his way,
to give his people knowledge of salvation
by the forgiveness of their sins.
In the tender compassion of our God
the dawn from on high shall break upon us,
to shine on those who dwell in darkness and the
shadow of death,
and to guide our feet into the way of peace.
Amen.

MORNING OFFERING
O Jesus, through the Immaculate Heart of Mary,
I offer you my prayers, works, joys and sufferings
of this day
for all the intentions of your Sacred Heart,
in union with the Holy Sacrifice of the Mass
throughout the world,
for the salvation of souls, the reparation for sins,
the reunion of all Christians,
and in particular for the intentions of the Holy
Father this month. Amen.

Evening Prayer
CANTICLE OF MARY (THE *MAGNIFICAT*)
My soul proclaims the greatness of the Lord;
my spirit rejoices in God my savior
for he has looked with favor on his lowly servant.
From this day all generations will call me blessed:
the Almighty has done great things for me
and holy is his name.
He has mercy on those who fear him
in every generation.
He has shown the strength of his arm,
and has scattered the proud in their conceit.
He has cast down the mighty from their thrones,
and has lifted up the lowly.
He has filled the hungry with good things,
and the rich he has sent away empty.
He has come to the help of his servant Israel
for he has remembered his promise of mercy,
the promise he made to our fathers,
to Abraham and his children forever. Amen.

GRACE BEFORE MEALS
Bless us, O Lord, and these your gifts,
which we are about to receive from your bounty,
through Christ our Lord. Amen.

GRACE AFTER MEALS
We give you thanks for all your benefits, almighty
God, who lives and reigns forever.
And may the souls of the faithful departed,
through the mercy of God, rest in peace.
Amen.

PRAYER OF ST. FRANCIS (PEACE PRAYER)
Lord, make me an instrument of your peace:
where there is hatred, let me sow love;
where there is injury, pardon;
where there is doubt, faith;
where there is despair, hope;
where there is darkness, light;
where there is sadness, joy.

O divine Master, grant that I may not so much seek
to be consoled as to console,
to be understood, as to understand,
to be loved as to love.

For it is in giving that we receive,
it is in pardoning that we are pardoned,
it is in dying that we are born to eternal life.
Amen.

Contrition and Sorrow
CONFITEOR
I confess to almighty God
and to you, my brothers and sisters,
that I have greatly sinned,
in my thoughts and in my words,
in what I have done and in what I have failed to
do,
through my fault, through my fault,
through my most grievous fault;
therefore I ask blessed Mary ever-Virgin,
all the Angels and Saints,
and you, my brothers and sisters,
to pray for me to the Lord our God. Amen.

ACT OF CONTRITION
O my God, I am heartily sorry for having offended
you, and I detest all my sins because of your
just punishments, but most of all because
they offend you, my God, who are all good and
deserving of all my love. I firmly resolve with the
help of your grace to sin no more and to avoid
the near occasion of sin. Amen.

Prayers before the Holy Eucharist

THE DIVINE PRAISES

Blessed be God.
Blessed be his holy name.
Blessed be Jesus Christ, true God and true man.
Blessed be the name of Jesus.
Blessed be his most Sacred Heart.
Blessed be his most precious Blood.
Blessed be Jesus in the most holy Sacrament of the altar.
Blessed be the Holy Spirit, the Paraclete.
Blessed be the great Mother of God, Mary most holy.
Blessed be her holy and Immaculate Conception.
Blessed be her glorious Assumption.
Blessed be the name of Mary, Virgin and Mother.
Blessed be St. Joseph, her most chaste spouse.
Blessed be God in his angels and in his saints.

ANIMA CHRISTI (SOUL OF CHRIST)

Soul of Christ, sanctify me.
Body of Christ, save me.
Blood of Christ, inebriate me.
Water from the side of Christ, wash me.
Passion of Christ, strengthen me.
O good Jesus, hear me.
Within your wounds hide me.
Permit me not to be separated from you.
From the malicious enemy defend me.
In the hour of my death call me.
And bid me come to you,
that with your saints I may praise you
forever and ever. Amen.

AN ACT OF SPIRITUAL COMMUNION

My Jesus, I believe that you are present in the Most Blessed Sacrament.
I love you above all things, and I desire to receive you into my soul.
Since I cannot at this moment receive you sacramentally, come at least spiritually into my heart.
I embrace you as if you were already there and unite myself wholly to you.
Never permit me to be separated from you. Amen.

Prayers to Mary, Mother of God

ANGELUS

Verse:	The Angel of the Lord declared unto Mary.
Response:	And she conceived of the Holy Spirit.

Hail Mary, full of grace,
the Lord is with thee.
Blessed art thou among women
and blessed is the fruit of thy womb, Jesus.
Holy Mary, Mother of God,
pray for us sinners,
now and at the hour of our death. Amen.

Verse:	Behold the handmaid of the Lord.
Response:	Be it done unto me according to your Word.

Hail Mary. . . .

Verse:	And the Word was made flesh,
Response:	And dwelt among us.

Hail Mary. . . .

Verse:	Pray for us, O holy Mother of God,
Response:	That we may be made worthy of the promises of Christ.

Let us pray. Pour forth, we beseech you, O Lord, your grace into our hearts: that we, to whom the Incarnation of Christ your Son was made known by the message of an Angel, may by his Passion and Cross be brought to the glory of his Resurrection. Through the same Christ our Lord. Amen.

MEMORARE

Remember, O most gracious Virgin Mary, that never was it known that anyone who fled to your protection, implored your help, or sought your intercession, was left unaided. Inspired by this confidence, I fly unto you, O Virgin of virgins, my mother; to you do I come, before you I stand, sinful and sorrowful. O Mother of the Word Incarnate, despise not my petitions, but in your mercy hear and answer me. Amen.

REGINA CAELI (QUEEN OF HEAVEN)

Queen of Heaven, rejoice, alleluia:
for the Son you were privileged to bear, alleluia,
is risen as he said, alleluia.
Pray for us to God, alleluia.

Verse: Rejoice and be glad, O Virgin Mary, Alleluia!

Response: For the Lord is truly risen, Alleluia.

Let us pray. O God, who gave joy to the world through the resurrection of your Son, our Lord Jesus Christ, grant, we beseech you, that through the intercession of the Virgin Mary, his Mother, we may obtain the joys of everlasting life. Through the same Christ our Lord. Amen.

SALVE, REGINA (HAIL, HOLY QUEEN)

Hail, holy Queen, Mother of mercy: Hail, our life, our sweetness and our hope. To you do we cry, poor banished children of Eve. To you do we send up our sighs, mourning and weeping in this valley of tears. Turn then, most gracious advocate, your eyes of mercy toward us; and after this our exile show unto us the blessed fruit of your womb, Jesus. O clement, O loving, O sweet Virgin Mary. Amen.

PRAYER TO OUR LADY OF GUADALUPE

God of power and mercy,
you blessed the Americas at Tepeyac
with the presence of the Virgin Mary of
    Guadalupe.
May her prayers help all men and women
to accept each other as brothers and sisters.
Through your justice present in our hearts
may your peace reign in the world. Amen.

THE ROSARY

THE JOYFUL MYSTERIES: Traditionally prayed on Mondays and Saturdays and on Sundays of the Christmas Season.

1. The Annunciation (Luke 1:26–38)
2. The Visitation (Luke 2:39–56)
3. The Nativity (Luke 2:1–20)
4. The Presentation in the Temple (Luke 2:22–38)
5. The Finding of Jesus after Three Days in the Temple (Luke 2:41–50)

THE LUMINOUS MYSTERIES: Traditionally prayed on Thursdays.

1. The Baptism at the Jordan (Matthew 3:13–17)
2. The Miracle at Cana (John 2:1–11)
3. The Proclamation of the Kingdom and the Call to Conversion (Mark 1:14–15)

4. The Transfiguration (Matthew 17:1–13)
5. The Institution of the Eucharist (Matthew 26:26–28)

THE SORROWFUL MYSTERIES: Traditionally prayed on Tuesdays and Fridays and on the Sundays of Lent.

1. The Agony in the Garden (Matthew 26:36–56)
2. The Scourging at the Pillar (John 18:28–19:1)
3. The Crowning with Thorns (John 19:2–3)
4. The Carrying of the Cross (John 19:17)
5. The Crucifixion and Death (John 19:18–30)

THE GLORIOUS MYSTERIES: Traditionally prayed on Wednesdays and Sundays, except on the Sundays of Christmas and Lent.

1. The Resurrection (Matthew 28:1–8)
2. The Ascension (Matthew 28:16–20/Acts 1:1–11)
3. The Descent of the Holy Spirit at Pentecost (Acts 2:1–13)
4. The Assumption of Mary (See CCC, no. 966)
5. The Crowning of the Blessed Virgin as Queen of Heaven and Earth (See CCC, no. 966)

How to pray the Rosary

1. Pray the *Sign of the Cross* and pray the *Apostles' Creed* while holding the crucifix.
2. Touch the first bead after the crucifix and pray the *Our Father*, pray the *Hail Mary* on each of the next three beads, and pray the *Glory Prayer* on the next bead.
3. Go to the main part of your rosary. Say the name of the Mystery and quietly reflect on the meaning of the events of that Mystery. Pray the *Our Father*, and then, fingering each of the ten beads, pray ten *Hail Marys*. Then touch the next bead and pray the *Glory Prayer*. (Repeat the process for the next four decades.)
4. Pray the *Salve Regina (Hail, Holy Queen)* and conclude by praying:

Verse: Pray for us, O holy Mother of God.

Response: That we may be made worthy of the promises of Christ.

Let us pray. O God, whose only-begotten

Son, by his life, death and Resurrection, has purchased for us the rewards of eternal life, grant, we beseech you, that meditating on these mysteries of the most holy rosary of the Blessed Virgin Mary, we may imitate what they contain and obtain what they promise, through the same Christ our Lord. Amen.

5. Conclude by praying the *Sign of the Cross*.

STATIONS, OR WAY, OF THE CROSS

The tradition of praying the Stations, or Way, of the Cross dates from the fourteenth century. The tradition, which is attributed to the Franciscans, came about to satisfy the desire of Christians who were unable to make a pilgrimage to Jerusalem. The traditional Stations of the Cross are:

FIRST STATION: Jesus is condemned to death
SECOND STATION: Jesus is made to carry his Cross
THIRD STATION: Jesus falls the first time
FOURTH STATION: Jesus meets his mother
FIFTH STATION: Simon helps Jesus to carry his Cross
SIXTH STATION: Veronica wipes the face of Jesus
SEVENTH STATION: Jesus falls the second time
EIGHTH STATION: Jesus meets the women of Jerusalem
NINTH STATION: Jesus falls the third time
TENTH STATION: Jesus is stripped of his garments
ELEVENTH STATION: Jesus is nailed to the Cross
TWELFTH STATION: Jesus dies on the Cross
THIRTEENTH STATION: Jesus is taken down from the Cross
FOURTEENTH STATION: Jesus is laid in the tomb.

In 1991 Pope St. John Paul II gave the Church a scriptural version of the Stations. The individual names given to these stations are:

FIRST STATION: Jesus in the Garden of Gethsemane—Matthew 25:36–41
SECOND STATION: Jesus, Betrayed by Judas, Is Arrested—Mark 14:43–46
THIRD STATION: Jesus Is Condemned by the Sanhedrin—Luke 22:66–71
FOURTH STATION: Jesus Is Denied by Peter—Matthew 26:69–75

FIFTH STATION: Jesus Is Judged by Pilate—Mark 15:1–5, 15
SIXTH STATION: Jesus Is Scourged and Crowned with Thorns—John 19:1–3
SEVENTH STATION: Jesus Bears the Cross—John 19:6, 15–17
EIGHTH STATION: Jesus Is Helped by Simon the Cyrenian to Carry the Cross—Mark 15:21
NINTH STATION: Jesus Meets the Women of Jerusalem—Luke 23:27–31
TENTH STATION: Jesus Is Crucified—Luke 23:33–34
ELEVENTH STATION: Jesus Promises His Kingdom to the Good Thief—Luke 23:39–43
TWELFTH STATION: Jesus Speaks to His Mother and the Disciple—John 19:25–27
THIRTEENTH STATION: Jesus Dies on the Cross—Luke 23:44–46
FOURTEENTH STATION: Jesus Is Placed in the Tomb—Matthew 27:57–60

Some parishes conclude with a prayerful meditation on the Resurrection.

The Way of Jesus: Catholic Practices

THE SEVEN SACRAMENTS
Sacraments of Christian Initiation
BAPTISM: The Sacrament by which we are freed from all sin and are endowed with the gift of divine life, are made members of the Church, and are called to holiness and mission.
CONFIRMATION: The Sacrament that completes the grace of Baptism by a special outpouring of the Gifts of the Holy Spirit, which seals and confirms the baptized in union with Christ and calls them to a greater participation in the worship and apostolic life of the Church.
EUCHARIST: The ritual, sacramental action of thanksgiving to God which constitutes the principal Christian liturgical celebration of and communion in the Paschal Mystery of Christ. This liturgical action is also traditionally known as the Holy Sacrifice of the Mass.

Sacraments of Healing
PENANCE AND RECONCILIATION: The sacrament in which sins committed after Baptism are forgiven,

which results in reconciliation with God and the Church. This sacrament is also called the Sacrament of Confession.

ANOINTING OF THE SICK: This sacrament is given to a person who is seriously ill or in danger of death or old age which strengthens the person with the special graces of healing and comfort and courage.

Sacraments at the Service of Communion

MARRIAGE (MATRIMONY): The sacrament in which a baptized man and a baptized woman enter the covenant partnership of the whole of life that by its nature is ordered toward the good of the spouses and the procreation and education of offspring.

HOLY ORDERS: The sacrament in which a bishop ordains a baptized man to be conformed to Jesus Christ by grace, to service and leadership in the Church as a bishop, priest, or deacon.

GIFTS OF THE HOLY SPIRIT

The seven gifts of the Holy Spirit are permanent dispositions which move us to respond to the guidance of the Spirit. The traditional list of these gifts is derived from Isaiah 11:1–3.

WISDOM: A spiritual gift which enables one to know the purpose and plan of God.

UNDERSTANDING: This gift stimulates us to work on knowing ourselves as part of our growth in knowing God.

COUNSEL (RIGHT JUDGMENT): This gift guides us to follow the teaching the Holy Spirit gives us about our moral life and the training of our conscience.

FORTITUDE (COURAGE): This gift strengthens us to choose courageously and firmly the good, despite difficulty, and also to persevere in doing what is right, despite temptation, fear or persecution.

KNOWLEDGE: This gift directs us to a contemplation, or thoughtful reflection, on the mystery of God and the mysteries of the Catholic faith.

PIETY (REVERENCE): This gift strengthens us to grow in respect for the Holy Trinity, for the Father who created us, for Jesus who saved us, and for the Holy Spirit who is sanctifying us.

FEAR OF THE LORD (WONDER AND AWE): This gift infuses honesty in our relationship with God.

FRUITS OF THE HOLY SPIRIT

The fruits of the Holy Spirit are the perfections that the Holy Spirit forms in us as the 'first fruits' of eternal glory. The Tradition of the Church lists twelve fruits of the Holy Spirit. They are: love, joy, peace, patience, kindness, goodness, generosity, gentleness, faithfulness, modesty, self-control and chastity.

VIRTUES

The Theological Virtues

Gifts from God that enable us to choose to and to live in right relationship with the Holy Trinity.

FAITH: The virtue by which the believer gives personal adherence to God (who invites his or her response) and freely assents to the whole truth that God revealed.

HOPE: The virtue through which a person both desires and expects the fulfillment of God's promises of things to come.

CHARITY (LOVE): The virtue by which we give love to God for his own sake and love to our neighbor on account of God.

The Cardinal Moral Virtues

The four moral virtues on which all other human virtues hinge.

FORTITUDE: The virtue by which one courageously and firmly chooses the good despite difficulty and also perseveres in doing what is right despite temptation.

JUSTICE: The virtue by which one is able to give God and neighbor what is due to them.

PRUDENCE: The virtue by which one knows the true good in every circumstance and chooses the right means to reach that end.

TEMPERANCE: The virtue by which one moderates the desire for the attainment of and pleasure in earthly goods.

THE NEW LAW

The Great, or Greatest, Commandment

'You shall love the Lord your God with all your heart, and with all your soul, and with all your mind. . . . You shall love your neighbor as yourself.'

Matthew 22:37, 39, based on
Deuteronomy 6:5 and Leviticus 19:18

THE NEW COMMANDMENT OF JESUS

'Love one another. Just as I have loved you, you also should love one another.' John 13:34

THE BEATITUDES

Blessed are the poor in spirit, for theirs is the kingdom of heaven.

Blessed are those who mourn, for they will be comforted.

Blessed are the meek, for they will inherit the earth.

Blessed are those who hunger and thirst for righteousness, for they will be filled.

Blessed are the merciful, for they will receive mercy.

Blessed are the pure in heart, for they will see God.

Blessed are the peacemakers, for they shall be called children of God.

Blessed are those who are persecuted for righteousness' sake, for theirs is the kingdom of heaven.

Blessed are you when people revile you and persecute you and utter all kinds of evil against you falsely on my account. Rejoice and be glad, for your reward is great in heaven, for in the same way they persecuted the prophets who were before you.

– Matthew 5:3–11

SPIRITUAL WORKS OF MERCY

Admonish and help those who sin.
Teach those who are ignorant.
Advise those who have doubts.
Comfort those who suffer.
Be patient with all people.
Forgive those who trespass against you.
Pray for the living and the dead.

CORPORAL WORKS OF MERCY

Feed the hungry.
Give drink to the thirsty.
Shelter the homeless.
Clothe the naked.
Visit the sick and those in prison.
Bury the dead.
Give alms to the poor.

THE TEN COMMANDMENTS, OR THE DECALOGUE

Traditional Catechetical Formula

FIRST: I am the LORD your God: you shall not have strange gods before me.

SECOND: You shall not take the name of the LORD your God in vain.

THIRD: Remember to keep holy the LORD's Day.

FOURTH: Honor your father and mother.

FIFTH: You shall not kill.

SIXTH: You shall not commit adultery.

SEVENTH: You shall not steal.

EIGHTH: You shall not bear false witness against your neighbor.

NINTH: You shall not covet your neighbor's wife.

TENTH: You shall not covet your neighbor's goods.

Scriptural Formula

FIRST: I am the LORD your God, who brought you out of the land of Egypt, out of the house of slavery; you shall have no other gods before me.

SECOND: You shall not make wrongful use of the name of the LORD your God, for the LORD will not acquit anyone who misuses his name.

THIRD: Observe the sabbath day to keep it holy. . . .

FOURTH: Honor your father and your mother. . . .

FIFTH: You shall not murder.

SIXTH: Neither shall you commit adultery.

SEVENTH: Neither shall you steal.

EIGHTH: Neither shall you bear false witness against your neighbour.

NINTH: Neither shall you covet your neighbor's wife.

TENTH: Neither shall you desire . . . anything that belongs to your neighbor.

– From Deuteronomy 5:6–21

PRECEPTS OF THE CHURCH

The Precepts are positive laws made by the Church that name the minimum in prayer and moral effort for the growth of the faithful in their love of God and neighbor.

FIRST PRECEPT: Participate in Mass on Sundays and on holy days of obligation and rest from work that impedes keeping these days holy.

SECOND PRECEPT: Confess sins at least once a year.

THIRD PRECEPT: Receive the Sacrament of the Eucharist at least during the Easter Season.

FOURTH PRECEPT: Fast and abstain on the days established by the Church.

FIFTH PRECEPT: Provide for the materials of the Church according to one's ability.

SOCIAL DOCTRINE OF THE CHURCH

These seven key principles are at the foundation of the social doctrine, or social teaching, of the Catholic Church:

1. *Life and dignity of the human person.* Human life is sacred and the dignity of the human person is the foundation of the moral life of individuals and of society.

2. *Call to family, community and participation.* The human person is social by nature and has the right to participate in family life and in the life of society.

3. *Rights and responsibilities.* The human person has the fundamental right to life and to the basic necessities that support life and human decency.

4. *Option for the poor and the vulnerable.* The Gospel commands us 'to put the needs of the poor and the vulnerable first'.

5. *Dignity of work and workers.* Work is a form of participating in God's work of Creation. 'The economy must serve people and not the other way around.'

6. *Solidarity.* God is the Creator of all people. 'We are one human family whatever our national, racial, ethnic, economic and ideological differences.'

7. *Care for God's creation.* Care of the environment is a divine command and a requirement of our faith.

FAITH GLOSSARY

Abbreviations:
CCC = *Catechism of the Catholic Church*
USCCA = *United States Catholic Catechism for*

A–B

actual grace(s): *see* **grace**.

apostasy: The total repudiation of the Christian faith. (CCC, Glossary)

Apostle(s): 'The title traditionally given to those specially chosen by Jesus to preach the Gospel and to whom he entrusted responsibility for guiding the early Church' (USCCA, 504). The names of the first Apostles, also called the Twelve, are Peter, Andrew, James, John, Thomas, James, Philip, Bartholomew (also known as Nathaniel), Matthew, Judas, Simon, and Jude (also known as Thaddeus). After the Ascension of Jesus, Matthias, who replaced Judas Iscariot, and Paul were also called to be Apostles.

apostolate: The activity of the Christian which fulfills the apostolic nature of the whole Church by working to extend the reign of Christ to the entire world. (CCC, Glossary)

apostolic constitution: The highest form of official document or teaching letter of the Pope addressed to the whole Church.

apostolic exhortation: A document written by the Pope to the Church encouraging its people to take some particular action.

apostolic succession: The passing on of the office of bishop from the Apostles to bishops, and from them to other bishops down each generation, by means of ordination. This office includes the sanctifying, teaching, and governing roles within the Church. (USCCA, 504)

Apostolic Tradition: Jesus entrusted his revelation and teachings to his Apostles. They passed it on by their preaching and witness.

Along with others, they began writing the message down in what became the New Testament. (USCCA, 504)

archbishop: A bishop appointed by the Pope to preside over an archdiocese. The archbishop, who has the title Metropolitan, has limited authority over the bishops, also called suffragan bishops, of the dioceses that belong to an archdiocese.

archdiocese: An archdiocese is a particular large or significant diocese over which an archbishop presides.

Ascension: The entry of Jesus' humanity into divine glory to be at the right hand of the Father; traditionally, this occurred forty days after Jesus' Resurrection. (USCCA, 504)

Assumption: The dogma that when the Blessed Virgin Mary's earthly life was finished, because she was sinless, she was kept from corruption and taken soul and body into heavenly glory. (USCCA, 505)

atonement: By his suffering and death on the Cross, Jesus freed us from our sins and brought about our reconciliation with God the Father. (USCCA, 505)

bishop: The highest of the three degrees of Holy Orders; a bishop is normally ordained to teach, to sanctify, and to govern a diocese or local church; a bishop is a successor of the Apostles. (USCCA, 505)

Body of Christ: A name for the Holy Eucharist. It is also a title for the Church, with Christ as her head, sometimes referred to as the Mystical Body of Christ. The Holy Spirit provides the members with the gifts needed to live as Christ's Body. (USCCA, 505)

breaking of bread: Jesus used this rite, part of a Jewish meal, when as master of the table he blessed and distributed the bread, above all at the Last Supper. It is by this action that his disciples will recognize him after his Resurrection, and it is this expression that the first Christians will use to designate their Eucharistic assemblies; by doing so they signified that all who eat the one broken bread, Christ, enter into communion with him and form but one body in him. (CCC, no. 1329)

C

canon of Scripture: 'The Church's complete list of sacred books of the Bible' (CCC, Glossary). The Catholic canon lists seventy-three books—forty-six in the Old Testament and twenty-seven in the New Testament.

canonization: The name for the solemn declaration by the pope that a deceased member of the faithful may be proposed as a model and intercessor to the Christian faithful and venerated as a saint, on the basis of the fact that the person lived a life of heroic virtue or remained faithful to God through martyrdom. (USCCA, 506)

catholic: One of the four marks or notes of the Church, taken from the Nicene Creed. The Church is catholic or universal both because she possesses the fullness of Christ's presence and the means of salvation, and because she has been sent out by Christ on a mission to the whole of the human race. (CCC, Glossary)

celibacy: The state or condition of those who have chosen to remain unmarried for the sake of the kingdom of heaven in order to give themselves entirely to God and to the service of his people. In the Latin Church, celibacy is obligatory for bishops and priests. In some Eastern Churches, celibacy is a prerequisite for the ordination only of bishops; priests may not marry after they have been ordained. (CCC, Glossary)

charism: A specific gift or grace of the Holy Spirit which directly or indirectly benefits the Church, given in order to help a person live out the Christian life, or to serve the common good in building up the Church. (CCC, Glossary)

charity (love): The Theological Virtue by which we give love to God for his own sake and love to our neighbor on account of God. (USCCA, 506) *See also* **faith; hope**.

chrism, sacred: Perfumed oil consecrated by a bishop at the annual Mass of the Chrism during Holy Week; it is used in those Sacraments which confer a permanent mark or character—Baptism, Confirmation, and Holy Orders. (USCCA, 506)

Church: The name given the 'convocation' or 'assembly' of the People God has called together from 'the ends of the earth.' In Christian usage, the word 'Church' has three inseparable meanings: the People that God gathers in the whole world; the particular or local church (diocese); and the liturgical (above all Eucharistic) assembly. The Church draws her life from the Word and the Body of Christ, and so herself becomes Christ's Body. In the Creed, the sole Church of Christ is professed to be one, holy, catholic, and apostolic. (CCC, Glossary)

college of bishops/collegiality: All the bishops of the Church with the Pope at their head form a single 'college,' which succeeds in every generation the 'college' of the Twelve Apostles, with Peter at their head, which Christ instituted as the foundation of the Church. This college of bishops together with, but never without, the Pope has supreme and full authority over the universal Church. (CCC, Glossary)

communion: The word 'communion' comes from the Latin *communio*, meaning 'one with each other' or 'sharing together'. The Church uses the word 'communion' to describe 'our fellowship and union with Jesus and other baptized Christians in the Church, which has its source and summit in the celebration of the Eucharist. In this sense, Church as communion is the deepest vocation of the Church' (CCC, Glossary).

common priesthood of the faithful: *see* **priesthood**.

Communion of the Saints: This refers to members of the Church through all time—those now in the Church and those members who have already gone before us and are either in Purgatory or heaven. (USCCA, 507)

compassion: In the Bible, the English word 'compassion' is a translation of a Greek word meaning 'womb' and of a Hebrew word that is also translated as 'mercy'. Compassion is the quality of a person who so closely identifies with the suffering and condition of another person that the suffering of the other becomes their own, 'enters their womb'. The Latin roots of the English word 'compassion' are *cum* and *passio*, which mean 'suffering with'.

conscience: 'Moral conscience, present at the heart of the person, enjoins [the person] at the appropriate moment to do good and to avoid evil. It also judges particular choices, approving those that are good and denouncing those that are evil.' When we listen to our conscience, we 'can hear God speaking'. (*See* CCC, no. 1777)

consecrated life: A permanent state of life recognized by the Church, entered freely in response to the call of Christ to perfection, and characterized by the profession of the evangelical counsels of poverty, chastity, and obedience. (CCC, Glossary)

covenant: A solemn agreement made between human beings or between God and a human being, involving mutual commitments or guarantees. The Bible refers to God's covenants with Noah, Abraham, and Moses as the leader of the chosen people, Israel. (CCC, Glossary)

conversion: Conversion means turning around one's life toward God and trying 'to live holier lives according to the Gospel' (Vatican II, *Decree on Ecumenism*, quoted in CCC, no. 821).

creation: The act by which the eternal God gave a beginning to all that exists outside of himself.

Creation also refers to the created universe or totality of what exists, as often expressed by the formula 'the heavens and the earth'. (CCC, Glossary)

Creator: Title for God; God alone is the 'Creator'. God—Father, Son and Holy Spirit—out of love for us created the world out of nothing, wanting to share divine life and love with us.

creed: A brief, normative summary statement or profession of Christian faith, for example, the Apostles' Creed, the Nicene Creed. The word 'Creed' comes from the Latin *Credo*, meaning 'I believe,' with which the Creed begins. Creeds are also called Symbols of Faith. (CCC, Glossary)

D–E

deacons: Men ordained by the bishop to serve. They receive the Sacrament of Holy Orders but not the ministerial priesthood. Through ordination, the deacon is conformed to the Christ who said he came to serve, not to be served. Deacons in the Latin Church may baptize, read the Gospel, preach the homily, assist the bishop or priest in the celebration of the Eucharist, assist at and bless marriages, and preside at funerals. They dedicate themselves to charitable endeavors, which was their ministerial role in New Testament times. (USCCA, 509)

Deposit of Faith: The heritage of faith contained in Sacred Scripture and Tradition, handed on in the Church from the time of the Apostles, from which the Magisterium draws all that it proposes for belief as divinely revealed. (USCCA, 509)

diocese: A 'particular church,' a community of the faithful in communion of faith and sacraments whose bishop has been ordained in apostolic succession. A diocese is usually a determined geographic area; sometimes it may be constituted as a group of people of the same rite or language. (CCC, Glossary)

discernment: The discipline of spiritual self-examination; the practice of looking for the presence and the workings of the Spirit in one's life. Discernment includes striving to understand the promptings of the Spirit, assessing our response or lack of response to the Spirit, and deciding to act in cooperation with the grace of the Holy Spirit.

disciple: Name given in the New Testament to all those men and women who followed Jesus and were taught by him while he was alive, and who, following Jesus' death, Resurrection, and Ascension, formed the Church with the Apostles and helped spread the Good News, or Gospel message. Contemporary members of the Church, as followers of Jesus, can also be referred to as disciples. (USCCA, 509–510)

divine inspiration: This is the divine assistance given to the human authors of the books of Sacred Scripture. Guided by the Holy Spirit, the human authors made full use of their talents and abilities while, at the same time, writing the truth that God intended. (USCCA, 516)

divine providence: God's loving care and concern for all he has made; he continues to watch over creation, sustaining its existence and presiding over its development and destiny. (USCCA, 510)

divine Revelation: God's communication of himself and his loving plan to save us. This is a gift of self-communication, which is realized by deeds and words over time and most fully by his sending us his own divine Son, Jesus Christ. (USCCA, 526)

Dogma/doctrine of the Church: The name given to divinely revealed truths proclaimed or taught by the Church's Magisterium; the faithful are obliged to believe these truths. (USCCA, 510)

domestic church: The Christian home is the place where children receive the first proclamation of the faith. For this reason the family home is rightly called 'the domestic church', a community of grace and prayer, a school of human virtues and of Christian charity. (CCC, no. 1666)

Eastern Churches: Churches of the East in union with Rome (the Western Church), but not of Roman rite, with their own liturgical, theological, and administrative traditions, such as those of the Byzantine, Alexandrian or Coptic, Syriac, Armenian, Maronite, and Chaldean rites. The variety of particular churches with distinctive traditions witnesses to the catholicity of the one Church of Christ, which takes root in distinct cultures. (CCC, Glossary)

ecclesial communities: The term applies to those bodies of Christians who do not have a valid episcopal leadership or hierarchy in direct succession from the Apostles. (*See* USCCA, 129) *See also* **apostolic succession**.

Ecumenical Council: A gathering of all the bishops of the world, in the exercise of their collegial authority over the universal Church. An ecumenical council is usually called by the successor of St. Peter, the Pope, or at least confirmed and accepted by him. (CCC, Glossary)

ecumenism: The efforts among all Christians to bring about the fulfilment of Christ's will for the unity of his followers. (USCCA, 511)

Eleven (the): The name given to the Apostles after Judas Iscariot betrayed Jesus and died and before Matthias was chosen to replace him.

eternal life: Living forever with God in the happiness of heaven, entered after death by the souls of those who die in the grace and friendship of God. (CCC, Glossary)

evangelical counsels: Those vows taken by men or women who enter religious life; there are three vows: poverty, chastity, and obedience. (USCCA, 511)

evangelization: This is the ministry and mission of proclaiming and witnessing Christ and his Gospel with the intention of deepening the faith of believers and inviting others to be baptized and initiated into the Church. (USCCA, 512)

exegesis: The process used by Scripture scholars to determine the literal and spiritual meanings of the biblical text. (USCCA, 512)

expiation: The act of redemption and atonement for sin which Christ won for us by the pouring out of his Blood on the Cross, by his obedient love 'even to the end' (John 13:1). The expiation of sins continues in the mystical Body of Christ and the communion of saints by joining our human acts of atonement to the redemptive action of Christ, both in this life and in Purgatory. (CCC, Glossary)

F–G

faith: One of the three theological virtues. Faith is 'both a gift of God and a human act by which the believer gives personal adherence to God (who invites his or her response) and freely assents to the whole truth that God has revealed' (USCCA, 512).

fruits of the Holy Spirit: The Tradition of the Church lists twelve fruits of the Holy Spirit: love, joy, peace, patience, kindness, goodness, generosity, gentleness, faithfulness, modesty, self-control and chastity. (USCCA, 513)

gifts of the Holy Spirit: These gifts are permanent dispositions that move us to respond to the guidance of the Spirit. The traditional list of these gifts is derived from Isaiah 11:1–3: wisdom, understanding, knowledge, counsel [right judgment], fortitude [courage], reverence (piety), and wonder and awe in God's presence (fear of the Lord). (USCCA, 513)

Gospel: The good news of God's mercy and love revealed in the life, death, and resurrection of Christ. It is the *Gospel* or good news that the Apostles, and the Church following them, are to proclaim to the entire world. The *Gospel* is handed on in the apostolic tradition of the Church as the source of all-saving truth and moral discipline. (CCC, Glossary)

Gospels: The four *Gospels* are the books written by the evangelists Matthew, Mark, Luke, and John which have for their central object Jesus Christ, God's incarnate Son: his life, teachings, Passion and glorification, and his Church's beginnings under the Spirit's guidance. (CCC, Glossary)

grace: The word 'grace' comes from the Latin word *gratia*, which means 'free'. Grace is the 'free and undeserved gift that God gives us to respond to our vocation to become his adopted children. As sanctifying grace, God shares his divine life and friendship with us in a habitual gift, a stable and supernatural disposition that enables the soul to live with God, to act by his love. As actual grace, God gives us the help to conform our lives to his will. Sacramental grace and special graces (charisms, the grace of one's state of life) are gifts of the Holy Spirit to help us live out our Christian vocation' (CCC, Glossary). *See also* **charism**.

H–I

heaven: Eternal life with God; communion of life and love with the Trinity and all the blessed. Heaven is the state of supreme and definitive happiness, the goal of the deepest longings of humanity. (CCC, Glossary)

hell: The state of definitive self-exclusion from communion with God and the blessed, reserved for those who refuse by their own free choice to believe and be converted from sin, even to the end of their lives. (CCC, Glossary)

heresy: A religious teaching that denies or contradicts truths revealed by God. (USCCA, 514)

hermit: One who lives the eremitical life. Through silence and solitude, in prayer and penance, the hermit or anchorite vows, although not necessarily publicly, to follow the evangelical counsels out of love for God and desire for the salvation of the world. (CCC, Glossary)

hierarchy: The Apostles and their successors, the college of bishops, to whom Christ gave the authority to teach, sanctify, and rule the Church in his name. (CCC, Glossary)

holiness: A state of goodness in which a person—with the help of God's grace, the action of the

Holy Spirit, and a life of prayer—is freed from sin and evil. (USCCA, 514)

holy days of obligation: 'Principal feast days on which, in addition to Sundays, Catholics are obliged by Church law to participate in the Eucharist; a precept of the Church' (CCC, Glossary). There are six Holy Days of Obligation in the United States of America: Solemnity of Mary, The Mother of God (January 1), Solemnity of The Ascension of the Lord (forty days after Easter), Solemnity of The Assumption of the Blessed Virgin Mary (August 15), Solemnity of All Saints (November 1), Solemnity of The Immaculate Conception of the Blessed Virgin Mary (December 8) and Solemnity of The Nativity of the Lord [Christmas] (December 25).

Holy Orders: The Sacrament in which a bishop ordains a man to be conformed to Jesus Christ by grace, to service and leadership in the Church. A man can be ordained a deacon, priest, or bishop. Through this Sacrament, the mission entrusted by Christ to his Apostles continues to be exercised in the Church. This Sacrament confers a permanent mark or character on the one who receives it. (USCCA, 514–515)

Holy See: The seat of the central administration of the worldwide Catholic Church; the name is taken from the seat or diocese of the Pope, Bishop of Rome and successor of St. Peter as Vicar of Christ and pastor of the universal Church. (CCC, Glossary) *See also* **Vatican**.

Holy Spirit: The Third Person of the Trinity who builds up, animates, and sanctifies the Church and her members. (USCCA, 515)

Holy Trinity, Triune God: One God in three Persons—Father, Son, Holy Spirit. (USCCA, 530)

hope: One of the three theological virtues 'through which a person both desires and expects the fulfillment of God's promises of things to come' (USCCA, 515). Hope is the desire and expectation of the salvation God promised. It is based on God's unwavering fidelity to keeping and fulfilling his promises. *See also* **charity (love); faith**.

hypostatic union: The union of the divine and human natures in the one divine Person (Greek: *hypostasis*) of the Son of God, Jesus Christ. (CCC, Glossary).

image of God: God has made us in his image by giving us the capacity for intelligence, love, freedom, and conscience. By Baptism, our bodies are made temples of the Holy Spirit. (USCCA, 515)

Immaculate Conception: The dogma proclaimed in Christian Tradition, that from the first moment of her conception, Mary—by the singular grace of God and by virtue of the merits of Jesus Christ—was preserved immune from original sin. (CCC, Glossary)

Incarnation: By the Incarnation, the Second Person of the Holy Trinity assumed our human nature, taking flesh in the womb of the Virgin Mary. There is one Person in Jesus and that is the divine Person of the Son of God. Jesus has two natures, a human one and a divine one. (USCCA, 515)

inculturation: Inculturation is a two-way process whereby the Gospel is woven into the various dimensions of human culture and experience, both personal and social, and authentic cultural values are in turn integrated into the Christian life.

indefectibility: Indefectibility means that the Church does not and cannot depart from proclaiming the authentic Gospel without error in spite of the defects of her members. The Lord Jesus ensures that his Church will remain until the Kingdom is fully achieved. (USCCA, 515)

inerrancy (of Scripture): The attribute of the books of Scripture whereby they faithfully and without error teach that truth which God, for the sake of our salvation, wished to have confided through the Sacred Scriptures. (CCC, Glossary) *See also* **inspiration**.

infallibility: This is the gift of the Holy Spirit to the Church whereby the pastors of the Church—the pope, and bishops in communion with him—can definitively proclaim a doctrine of faith and morals, which is divinely revealed for the belief of the faithful. This gift flows from the grace of the whole body of the faithful not to err in matters of faith and morals. The pope teaches infallibly when he declares that his teaching is *ex cathedra* (literally, 'from the throne'); that is, he teaches as supreme pastor of the Church. (USCCA, 516)

inspiration: *see* **divine inspiration**.

K–L–M–N

Kingdom [Reign] of God: The actualization of God's will for human beings proclaimed by Jesus Christ as a community of justice, peace, mercy, and love, the seed of which is the Church on earth, and the fulfillment of which is in eternity. (USCCA, 517)

laity: Members of the Church, distinguished from the clergy and those in consecrated life, who have been incorporated into the People of God through the Sacrament of Baptism. (USCCA, 517)

last judgment: The moment at the end of time when everyone will appear before Christ and receive an eternal recompense in accord with their earthly life. (USCCA, 517)

Law of Love: The heart of God's Law revealed in Leviticus 19:18 and Deuteronomy 6:4–5 which was fulfilled in Jesus Christ and expressed in his teaching his disciples the New Commandment in John 13:34–35.

lay ecclesial ministers: Laypersons to whom the hierarchy 'entrust responsibilities for leadership in particular areas of ministry and thereby draw certain lay persons into a close mutual collaboration with the pastoral ministry of bishops, priests, and deacons. These men and women of every race and culture who serve in parishes, schools, diocesan agencies and Church institutions are identified by many different position titles' (*Co-Workers in the Vineyard of the Lord*, Introduction, page 7).

laypeople: *see* **laity**.

lectio divina: A manner of praying with Scripture; the person praying either reflectively reads a passage from Scripture or listens attentively to its being read, and then meditates on words or phrases that resonate. (USCCA, 517–518)

liturgical year: The calendar that guides the liturgies and prayers of the Church. It commences on the First Sunday of Advent and ends with the celebration of Christ the King. It includes Advent, the Christmas Season, Lent, the Easter Season, and Ordinary Time, as well as various Feasts of Mary, the Apostles, and many other saints. (USCCA, 518)

Liturgy of the Church: Liturgy 'refers especially to the public worship of the Church, including the Mass and the Liturgy of the Hours' (USCCA, 518). 'The word "liturgy" originally meant a "public work" or a "service in the name of/on behalf of the people". In Christian Tradition it means the participation of the People of God in "the work of God" ' (CCC, no. 1069). 'In the liturgy of the Church, God the Father is blessed and adored as the source of all the blessings of creation and salvation with which he has blessed us in his Son, in order to give us the Spirit of filial adoption' (CCC, no. 1110).

Liturgy of the Hours: The public daily prayer of the Church which extends the praise given to God in the Eucharistic celebration. (USCCA, 518)

Lord's Day (The): A name used synonymously for Sunday, the day of the Lord Jesus' Resurrection. (USCCA, 518)

Magisterium: The living teaching office of the Church, whose task it is to give authentic interpretation of the word of God, whether in its written form (Sacred Scripture) or in the form of Tradition. The Magisterium ensures the Church's fidelity to the teaching of the Apostles in matters of faith and morals. (CCC, Glossary)

Marriage: A covenant or partnership of life between a man and woman, which is ordered to the well-being of the spouses and to the procreation and upbringing of children. When validly contracted between two baptized people, marriage is a sacrament (Matrimony). (CCC, Glossary)

martyr: From the Greek word *martyr*, which means 'witness'. In a Christian context, a martyr is 'a witness to the truth of the faith, in which the martyr endures even death to be faithful to Christ' (CCC, Glossary).

Matrimony: *see* **Marriage.**

Mediatrix: The title 'Mediatrix' was given to Mary to express her unique relationship to Christ and to the Church. The word 'mediator' means 'one who links or reconciles separate or opposing parties. Thus Jesus Christ is the "one *mediator* between God and the human race" (1 Timothy 2:5). . . . Mary too is sometimes called *Mediatrix* in virtue of her cooperation in the saving mission of Christ, who alone is the unique mediator between God and humanity' (CCC, Glossary).

mercy: The loving kindness, compassion, or forbearance shown to one who offends; for example, the mercy of God to us sinners. (CCC, Glossary)

Messiah: The Messiah is the one whom God sent to inaugurate his kingdom definitively. 'The word "Christ" comes from the Greek translation of the Hebrew *Messiah*, which means "anointed". [Christ] became the name proper to Jesus only because he accomplished perfectly the divine mission that "Christ" signifies. . . . It was necessary that the Messiah be anointed by the Spirit of the Lord at once as king and priest, and also as prophet. Jesus fulfilled the messianic hope of Israel in his threefold office of priest, prophet and king' (CCC, no. 436).

mezuzah: In Jewish homes today we often find a small decorative rectangular object nailed to the doorpost. This is called a *mezuzah*, and it contains a tiny scroll. On the scroll are the words of the *Shema*, the Jewish prayer quoting Deuteronomy 6:4–9, which begins: 'Hear, O Israel: The LORD is our God, the LORD alone. You shall love the LORD your God with all your heart, and with all your soul, and with all your might.' Devout Jews observe the tradition of praying the *Shema* each time they exit and enter their homes as a reminder to love and honor God above all.

ministerial priesthood: This priesthood, received in the Sacrament of Holy Orders, differs in essence from the priesthood of the faithful. The ministerial priesthood serves the priesthood of the faithful by building up the Church in the name of Christ, who is head of the Body, by offering prayers and sacrifices to God on behalf of people. A priest is given the power to consecrate the Eucharist, forgive sins, and administer the other Sacraments, except Holy Orders. (USCCA, 519–520)

miracle: A sign or wonder, such as a healing or the control of nature, which can only be attributed to divine power. The miracles of Jesus were messianic signs of the presence of God's kingdom. (CCC, Glossary)

missionary/missioner: One of the faithful, either clergy, religious or layperson, who fulfills the Church's mandate to evangelize outside their native land or in another part of their native land other than in which they live.

Mystical Body of Christ: The Church.

New Evangelization: Proclaiming and witnessing Christ and his Gospel either to those who have already been initiated into the Church but who have lost their deep sense of commitment to Jesus Christ and connection with the Christian community, or to those who have never heard the Gospel proclaimed.

O–P

oral tradition: The passing on of Revelation by word of mouth before it was written down by the inspired human authors of Sacred Scripture.

Ordinary, local: The bishop of a diocese. In general the term 'ordinary' also applies to all who, even for a time only, have been given authority to preside over and serve a particular Church or other church community.

original holiness: The 'grace of original holiness was to share in divine life' (CCC. no. 375).

original justice: The inner harmony of the human person, the harmony between man and woman, and finally the harmony between the first couple and all creation, comprised the state of 'original justice'. (CCC, no. 376)

Original Sin: The personal sin of disobedience by the first human beings, resulting in the deprivation of original holiness and justice and the experience of suffering and death. (USCCA, 522)

Orthodox Churches: Eastern Churches not in full communion with the Catholic Church. Christians of the Orthodox Churches are separated from the Catholic Church (schism), yet are in an imperfect but deep communion with the Catholic Church by reason of our common Baptism, the profession of the Creed, and the possession of true sacraments by reason of the apostolic succession of their priesthood. (CCC, Glossary)

parable(s): A characteristic feature of the teaching of Jesus. Parables are simple images or comparisons that confront the hearer or reader with a radical choice about his invitation to enter the Kingdom of God. (CCC, Glossary)

Paschal Mystery: Christ's work of redemption accomplished principally by his Passion, death, Resurrection, and glorious Ascension, whereby 'dying he destroyed our death, rising he restored our life' (CCC, no. 1067). The Paschal Mystery is celebrated and made present in the liturgy of the Church, and its saving effects are communicated through the sacraments, especially the Eucharist, which renews the paschal sacrifice of Christ as the sacrifice offered by the Church. (CCC, Glossary)

Passion (the): The suffering and death of Jesus. Passion or Palm Sunday begins Holy Week, during which the annual liturgical celebration of the Paschal Mystery of Christ takes place. (CCC, Glossary)

Passions (moral): The emotions or dispositions which incline us to good or evil actions, such as love and hate, hope and fear, joy and sadness, and anger. (CCC, Glossary)

Pentecost: The 'fiftieth day' at the end of the seven weeks following Passover (Easter in the Christian dispensation). At the first Pentecost after the Resurrection and Ascension of Jesus, the Holy Spirit was manifested, given and communicated as a divine Person to the Church, fulfilling the paschal mystery of Christ according to his promise. (CCC, Glossary)

People of God: A synonym for the Church, taken from the Old Testament people whom God chose, Israel. Christ instituted the new and eternal covenant by which a new priestly, prophetic, and royal People of God, the Church, participates in these offices of Christ and in the mission and service which flow from them. (CCC, Glossary)

Perpetual Virginity of Mary: Mary was a virgin in conceiving Jesus, in giving birth to him, and in remaining always a virgin ever after. (USCCA, 523)

piety: One of the seven gifts of the Holy Spirit which leads one to devotion to God. Filial piety connotes an attitude of reverence and respect by children toward their parents. Piety also refers to the religious sense of a people, and its expression in popular devotions. (CCC, Glossary)

prayer: 'The raising of one's mind and heart to God in thanksgiving and in praise of his glory. It can also include the requesting of good things from God. It is an act by which one enters into awareness of a loving communion with God' (USCCA, 523–524). The five *forms* of Christian prayer are: prayer of blessing and adoration, of intercession, of petition, of praise, and of thanksgiving. The three *expressions* of Christian prayer are: vocal prayer, meditation and contemplation.

precepts of the Church: Laws made by the Church that indicate basic requirements for her members. (USCCA, 524)

presbyter: Another name for an ordained priest; 'An "elder" or priest, a member of the order of priesthood; the presbyterate is one of the three degrees of the Sacrament of Holy Orders' (CCC, Glossary).

priest: A baptized man ordained through the Sacrament of Holy Orders. 'Priests are united with the bishops in priestly dignity and at the same time depend on them in the exercise of their pastoral functions; they are called to be the bishops' prudent co-workers' (CCC, no. 1595). With the bishop, priests form a presbyteral (priestly) community and assume with him the pastoral mission for a particular parish. They serve God's People in the work of sanctification by their preaching, teaching, and offering the Sacraments, especially the Eucharist and the forgiving of sins. (USCCA, 524) *See also* **ministerial priesthood**.

priesthood: *see* **ministerial priesthood; priesthood of the faithful; priesthood of Christ; presbyter**.

priesthood of Christ: The unique high priest, according to the order of Melchizedek. Christ fulfilled everything that the priesthood of the Old Covenant prefigured. He offered himself once and for all, in a perfect sacrifice upon the cross. His priesthood is made present in a special way in the Church through the ministerial priesthood, conferred through the Sacrament of Holy Orders. (CCC, Glossary)

priesthood of the faithful: Christ gives the faithful a share in his priesthood through the Sacraments of Baptism and Confirmation. This means that all baptized and confirmed members of the Church share in offering prayer and sacrifice to God. The priesthood of the faithful differs in essence from the ministerial priesthood. (USCCA, 524)

prophet: One sent by God to form the people of the Old Covenant in the hope of salvation. The prophets are often authors of books of the Old Testament. The prophetic books constitute a major section of the Old Testament of the Bible. John the Baptist concludes the work of the prophets of the Old Covenant. (CCC Glossary)

Protestant: A person who believes in Christ and has been baptized, but who does not profess the Catholic faith in its entirety, but rather is a member of a Protestant church or ecclesial community whose roots are in the Reformation, begun in the sixteenth century. (CCC, Glossary)

Protoevangelium: The proto– or 'first' Gospel: the passage in Genesis (3:15) that first mysteriously announces the promise of the Messiah and Redeemer. (CCC, Glossary)

purgatory: A state of final purification after death and before entrance into heaven for those who died in God's friendship, but were only imperfectly purified; a final cleansing of human imperfection before one is able to enter the joy of heaven. (CCC, Glossary)

R–S

racism: Unjust discrimination on the basis of a person's race; a violation of human dignity, and a sin against justice. (CCC, Glossary)

Real Presence: The unique presence of Christ in the Eucharist. 'When the bread is consecrated, it is changed into Christ's Body. When the wine is consecrated, it is changed into Christ's Blood. Jesus Christ is substantially present in a way that is entirely unique. This happens through the power of the Holy Spirit and the ministry of the priest or bishop acting in the person of Christ during the Eucharistic prayer' (USCCA, 525).

redemption: Redemption is the salvation won for us by Jesus by his paying 'the price of his own sacrificial death on the Cross to ransom us, to set us free from the slavery of sin' (CCC, Glossary).

relativism: Any teaching that denies the existence of absolute values and teaches that all points of view are equal and 'relative' to the individual.

religion: A set of beliefs and practices followed by those committed to the service and worship of God. The first commandment requires us to believe in God, to worship and serve him, as the first duty of the virtue of religion. (CCC, Glossary)

Resurrection: 'This is the triumph of Jesus over death on the third day after his crucifixion. Christ's body is real, but glorified, not restrained by space or time' (USCCA, 525). The Resurrection confirms the 'saving', 'redeeming' and 'liberating' power of Jesus and the truth of his divinity.

Revelation: *see* **divine Revelation**.

Sabbath: In Scripture, the Sabbath was the seventh day of the week that the people of Ancient Israel were to keep holy by praising God for the creation and the covenant and by resting from their ordinary work. For Christians, the observance of the Sabbath has been transferred to Sunday, the day of the Lord's Resurrection. (USCCA, 526)

sacrament: 'An efficacious sign of grace, instituted by Christ and entrusted to the Church, by which divine life is dispensed to us by the work of the Holy Spirit' (USCCA, 526). The Seven Sacraments are classified in three groups: the three Sacraments of Christian Initiation (Baptism, Confirmation, and Eucharist), the two Sacraments of Healing (Penance and Reconciliation, and Anointing of the Sick), and the two Sacraments at the Service of Communion (Marriage and Holy Orders).

sacramental graces: Graces of the Holy Spirit to help us live out our Christian vocation. (CCC, Glossary)

Sacraments at the Service of Communion: The term *communion* refers to the Community of the Church. Holy Orders and Matrimony are the Sacraments at the Service of Communion (the community of the Church). This means that they are primarily directed toward the salvation of others. If they benefit the personal salvation of the ordained or married person, it is through service to others that this happens. (USCCA, 527)

sacred chrism: *see* **chrism, sacred.**

Sacred Scripture: *see* **Scripture, Sacred.**

Sacred Tradition: *see* **Tradition, Sacred.**

sacrifice: A ritual offering made to God by a priest on behalf of the people, as a sign of adoration, gratitude, supplication, and communion. The perfect sacrifice was Christ's death on the cross; by this sacrifice, Christ accomplished our redemption as high priest of the new and eternal covenant. The sacrifice of Christ on the cross is commemorated and mysteriously made present in the Eucharistic sacrifice of the Church. (CCC, Glossary)

salvation: The forgiveness of sins and restoration of friendship with God, which can be done by God alone. (CCC, Glossary)

sanctifying grace: Sanctifying grace is a habitual gift of God's own divine life, a stable and supernatural disposition that enables us to live with God and to act by his love. (USCCA, 514)

schism: Schism is the refusal to submit to the pope's authority as head of the Church. (USCCA, 342)

Scripture, Sacred (Bible): The inspired written Word of God. 'The books that contain the truth of God's revelation and that were composed by human authors, inspired by the Holy Spirit, and recognized by the Church' (USCCA, 527).

sensus fidelium/sensus fidei: A supernatural appreciation of the faith (*sensus fidei*) shown by the universal consent in matters of faith and morals manifested by the whole body of the faithful under the guidance of the Magisterium. (CCC, Glossary)

sin: Sin is an offense against God as well as against reason, truth, and right conscience; it is a failure in genuine love for God and neighbor caused by a perverse attachment to certain goods. It wounds the nature of man and injures human solidarity. It has been defined as 'an utterance, a deed, or a desire contrary to the eternal law' [CCC, no. 1849]. (USCCA, 528)

social sin: Sins that produce unjust social laws and oppressive institutions. They are social situations and institutions contrary to divine goodness. Sometimes called 'structures of sin' they are the expression and effect of personal sins. (USCCA, 528)

social teaching (social doctrine) of the Church: The teaching (social doctrine) of the Church on the truth of revelation about human dignity, human solidarity, and the principles of justice and peace; the moral judgments about economic and social matters required by such truth and about the demands of justice and peace. (CCC, Glossary)

Son of Man: The title used by our Lord of himself in the Gospel. This title connotes a relationship with the eschatological figure of the 'Son of man appearing in clouds and glory' in the prophecy of Daniel (see *Mark* 13:26; *Daniel* 7:13). (CCC, Glossary)

steward: Someone who has the responsibility of caring for what belongs to another person or group of people. In the biblical accounts of creation, God designates humanity to have the responsibility to have *dominion* over, or serve as the stewards of, his creation. The root word for 'dominion' is *domus*, which means household. God has entrusted the care of creation, his household, to humanity.

synod: A meeting of bishops of an ecclesiastical province or patriarchate (or even from the whole world, for example, Synod of Bishops) to discuss the doctrinal and pastoral needs of the church. A *diocesan* synod is an assembly of priests and other members of Christ's faithful who assist the bishop by offering advice about the needs of the diocese and by proposing legislation for him to enact. The words 'synod' and 'council' are sometimes used interchangeably. (CCC, Glossary)

T–U–V–W

temptation: An attraction, either from outside oneself or from within, to act contrary to right reason and the commandments of God. (CCC, Glossary)

theosis: *Theosis* means 'divinization' or 'the process of becoming like God'. From the Greek word *theos*, meaning 'God', *theosis* is a central concept for many Eastern Catholics. St. Athanasius, Father of the Church, expressed this belief in about AD 319 when he wrote, 'The Son of God became man so that we might become God.'

Theotokos: A Greek term meaning 'God-bearer'; Mary is *Theotokos*. She is the Mother of God. Her Son, Jesus, is the Incarnate Son of God, in whom the divine nature and a human nature are united in the one divine Person, Jesus Christ.

tithe: An ancient word for 'ten' that refers to the practice of giving over one tenth of one's earnings for sacred purposes. The Bible often mentions and mandates tithing; for example, Deuteronomy 14:22–29 lists as a law of the Torah that people give over one tenth of their harvest of grain, wine, oil and first-born animals. Some of these were to be used in sacred banquets, some to support the priests, and some to go to the poor.

Tradition (Sacred): The living transmission of the message of the Gospel in the Church, flowing from the oral preaching of the Apostles and the written message of salvation under the inspiration of the Holy Spirit (Scripture). Tradition is preserved and handed on as the Deposit of Faith under the guidance of the bishops, successors to the Apostles. (USCCA, 530)

transcendence: A term used to name the mystery of God who is so 'beyond' the universe, and so different from anything else that exists, that God cannot be directly experienced by human beings. A shorthand way of saying that God is transcendent is: God is the absolute Other.

Transfiguration: The mysterious event in which Jesus, seen speaking with Moses and Elijah on the mountain, was transformed in appearance—in the sight of Peter, James and John—as a moment of disclosure of his divine glory. (CCC, Glossary).

Twelve (the): The Apostles chosen by Jesus before his Death, Resurrection and Ascension. From among the Twelve, Jesus appointed St. Peter to be the leader of the Apostles (*see* John 21:15–19). *See also* **Apostles**.

Urbi et orbi: Phrase meaning 'to the city and to the world'; the annual Christmas, World Day for Peace (January 1) and Easter messages the Pope proclaims. These *Urbi et Orbi* proclamations usually focus on bringing the light of Christ and the Gospel to key issues facing the world.

Vatican/Vatican City: The territorial seat of the papacy that is situated within the city of Rome; the smallest sovereign state in the world. The Vatican is also referred to as the Holy See. It is the location of the central governing body, the Curia, of the Catholic Church. *See also* **Holy See**.

virtue: A habitual and firm disposition to do the good. The moral virtues are acquired through human effort aided by God's grace; the theological virtues are gifts of God. (CCC, Glossary)

vocation: The term given to the call to each person from God; everyone has been called to holiness and eternal life, especially in Baptism. Each person can also be called more specifically to the priesthood or to religious life, to married life, and to single life, as well as to a particular profession or service. (USCCA, 531)

wisdom: A spiritual gift which enables one to know the purpose and plan of God; one of the seven gifts of the Holy Spirit. Wisdom is also the name of one of the books of the Old Testament. (CCC, Glossary)

Acknowledgments

Scripture quotations taken from or adapted from the New Revised Standard Version Bible: Catholic Edition, copyright © 1989, 1993, Division of Christian Education of the National Council of Churches of Christ in the U.S.A.; all rights reserved.

Excerpts from the English translation of the *Catechism of the Catholic Church* for use in the United States, second edition, copyright © 1997, United States Catholic Conference, Inc., Libreria Editrice Vaticana; all rights reserved.

Excerpts from the *United States Catholic Catechism for Adults*, copyright © 2006, United States Conference of Catholic Bishops, Washington D.C.; all rights reserved.

Excerpts from documents of Vatican II from A. Flannery (ed.), *Vatican Council II: Constitutions, Decrees, Declarations* (New York/Dublin: Costello Publishing/Dominican Publications, 1996).

Excerpts from *Catholic Household Blessings & Prayers*, Revised Edition, copyright © 2007, Bishops Committee on the Liturgy, United States Conference of Catholic Bishops, Washington, D.C.

Quotation, p. 20, from United States Conference of Catholic Bishops, *A Catholic Framework for Economic Life*, 1996.

Quotations, pp. 28 and 32, from Pope Benedict XVI, *Jesus of Nazareth: The Infancy Narratives* (New York: Random House, 2012; translation copyright © Libreria Editrice Vaticana, 2012).

Quotation by Justin Meggitt, p. 34, from *Paul, Poverty, and Survival* (Edinburgh, United Kingdom: T&T Clarke, 1998).

Excerpt from song 'What Color Is God's skin?', p. 50, written by David Finley Stevenson and Thomas E. Wilkes, published by Sobel Global Music o/b/o Up With People (ASCAP); used with permission.

Quotation, p. 91, from United States Conference of Catholic Bishops, *To the Ends of the Earth: A Pastoral Statement on World Mission*, no. 44.

Quotation, p. 127, from Catholic Relief Services website: *http://crs.org/about/mission-statement/*

Information on the Maryknoll Lay Missioners, pp. 136–7, from the Maryknoll Lay Missioners' website: *www.maryknolllaymissioners.org/*; used with permission of the Maryknoll Lay Missioners.

Material on Jules Naudet, p. 142, adapted from *A Global Search for God* by Bill McGarvey, found at *http://www.bustedhalo.com/features/a-global-search-for-god*; reprinted with permission from BustedHalo.com.

Excerpt from 'We Are One Body' by Dana Scallon, p. 145, from the album *Say Yes*, published by Heartbeat Records, 1993.

Quotation from Cardinal Dulles S.J., p. 154, from 'Long Road to Rome' in *Crisis Magazine*, July–August 2001.

Excerpt, p. 163, from Pope Benedict XVI's 2012 Christmas *Urbi et Orbi* message, copyright © 2012, Libreria Editrice Vaticana.

Excerpts, p. 164, from Pope Francis' *Evangelii Gaudium* (The Joy of the Gospel), copyright © Libreria Editrice Vaticana.

Song within prayer service, p. 174, by Fr Robert Lebel; 'Light of the World' (85656) copyright © 2001, World Youth Day 2002; all rights reserved; published by OCP, 5536 NE Hassalo, Portland, OR 97213, (p) 2001, OCP; all rights reserved; used with permission.

Excerpt, p. 180, from the English translation of the *Rite of Baptism for Children*, copyright © 1969 International Committee on English in the Liturgy, Inc. (ICEL).

Quotation, p. 189, from *Co-Workers in the Vineyard of the Lord*, copyright © 2005, United States Conference of Catholic Bishops, Washington D.C.

Quotation within 'The story of the Johnson family', pp. 192–3, from the Lay Mission-Helpers website: *www.laymissionhelpers.org*; used with permission.

Excerpts, pp. 199–200, from Pope Benedict XVI's 2012 World Day of Peace address, copyright Libreria Editrice Vaticana.

Prayer Reflection, pp. 211–12, adapted from 'Dialogued Prayer on the Beatitudes' found at Catholic Forum: *www.catholic-forum.com/saints/litany15.htm*

Excerpt, p. 241, from 'I'm Gonna Sit Right Down and Write Myself a Letter', written by Fred E. Ahlert and Joe Young, 1935.

Excerpt, p. 244, from Pope St. John Paul II's address to youth at Toronto World Youth Day 2002 from the Vatican website: *www.vatican.va*

Image credits

Main cover image: Cathedral stained-glass window by PhotoSergio. *Top:* Photo by Yellow Dog Productions/ Getty Images. *Center:* Palm Sunday service in Vatican City (Photo by Franco Origlia/Getty Images)

p. 7: Photo: Andreas Praefcke

p. 14: Photo: Wolfgang Sauber

p. 16: Photo: Jean-Christophe Benoist

p. 18: Photo © Nik Wheeler/CORBIS

p. 21 (top): Photo: akg-images

p. 27: Photo by Franco Origlia

p. 29: Photo: Sailko

p. 42: Photo: akg-images/ullstein bild

p. 54: Map by Lir Mac Cárthaigh

p. 56: Photo: Mattias Kabel

p. 58: Photo: Matt Cardy - WPA Pool/Getty Images

p. 59: Photo: Marie-Lan Nguyen

p. 61: Photo: Amos Ben Gershom/GPO via Getty Images

p. 66: Photo: Kleuske

p. 78: Photo: Lothar Wollen

p. 87: Photo: Peter MacDiarmid/Getty Images

p. 94: Photo: Marie-Lan Nguyen

p. 97: Patriarch Kirill I (Photo: ALEXANDER NEMENOV/ AFP/Getty Images); Pope Francis (Photo: Buda Mendes/Getty Images)

p. 101: Photo © Corbis

p. 111: Walt Disney Pictures/Phil Bray/Album/akg-images

p. 122: *The Golden Rule*. Printed by permission of the Norman Rockwell Family Agency, copyright © 1961 The Norman Rockwell Family Entities

p. 125: *St. Francis of Assisi* by El Greco (Musee des Beaux-Arts, Lille, France/Giraudon/The Bridgeman Art Library)

p. 127: Photo: Spencer Platt/Getty Images for Caritas

p. 131: Photo: Erzalibillas

p. 132: IMAGINE ENTERTAINMENT/Ronald Grant Archive/Mary Evans

p. 133: Photo: Wolfgang Sauber

p. 135: Photo: Jeff J Mitchell/Getty Images

p. 144: Photo: Alexandra Beier/Getty Images

p. 147: Photo: GFreihalter

p. 148: Photo: GFreihalter

p. 151: Photo © Robertus Pudyanto/Demotix/Corbis

p. 154: Photo: THOMAS COEX/AFP/Getty Images

p. 161: Photo: Giuseppe Ciccia/NurPhoto/Corbis

p. 166: Photo: Christine Sine

p. 170: Photo: Watanabe/Pix Inc./Time & Life Pictures/ Getty Images

p. 172: Photo of Pope John Paul II © Ralf-Finn Hestoft/ CORBIS; Photo of World Youth Day © P Deliss/ Godong/Corbis

p. 179: Photo: Andreas F. Borchert

p. 182: Photo: Franco Origlia/Getty Images

p. 183: Photo courtesy of Luigi Coronel (*www. prieststuff.com*)

p. 185: Photo courtesy of Susan Kehoe (*http:// adeaconswife.com*)

p. 210: Photo: Ralf Roletschek

p. 211: Photo: Yelkrokoyade

p. 221: Russian icon of Sophia, 17th century (panel) (Mark Gallery, London, UK/The Bridgeman Art Library)

p. 226: Photo: Design Pics/Con Tanasiuk

p. 228: Photo: LIU JIN/AFP/Getty Images

p. 229: Photo: Ralph Hammann

p. 232: Photo: akg-images

p. 235: Photo of the Transfiguration: Anagoria

p. 238: Photo: IAM/akg-images

p. 239: Photo: Reinhardhauke

Index

STUDENT NOTES